ATTAINING THE WORLDS BEYOND

A Guide to Spiritual Discovery

ATTAINING
THE WORLDS BEYOND

A Guide to Spiritual Discovery

BY

RABBI MICHAEL LAITMAN

COMPILED BY BENZION GIERTZ

LAITMAN
Kabbalah
Publishers

Executive Editor: Benzion Giertz

Laitman Kabbalah Publishers Website:
www.kabbalah.info
Laitman Kabbalah Publishers Email:
info@kabbalah.info

ISBN: 0-9731909-0-6
Second Edition: November 2003

Contents

Contents

Contents

It is beyond human comprehension to understand the essence of such spiritual qualities as total altruism and love. Even the existence of such feelings is beyond our comprehension; we seem to require an incentive to perform any act that does not promise us some form of personal gain. That is why a quality such as altruism can only be imparted to us from Above, and only those of us who have experienced it can understand it.

Rabbi Michael Laitman

Introduction

If you listen with your heart to one famous question, I am sure that all your doubts as to whether you should study Kabbalah will vanish without a trace. This question is a bitter and a fair one, asked by all born on earth: "What is the meaning of my life?"

Rabbi Yehuda Ashlag, Introduction to Talmud Esser Sefirot

Among all the texts and notes that were used by my Rabbi, Baruch Shalom Halevi Ashlag, there was one particular notebook he always carried. This notebook contained all the transcripts of his conversations with his father, Rabbi Yehuda Leib Halevi Ashlag, the Rabbi of Jerusalem, and a Kabbalist. He was the author of a 21-volume commentary on the book of Zohar, as well as the author of a six-volume commentary on the texts of the Kabbalist, Ari, and of many other works on Kabbalah.

Not feeling well on the Jewish New Year in September 1991, my Rabbi called me to his bedside and handed me his notebook, saying, "Take it and learn from it." The following morning, my teacher perished in my arms, leaving me and many of his other disciples without guidance in this world.

He used to say, "I want to teach you to turn to the Creator, rather than to me, because He is the only strength, the only Source of all that exists, the only One who can really help you, and He awaits your prayers for help. When you seek help in your search for freedom from the bondage of this world, help in elevating yourself above this world, help in finding the self, and help in determining your purpose in life, you must turn to the Creator, who sends you all those aspirations in order to compel you to turn to Him."

In this text, I attempt to convey some of the ideas from his notebook as I perceived them. It is impossible to fully relate to what is written there, as each of us can only understand what we read within the limits of our immediate grasp, since each of us is limited by the qualities of our individual souls. Therefore, in the course of interacting with the Supreme Light, each of us will interpret these ideas as our souls perceive them.

May the thoughts of Rabbi Yehuda Ashlag penetrate this world through the words of his eldest son, my Rabbi, and may they help all of us unite with the Creator in the course of our lives here in this world!

Rabbi Michael Laitman

How To Read the Text

The need for this text became apparent to me from the questions that I received from my students, and from the questions that were asked during various lectures and radio programs, as well as from the letters that continue to flood in from all over the world.

The difficulty of explaining and teaching Kabbalah lies in the fact that the spiritual world has no counterpart in our world. Even if the object of our studies becomes clear, our understanding of it is only temporary. What we learn is grasped by the spiritual component of our ability to understand, which is constantly renewed from Above.

Thus, a subject we initially understand may appear unclear at a later date. Depending on our mood and our spiritual state, the text can appear as either full of deep meaning, or entirely meaningless.

Do not despair if what was so clear yesterday becomes very confusing today. Do not give up if the text appears to be vague, strange, or illogical.

Kabbalah is not studied for the sake of acquiring theoretical knowledge, but to help us see and perceive what is hidden from us.

When, after we have contemplated and acquired spiritual strength, we begin to see and perceive, then our ability to attain the resulting spiritual lights and levels will bring us to true knowledge.

Until we can comprehend the Upper Light and can perceive what it presents to us, we will not understand how the universe is built and how it works, since there are no analogies to these concepts in our own world. This text can help ease our first steps toward perceiving the spiritual forces. At later stages, we will be able to progress only with the help of a teacher.

This text should not be read in an ordinary fashion. Rather, we should concentrate on a paragraph, think about it, and attempt to understand examples that reflect in the issues discussed. We may then try to apply these issues to our own personal experiences.

We should patiently and repeatedly read and think about each sentence as we try to penetrate the author's feelings. We should also read slowly, trying to extract the nuances of what is written, and if need be, return to the beginning of each sentence.

This method can either help us delve into the material with our own feelings, or recognize that our feelings are lacking regarding a particular issue. If the latter is the case, it is a crucial prerequisite for us to move forward spiritually.

This text is not written for quick reading. Though it deals with one subject only, "How to relate to the Creator," it deals with it in different ways. This allows each of us to find the particular phrase or word that will transport us into the depths of the text.

Although the desires and actions of egoism are described in the third person, until we can separate our personal consciousness from our desires, we should consider the aspirations and desires of egoism our own. The word "body" in the text does not relate to the physical self, but to "egoism" our desire to receive.

To get the most out of this material, I recommend reading the same passages at different times and in different states of mind. By doing so, you can better acquaint yourself with your reactions and attitudes towards the same text on different occasions.

Disagreeing with the material is always positive, as is agreeing with it. The most important aspect of reading the text is your response to it. A feeling of disagreement indicates you have reached the preliminary stage (*achoraim*, the backside) of understanding, which prepares you for the next stage of perception (*panim*, face).

It is precisely through this slow meaningful manner of reading that you can develop feelings, or "vessels" (*kelim*). These are necessary for us to receive spiritual sensations. Once the vessels are in place, the Upper Light will be able to enter them. Prior to their formation, the Light merely exists around you, surrounding your soul, although you cannot perceive it.

This text is not written to enhance your knowledge. Nor is it meant to be memorized. In fact, we must never test ourselves on the material.

It is even better if we forget the contents altogether, so that the second reading will seem fresh and entirely unfamiliar. By forgetting the material, it implies that we have grasped the previous sensations and that they have now subsided, leaving a space to be filled by sensations we have yet to experience. The process of developing new sensory organs is constantly renewed and accumulated in the spiritual, unperceived sphere of our souls.

The most important aspect of our reading is the way we feel about the material while reading it, not afterwards.

Once we experience these feelings, they become revealed within the heart and mind, and manifest themselves whenever they are needed in the continuous process of the soul's development.

Rather than rushing to complete reading the text, it is recommended to concentrate on the sections that appeal to us the most. Only then will the text be able to help and guide us in our search for personal spiritual ascent. The goal of this text is to help us become interested in the mysteries of life, such as:

Why were we born into this world? Can we enter the spiritual worlds from here? Can we ever understand the purpose of the creation? Is it possible to perceive the Creator, eternity and immortality? How can we begin to grow spiritually?

If you listen with your heart to one famous question, I am sure that all your doubts as to whether you should study Kabbalah will vanish without a trace. This question is a bitter and a fair one, asked by all born on earth: "What is the meaning of my life?"

Rabbi Yehuda Ashlag

1

Perceiving the Creator

Generations come and go, yet every generation and every individual asks the same question about the meaning of life. This happens especially at times of war and global suffering, and during periods of misfortune that befall each of us at some point in our lives. What is the purpose of life, which is so costly to us? And shouldn't the absence of suffering be deemed as happiness?

In the Talmud's, *Ethics of the Fathers,* it says: "Against your will you are born, against your will do you live, and against your will you will die."

Each generation has had its share of misfortune. There are some among us who have lived through the Depression, through war, and through postwar turbulence. But I see my generation, being full of problems and suffering, unable to establish itself, and unable to find itself.

In this atmosphere, the question regarding the meaning of our lives stands out particularly clearly. At times it seems that life is more difficult than death itself; therefore, it is no surprise that *Ethics of the Fathers* states, "Against your will do you live."

Nature created us, and we are forced to exist with the qualities that were imposed upon us. It is as if we were only semi-intelligent beings: intelligent only to the degree that we are aware that our actions are determined by our inherent characteristics and qualities, and that we cannot go against them. If we are at the mercy of nature, then there is no predicting where this wild, unreasonable nature can lead us.

Our natures are responsible for constantly causing conflicts between individuals and entire nations, who, like wild animals, are engaged in a vicious struggle of the instincts. Yet, subconsciously, we cannot accept a comparison of ourselves with primitive beasts.

If, however, the Divine Force that created us does exist, then why do we not perceive it, why does it conceal itself from us? For if we knew what It required of us, we would not commit those mistakes in our lives for which we are punished by suffering!

How much easier would life be if the Creator were not concealed from human beings, but were clearly perceived and seen by each and every one of us!

Then, we would have no doubt of His existence. We would be able to observe the effects of His Providence on the surrounding world; realize the cause and purpose of our creation; clearly see the consequences of our actions and His response to them; be able to discuss all of our problems in a dialogue with Him; ask for His help; seek His protection and advice; complain to Him about our troubles, and ask Him to explain why He treats us as He does.

Finally, we would consult with Him for advice concerning the future; we would constantly be in contact with Him and we would be correcting ourselves in accordance with His advice. In the end, He would be pleased and we would benefit as well.

Just as a child is aware of its mother from the moment of its birth, so we would be aware of the Creator. We would learn the correct way of life by observing His reactions to our actions, and even to our intentions. We would perceive the Creator to be just as close as any mother, since we would see

Him as the Source of our birth, as our parent, and as the cause of our existence and that of all future life.

If the above were so, we would have no need for governments, schools, or educators. The existence of all nations would essentially focus on a wonderful and simple coexistence for the sake of a common cause apparent to all: our spiritual unification with the openly visible and perceivable Creator.

Everyone's actions would be guided by clear spiritual laws, called "the commandments," and everyone would obey them because disobeying the commandments would obviously mean inflicting harm on the self, equivalent to jumping into a fire or off a cliff.

If we could clearly perceive the Creator and His Providence, we would have no difficulty in performing the hardest of tasks, for the personal benefit derived from these tasks would be apparent. It would be as if we were giving all our possessions to a stranger without thinking twice about the present or future.

Yet, this would present absolutely no problem, since being aware of the Divine Rule would enable us to see the benefits of acting selflessly. We would know that we were in the power of the kind and eternal Creator.

Just imagine how natural it would be (and also how unnatural and impossible it is in the present condition of Divine concealment) to give ourselves fully to the Creator, to surrender all of our thoughts and desires to Him without reservation, and to be what He wants us to be.

We would not have the least concern for ourselves, and would give no thought to ourselves. In fact, we would cease to be aware of our own selves and would transfer all our feelings from ourselves to Him, trying to approach Him and to live by His thoughts and His Will.

From the above, it should be clear that the only element lacking in our world is our perception of the Creator.

The attainment of such a perception should be our sole purpose in this world. This is the one goal we should spare no effort to achieve, for only when we can perceive the Creator can we receive His help. This would save us from both the calamities of this life and from a spiritual death, thereby according us spiritual immortality without having to return to this world.

The method of searching for our perception of the Creator is known as "Kabbalah." Our perception of the Creator is called "faith." However, we often mistakenly believe that faith implies groping in the dark, without seeing or perceiving the Creator.

In fact, faith means exactly the opposite. According to Kabbalah, the Light of the Creator that fills a person, the Light of the connection to the Creator, the Light that gives a feeling of unification with Him (*Ohr Hassadim*) is known as "the Light of Faith," or simply, faith.

Faith, the Light of the Creator, gives us a sensation of being linked to the eternal. It brings us an understanding of the Creator, a feeling of complete communication with Him, as well as a sense of absolute security, immortality, greatness and strength. It becomes clear that deliverance from our temporal existence and from our suffering (caused by our futile pursuit of transient pleasures) lies only in our attaining faith, through which we will be able to perceive the Creator.

In general, the only cause of our misfortunes, and of the worthless and temporal nature of our lives, is our failure to perceive the Creator. Kabbalah impels us towards Him by teaching us: "Taste and see that the Creator is good." The aim of this text is to guide you through the initial stages of the path to perceiving the Creator.

Window to the Heart

It is clear that, since the creation of the world, humanity has suffered torment and pain in such magnitude, it has often been worse than death itself. Who, if not the Creator, is the Source of that suffering?

Throughout history, how many individuals have been willing to suffer and endure any pain in order to attain superior wisdom and to achieve spiritual elevation? How many of them voluntarily subjected themselves to unbearable agonies for the sake of finding at least a drop of spiritual perception and understanding of the Higher Force, and for the sake of uniting with the Creator to become His servant?

Yet they all lived out their lives without ever receiving a response, and without any visible achievements. They left this world with nothing, just as they had come into it.

Why did the Creator ignore their prayers? Why did He turn away from them and scorn their suffering? All of these human beings subconsciously realized that there is a higher purpose to the universe, and to every event that takes place. This realization is called the "drop of unification" of an individual with the Creator.

In fact, despite their immersion in egoism and their unbearable torment when they sensed the Creator's rejection, they suddenly felt a window opening in their hearts, which until then had been closed to the truth. Up until that moment, their hearts had been incapable of feeling anything but their own pain and desires.

This window revealed that they were deemed worthy to experience and feel that longed-for "drop of unification," penetrating each heart through its broken walls. Hence, all their qualities were altered to the opposite, to resemble the qualities of the Creator.

Only then did they realize that they could unite with the Creator only while in the depth of their suffering. Only then could they grasp Oneness with the Creator, since His Presence was there, as well as the "drop of unification" with Him. At the moment of experiencing this insight, the Light became evident to them and filled their wounds.

Precisely because of these wounds of perception and cognizance, and because of the terrible, soul-tormenting contradictions, the Creator Himself filled these people with such an unbounded, wonderful bliss that nothing more perfect could be imagined. All of this was given to make them feel there was some value to their suffering and agony. It was required in order for them to experience the Ultimate Perfection.

Once having achieved this state, every cell in their bodies convinced them that anyone in our world would be willing to go through unthinkable torment to experience, at least once in a lifetime, the bliss of being united with the Creator.

Why, then, is the Creator silent in response to human pleas for relief?

This can be explained as follows: people are much more concerned with their own progress than with glorifying the Creator. Thus, their tears are empty, and they leave this world just as they entered it, with nothing.

The final fate of every animal is eradication, and people who have not perceived the Creator are as animals. On the other hand, if one concerns oneself with glorifying the Creator, He will reveal Himself to that person.

The "drops of unification," which fulfill the purpose of creation, flow into the hearts of those who are concerned with the Creator's glory and love. They flow into those who, rather than complain about the unfairness of Divine Rule, are completely convinced in their hearts that all the Creator has done is ultimately for their own good.

The spiritual cannot be divided into separate parts; we can comprehend the whole only a part at a time, until we comprehend it all.

Therefore, the success of our spiritual endeavors depends on the purity of our yearning. The spiritual Light flows only into those parts of our hearts that have been cleansed of egoism.

When we look objectively at the nature of our existence and at all that surrounds us, we can more fully appreciate the wonder of creation. According to Kabbalists, who communicate directly with the Creator, His existence has important implications for us. If the Creator in fact exists, and if He generates all the circumstances that affect our lives, then there is nothing more logical than trying to maintain as close a contact with Him as possible.

However, if we tried hard and actually succeeded in doing so, we would feel as if we were suspended in air, without any support, since the Creator is concealed from our perception. Without seeing, feeling, hearing, or receiving some sensory input, we would be engaged in a one-way effort, screaming into empty space.

Then why did the Creator make us in such a way that we cannot perceive Him? Moreover, why should He hide from us? Why, even when we appeal to Him, does He appear not to respond, preferring instead to affect us in a way that is hidden from us, concealed behind nature and our environment?

If He desired to correct us, that is, to correct His own "error" in creation, He could have done so long ago, either directly or indirectly. If He revealed Himself to us, we would all see and appreciate Him to the degree allowed by our senses and the intelligence with which He created us. Surely then we would know what to do and how to act in this world, which was supposedly created for us.

Furthermore, paradoxically, as soon as we strive to reach the Creator, to perceive Him, to come closer to Him, we feel our yearning for the Creator vanish, disappear. But if the Creator directs all of our sensations, why then does He specifically dissolve this yearning in those who desire to perceive Him.

And not only that: Why does he put all possible manner of obstacles in our path? Those of us who attempt to come closer are often met with His rejection. Indeed, He may even inflict years of suffering on those who seek Him.

Occasionally, we might even feel that the pride and arrogance that we are told to rid ourselves of, is infinitely more characteristic of the Creator! After all, if the Creator is merciful, especially to those who seek Him, why don't we receive a response to our tears and appeals?

If we can alter something in our lives, it means that He has given us the free will to do it. But for reasons we do not understand, He did not endow us with sufficient knowledge to avoid the suffering that accompanies our existence and our spiritual development.

On the other hand, if there is no free will, then what can be more harsh than making us senselessly suffer for years in the cruel world that He created? Certainly, such grievances are infinite in number. And if the Creator is the cause of our condition, then we have much to criticize and blame Him for, which we do, when we experience pain and suffering.

The Creator sees all that goes on in our hearts.

When we are displeased with something, the feeling of dissatisfaction can be interpreted as blaming the Creator, even if the blame is not directly addressed to the Creator, or even when we do not believe in the existence of the Creator.

Each of us is correct in maintaining whatever our beliefs are in our present condition, regardless of what that belief is. This is because we maintain only what we feel to be true at that moment, as well as what we have analyzed with our own minds.

However, those of us with vast life experience know how drastically our views can change throughout the years. We cannot say that we were wrong before, but now we are right; we must realize that today's point of view may be proven wrong tomorrow. Therefore, the conclusions that we draw from any situation are correct for that particular situation; yet, they can be directly opposite to the conclusions we will draw in other situations.

By the same token, we cannot assess other worlds or their laws, or judge them based on our own current criteria—the criteria of our world. We do not possess supernatural intelligence or perception, and we err constantly even within the boundaries of our own world. Thus, we cannot draw conclusions about the unknown and pass judgment on it.

Only those of us who possess the requisite supernatural qualities can make correct judgments concerning what exists above and beyond the natural. Those who possess both supernatural qualities and our own qualities can more closely describe the supernatural to us. Such a person is known as a Kabbalist—a person of our world, created with the same qualities as each of us, but also endowed with other qualities from Above that permit this person to describe to us what goes on in the other worlds.

This is why the Creator has allowed certain Kabbalists to reveal their knowledge to vast numbers of people in society, in order to help others communicate with Him. In a language we can understand, Kabbalists explain that the structure and function of reason in the spiritual, heavenly worlds are based on laws that are different from—and opposite in nature to—our own laws.

Faith above Reason

There is no boundary separating our world from the heavenly, spiritual world. But because the spiritual world is, according to its properties, an "anti-world," it is placed so far beyond our perception that after we are born into this world, we completely forget all about our past condition.

Naturally, the only way for us to perceive this "anti-world" is by acquiring its essence, its reason, and its qualities. How must we alter our present nature in order to acquire a completely opposite one?

The basic law of the spiritual world is summarized in two words: "absolute altruism."

How can we acquire this quality? Kabbalists suggest that we undergo a transformation within ourselves. It is only through this inner act that we are able to perceive the spiritual world and start living in both worlds simultaneously.

Such a transformation is called "faith above reason." The spiritual world is an altruistic one. Every desire and action that exists in that realm is not dictated by human reason or egoism, but by faith; i.e., by a sense of the Creator.

If common sense is a vital tool for our actions, then it would seem that we are not able to completely free ourselves of intellect. However, given that our intellect does not reveal how we can escape from circumstances that the Creator places before us in a hidden fashion, it will not assist us in solving our problems.

Instead we will remain afloat without support and without logical answers to what is happening to us. In our world, we are guided only by our own reasoning. In everything we do, reason—meaning purely egoistic "reasonable" calculation—is the basis for all our desires and actions.

Our reason calculates the amount of pleasure we expect to experience, and matches it against the amount of pain required to exert ourselves to achieve that pleasure. We then subtract one from the other to assess the cost, and then decide whether we will strive toward pleasure or choose tranquility.

Such a "reasonable" approach to our surroundings is called "faith within reason." In this case, our reason determines how much faith we will expend.

Often we act without any calculation of benefit or cost of effort, as in cases of fanaticism or conditioned behavior. Such "blind" acts are called acts of "faith beneath reason," because they are determined by blindly following decisions made by someone else, rather than by reason or calculation.

Our actions can also be dictated by our upbringing, having become second nature to such an extent that we must make an effort not to act mechanically, through sheer force of habit.

In order to make the transition from following the laws of our world, to following the laws of the spiritual world, we must meet certain conditions. First, we must completely discard the arguments of reason, and forsake using our intellect to determine our actions. As if suspended in midair, we should attempt to hold on to the Creator with both hands, thus allowing the Creator, and only the Creator, to determine our actions.

Figuratively speaking, we should replace our own minds with the Creator's, and act contrary to our own reason. We must place the Creator's Will above our own. Once we are capable of doing this, our behavior will represent "faith above reason."

Having completed the first stage, we will be able to perceive both this world *and* the spiritual world. We will subsequently discover that both worlds function according to the same spiritual law of "faith above reason."

Our willingness to suppress our own reason and be guided only by the desire to give ourselves to the Creator forms the spiritual vessel in which we will receive all of our spiritual understanding. The capacity of that vessel; i.e. the capacity of our spiritual reason, is determined by how much earthly, selfish reasoning we are attempting to suppress.

In order to increase the capacity of our spiritual vessels, the Creator places increasingly greater obstacles in our spiritual path. This strengthens our egoistic desires, as well as our doubts regarding the Creator's Rule.

These, in turn, enable us to gradually overcome these obstacles, and to develop stronger altruistic desires. By doing so, we are provided the opportunity to increase the capacity of our spiritual vessels.

If we can mentally grip the Creator with both hands (that is, ignore the critical approach of human reason and rejoice in the fact that such an opportunity has presented itself), and if we can endure this condition for at least an instant, we will see how wonderful the spiritual state really is. This state can be reached only when we have attained the eternal Truth.

This Truth will not alter tomorrow, as was the case with all former beliefs, because now we are united with the Creator, and can view all events through the prism of the eternal

Truth. Progress is only possible along three simultaneous, parallel lines. The right line is faith; the left line is cognition and comprehension.

These two lines never diverge, for they are mutually opposed to each other.

Therefore, the only way to balance them is by means of a middle line, which consists of both the right and left lines at the same time. This middle line connotes spiritual behavior, where reason is used in accordance with one's degree of faith.

All spiritual objects are coiled around the Creator; they are layered onto Him in the order from which they emerged from Him. Everything in the universe that is layered around the Creator exists only relative to the creations, and all are products of the original created being, called "*Malchut*."

That is, all worlds and all created beings, except for the Creator, are a single *Malchut* entity, meaning the root or the original Source of all beings. *Malchut* eventually fragments into many small parts of itself. The total of the constituent parts of *Malchut* is known as "*Shechina*."

The Light of the Creator, His Presence, and the Divine filling of *Shechina* are all known as "*Shochen*." The time required for the complete filling of all parts of *Shechina* is called the "time of correction."

During this time, the created beings implement internal corrections on their respective parts of *Malchut*. Each being corrects the part from which it was created; meaning it corrects its own soul .

Until the moment the Creator can fully merge with His created beings by revealing Himself entirely to them, or "until the *Shochen* fills the *Shechina*," the condition of the *Shechina*, (the root of the souls) is known as "the exile of the *Shechina* from the Creator" (*Galut HaShechina*). In this condition, there is no perfection in the Higher Worlds Even in our world, the lowest of all, every being must also fully perceive the Creator. But most of the time we are occupied with satisfying our petty personal desires characteristic of this world, as well as blindly following the demands of the body.

There is a condition of the soul called "*Shechina* in the dust," when spiritually pure pleasures are considered to be superfluous and absurd. This state is also described as the "suffering of the *Shechina*."

All human suffering stems from the fact that we are compelled from Above to completely reject all common sense and proceed blindly, placing faith above reason.

Yet, the more reason and knowledge we possess, and the stronger and more intelligent we become, the harder it is for us to follow the path of faith.

Consequently, as we attempt to reject our common sense, we increase our suffering.

Those of us who have chosen the path of spiritual development described above cannot agree with the Creator. In our hearts, we condemn the need for such a way; thus, we have difficulty justifying the Creator's methods. Yet, we cannot sustain such a condition for a prolonged period of time unless the Creator decides to help us and reveals the whole picture of creation to us.

When we feel that we are in an elevated spiritual state, and that all of our desires are concentrated only on the Creator, we are ready to delve into the appropriate Kabbalah texts to try to penetrate their inner meaning. Although we might feel that we cannot understand anything, despite our efforts, we must continue to return to the study of Kabbalah again and again, and not despair if we fail to understand the subject.

How can we benefit from these efforts? In fact, our efforts to comprehend the mysteries of Kabbalah are equal to our prayers asking the Creator to reveal Himself to us. This yearning for a connection is strengthened when we seek to understand the concepts of Kabbalah.

The strength of our prayers is determined by the strength of our yearning. In general, when we invest effort into attaining something, our desire to attain it increases. The strength of our desire can be judged by how much suffering we feel from the absence of the desired object. Suffering, not expressed in words but felt only in the heart, is in itself a prayer.

Proceeding from the above, we can recognize that only after strenuous, yet unsuccessful, efforts to attain what we desire, can we pray so sincerely that we receive it. If, during our attempts to delve into the texts, our hearts are still not quite free from extrinsic thoughts, then our minds will not be able to devote themselves exclusively to study, since the mind obeys the heart.

In order for the Creator to accept our prayers, they should come from the depths of our hearts. That is, all our desires must be concentrated in that prayer. For this reason, we must delve into the text hundreds of times, even without understanding it, in order to achieve our true desire: to be heard by the Creator.

A true desire leaves no room for any other desires. While studying Kabbalah, we will examine the actions of the Creator and thus can progress toward Him. Gradually, then, we will become worthy of comprehending what we are studying.

Faith, or the awareness of the Creator, must be such that we feel that we are in the presence of the King of the Universe. Then, undoubtedly, we will become imbued with the necessary feelings of love and fear. Until we attain such faith, we must continuously strive for it. For it is only faith that will allow us to enjoy a spiritual life and prevent us from sinking to the depths of egoism, once again becoming pleasure seekers.

Our need to become aware of the Creator must be cultivated until it becomes permanently entrenched in our being. It must resemble a permanent attraction towards a loved one, without whom life seems unbearable.

Everything that surrounds human beings deliberately dulls the need for Divine Awareness, and sensing pleasure from anything external instantly reduces the pain of spiritual emptiness. Therefore, while enjoying the pleasures of this world, it is vital that we keep them from obliterating our need to perceive the Creator, as these pleasures rob us of spiritual sensations.

A desire to perceive the Creator is characteristic only of human beings. It is not true, however, of *all* human beings. This desire stems from our need to understand what we are, to comprehend ourselves, our purpose in the world, and our origins. It is the quest for answers about ourselves that leads us to seek the Source of life.

2

Spiritual Path

Our need to perceive the Divine makes us spare no effort in attempting to solve all of nature's mysteries, leaving no stone unturned either in ourselves or in our environment. But only the yearning to perceive the Creator is a true yearning, since He is the Source of everything and, above all, He is our Creator. Therefore, even if a human being existed alone in this world, or in other worlds, one's search for the self would inevitably lead to a search for the Creator.

There are two lines that reveal the Creator's influence on His creations. The right line represents His personal Providence over each of us, regardless of our actions. The left line represents the Providence over each of us, depending on our actions. It stands for punishment for evil deeds and reward for good ones.

When we choose a certain time to proceed along the right line, we must tell ourselves that everything in the world happens only because the Creator wants it to happen. Everything proceeds according to His Plan, and nothing depends on us.

From this point of view, we have neither faults nor merits. Our actions are determined by the aspirations that we receive from the outside.

We must therefore thank the Creator for all that we receive from Him. Moreover, realizing that the Creator leads us to eternity, we can develop feelings of love for Him. We can move forward with a proper combination of the right and left lines, aiming exactly at the middle. That is, we can advance only along the line that is exactly halfway between them.

Yet, even if we begin to advance from a correct starting point, if we don't know exactly how to continually check and correct our course, we are sure to deviate from the correct path. Furthermore, if we make even the slightest deviation at any point along the journey, then our error will increase with every step as we continue moving forward. Consequently, we will get farther and farther from our set goal.

Before our souls descend into this world, they are a part of the Creator, a tiny element of Him. This element is known as "the root of the soul." The Creator places the soul into the body so it can elevate the body's desires when the soul rises and merges with the Creator again.

In other words, the soul is placed into the body when a person is born into this world to overcome the desires of the body. By overcoming the desires of the body, the soul ascends to the same spiritual level it descended from, experiencing far greater pleasures than it had in its initial state when it was part of the Creator. At this point, a tiny element is transformed into a whole spiritual body, and is 620 times greater than was the original element before it descended into this world.

Thus, in its complete state, the spiritual body of the soul consists of 620 parts, or organs. Each part is considered to be a spiritual law or spiritual act (*mitzvah*). The Light of the Creator or the Creator Himself (which are the same) that fills every part of the soul is called "Torah."

When we ascend to a new spiritual level, it is called "fulfilling a spiritual law."

As a result of this elevation, new altruistic aspirations are created and the soul receives the *Torah*, the Light of the Creator.

The true path to this goal proceeds along the middle line. This implies combining three concepts into one: the human being, the path to follow, and the Creator. Indeed, three objects exist in the world : the human being, who is striving to return to the Creator, the path one needs to follow in order to reach the Creator, and the Creator, the goal toward which the human being is striving.

As has been said many times, there is nothing that truly exists except the Creator, and we are but His creations, endowed with a sense of our own existence. We come to recognize this clearly in the course of our spiritual ascent.

All of our perceptions, or rather, the perceptions we see as our own, are but responses to the Divine Acts He has produced in us. In the end, our feelings are only what He wants us to feel.

As long as we have not yet fully comprehended this truth, we will see not one, but three separate concepts: the self, the path to the Creator, and the Creator Himself. However, once we have reached the final stage of spiritual development, once we have ascended to the same level from which our souls descended—only this time with all our desires corrected—we can receive the Creator completely into our spiritual body.

Then, we will receive all the Light of the Creator and the Creator Himself. In this manner, the three objects that once existed separately in our perception: ourselves, our spiritual path, and the Creator merge to become a single entity—the spiritual body filled with Light.

Therefore, to ensure that we proceed correctly, we must conduct regular checks while advancing on the spiritual path. This will ensure that we strive for all three objects with an equally powerful desire from the very outset, regardless of the fact that we perceive the three objects to be separate.

From the outset, we must work to blend them into one; at the end of the path, this will be apparent. They are, in fact, apparent now, even though we are unable to see them as such, due to our own imperfections.

If we strive for one of the three objects more than for the others, we will immediately deviate from the true path. The simplest way to check whether we are still on the true path is to determine whether we are striving to comprehend the characteristics of the Creator in order to become one with Him.

"If I am not for me, then who is for me? And if I am only concerned with myself, then what am I?" These contradictory statements reflect the conflicting attitudes we face when considering our efforts to attain a set personal goal. On the one hand, we must believe that there is no one to turn to for help but ourselves, and act with the certainty that our good deeds will be rewarded and our evil deeds will be punished.

We, as individuals, must believe that our own actions have direct consequences, and that we build our own futures. On the other hand, we must say to ourselves, "Who am I, to be able to defeat my own nature by myself? Yet, no one else can help me, either."

Providence of the Creator

If everything happens according to the Creator's Plan, then what good are our efforts? As a result of our own work, based on the principle of reward and punishment, we acquire from Above an understanding of the Creator's Rule. We then rise to a level of consciousness where we clearly see that it is the Creator who rules everything and that everything is predetermined.

First, however, we must reach this stage, and until we do, we cannot determine that everything is in the hands of the Creator. Also, until we reach that stage, we cannot live or act according to its laws, for this is not how we understand the world to operate. Therefore, we can act only according to the laws of which we are aware.

Only when we have put forth efforts based on the principle of "reward and punishment" do we become worthy of the Creator's complete trust. Only then do we have the right to see the true picture of the world, as well as the way it operates. And when we arrive at this stage, and realize that everything depends on the Creator, we long for Him.

One cannot oust selfish thoughts and desires from one's heart and leave it empty. Only by filling the heart with spiritual, altruistic desires instead of selfish ones can we replace the old aspirations with opposite ones, and in this way obliterate egoism.

Those of us who love the Creator are sure to feel revulsion toward egoism, since we know from personal experience how much harm the ego can cause.

However, we may not have the means to rid ourselves of the ego, and will eventually realize that it is beyond our power to oust egoism, since it was the Creator who had endowed us, His creations, with this quality.

Although we cannot rid ourselves of egoism by our own efforts, the sooner we realize that egoism is our enemy and our spiritual exterminator, the stronger will be our hatred of it. Eventually, this hatred will bring the Creator to help us overcome the enemy; in this way, even our egoism will serve the purpose of spiritual elevation.

The Talmud says, "I created the world only for the completely righteous and for the complete sinners." It is understandable why the world would be created for the absolutely righteous, but why wasn't the world also created for those who are neither absolutely righteous nor absolute sinners?

We inadvertently perceive Providence according to the way it affects us. It is "good" and "kind" if it is agreeable to us, and "harsh" if it causes us suffering. That is, we consider the Creator either good or bad, depending on how we perceive our world.

Thus, there are only two ways for human beings to perceive the Providence of the Creator over the world. Either we perceive the Creator and see life as wonderful, or we deny the Creator's Providence over the world, and assume the world is ruled by "forces of nature."

Though we may realize that the latter scenario is unlikely, our emotions, rather than our reason, determine our attitude toward the world. Hence, when we observe the disparity between our emotions and our reason, we begin to consider ourselves as sinners.

When we understand that the Creator wants to bestow only benefit and good, we realize this is possible only by drawing closer to Him. Thus, if we feel distanced from the Creator, we perceive this as "bad," and then we consider ourselves to be sinners.

But if we feel ourselves to be so evil that we cry out to the Creator to save us, asking the Creator to reveal Himself to give us the power to break out from the prison of our egoism into the spiritual world, then the Creator will help us instantly.

It is for this form of human condition that this world and the Higher Worlds were created.

When we reach the level of absolute sinner, we can cry out to the Creator and eventually rise to the level of the absolutely righteous.

Thus, we can only become worthy of perceiving the Creator's greatness after we have rid ourselves of all conceit and realized the impotence and the baseness of our personal desires.

The more importance we ascribe to becoming close to the Creator, the more we perceive Him and the better we can discern the Creator's various nuances and manifestations in our daily lives. This deep, impressive awe of Him will give rise to feelings in our hearts, and as a result joy will flow in.

We can see that we are no better than those around us, and yet we can also see that, unlike us, others have not earned the Creator's special attention. Moreover, others are not even aware that the possibility of communicating with the Creator exists. Nor do they really care to perceive the Creator and understand the meaning of life and spiritual progress.

On the other hand, we are not clear how we merited such a special relationship with the Creator, in that we are granted, if only just occasionally, the opportunity to concern ourselves with the purpose of life and our bond with the Creator.

If, at that point, we can appreciate the uniqueness of the Creator's attitude toward us, then we can experience boundless gratitude and joy. The more we can appreciate individual success, the more deeply we can thank the Creator.

The more nuance of feeling we can experience at each particular point and instant of contact with the Creator, the better we can appreciate the greatness of the spiritual world that is revealed to us, as well as the greatness and might of the omnipotent Creator. This results in stronger confidence with which we can anticipate our future unification with Him.

When contemplating the vast difference between the characteristics of the Creator and those of His created beings, it is easy to arrive at the conclusion that the Creator and created can only become compatible if the created beings alter their absolutely egoistic nature. This is only possible if the created nullify themselves as if they do not exist; thus, there is nothing to separate them from their Creator.

Only if we feel that, without receiving a spiritual life, we are dead (as when life has left the body), and only if we feel a compelling desire for a spiritual life, can we receive the possibility of entering this spiritual life, to breathe spiritual air.

Realizing the Creator's Rule

How can we rise to a spiritual level where we have completely eradicated self-interest and self-concern? How can our desire to devote ourselves to the Creator become our only goal, so much so that without attaining this goal, we feel as if we were dead?

Rising to this level takes place gradually and is processed in the form of feedback. The more effort we make in our quest for a spiritual path, both in studying and in emulating spiritual objects, the more convinced we will become of our utter inability to achieve this goal by ourselves. The more we study texts that are important for our spiritual development, the more confusing and disorganized the material will appear. The better we try to treat our instructors and peers, if we are indeed advancing spiritually, the clearer it will become that all our actions are dictated by egoism.

Such results follow the principle: *Force him until he says, "I do."* We can rid ourselves of egoism only if we grasp that egoism causes death by holding us back from realizing true, eternal life, filled with delight.

Developing a hatred toward egoism will eventually lead to our liberation from it.

Most important is our desire to give ourselves fully to the Creator by realizing His greatness. (Giving oneself to the Creator means to separate from the "I").

At this point, we must decide which is a more worthy goal: to attain transient values or eternal ones. Nothing that we have created remains forever; all is transient. Only spiritual structures such as altruistic thoughts, acts, and feelings are eternal.

Therefore, by striving to emulate the Creator in our thoughts, desires and efforts, we are, in fact, building the structure of our own eternity. However, dedicating ourselves to the Creator is only possible when we realize the Creator's greatness.

It is the same in our world: If we consider someone great, we are happy to be of service to that person. We may even feel that the recipient of our gift has done us a favor by accepting it, rather than the other way around.

This example shows that the *intention* of an action can change the external form of a mechanical act—giving or taking—to its opposite. Therefore, the more praiseworthy we regard the Creator, the more readily will we give Him all of our thoughts, desires and efforts.

But in doing so, we actually feel that we are receiving from, rather than giving to, Him. We feel that we are being given an opportunity to render a service, an opportunity that is only bestowed upon a few worthy ones in each generation. This can further be clarified by the example provided in the following short play.

3

The Dining Table

Act One

In a brightly lit house with spacious rooms, a pleasant-looking man is busy in the kitchen. He is preparing a meal for his long-awaited guest. While hovering over the pots and pans, he reminds himself of the delicacies his guest so enjoys.

The host's joyous anticipation is very evident. Gracefully, with the moves of a dancer, he fills the table with five different courses. Next to the table are two cushioned chairs.

There is a knock on the door, and the guest enters. The host's face brightens at the sight of the guest and he invites him to sit at the dining table. The guest sits down and the host looks at him fondly.

The guest regards the delicacies in front of him and sniffs them from a courteous distance. It is apparent that he likes what he sees, but he expresses his admiration with tactful restraint, not revealing that he knows the food is meant for him.

Host: Do sit down. I've made these things especially for you because I know how much you like them. We both know how familiar I am with your tastes and dining habits. I know you're hungry and I know how much you can eat, so I've prepared everything exactly the way you like it, in the exact amount that you can finish without leaving a crumb.

Narrator: If there were any food left when the guest was satiated, both Host and Guest would be unhappy. The host would be unhappy because that would mean he wants to give his guest more than his guest wants to receive.

The guest would be disappointed at not being able to fulfill the host's wish that he would consume it all. The guest would also regret if he were full while there were still more delicacies left over, and was unable to enjoy any more of them. It would mean that the guest lacked enough desire for all the pleasure being offered.

Guest (solemnly): Indeed, you have prepared exactly what I'd like to see and eat at my dinner table. Even the amount is just right. This is all I could ever want out of life: to enjoy all this. For me, it would be the ultimate divine pleasure.

Host: Please, have it all and enjoy it. It will delight me.
The guest begins to eat.

Guest (obviously enjoying and with his mouth full, yet looking somewhat troubled): Why is it that the more I eat, the less I enjoy the food?

The pleasure I receive extinguishes the hunger and I enjoy it less and less. The nearer I get to feeling full, the less I enjoy my meal.

And when I've received all the food, I'm left with nothing but the memory of the pleasure, not the pleasure itself. The pleasure was there only while I was hungry. When the hunger faded away, so did the joy. I received what I longed for, and here I am left with neither pleasure nor joy. I don't want anything any more, and I have nothing to bring me joy.

Host (a little resentful): I've done all I could to please you. It isn't my fault that the very receiving of pleasure extinguishes the sensation of delight because the yearning is gone. In any case, you're now full of what I have prepared for you.

Guest (defending himself): By receiving all that you've prepared for me, I can't even thank you because I've stopped enjoying the abundance you've given me. The main thing I feel is that *you* have given me a great deal, while *I* have given you nothing in return. As a result, you've caused me to feel shame by thoughtlessly showing that you are the giver and I am the taker.

Host: I didn't show you that you're the taker and I'm the giver. But the very fact that you've received something from me without returning anything made you feel guilty, despite the fact that kindness is my nature.

I want nothing more than to have you accept my food. I can't change that. For example: I raise fish. They don't care who feeds and nourishes them. I also tend to Bob, my cat. He, too, couldn't care less whose hand fed him. But Rex, my dog, *does* care. He will not take food from just anyone.

Narrator: People are built in such a way that there are some who receive without sensing that someone is giving to them, and they just take. Some even steal with no remorse! But when people develop a sense of self, they know when they are being given to, and it awakens their awareness that they are the takers. That brings with it shame, self-reproach and agony.

Guest (somewhat appeased): But what can I do to receive pleasure on the one hand, without perceiving myself as the taker? How can I neutralize the feeling within me that you are the giver and I'm the taker? If there's a give-and-take situation, and it brings up this shame in me, what can I do to avoid it?

Perhaps you can act in such a way that I will not feel like the receiver! But that's possible only if I'm unaware of your existence (just like your fish) or if I sensed you, but did not understand that you were giving to me (like a cat or an underdeveloped human).

Host (narrowing his eyes in concentration and speaking thoughtfully): I think there's a solution after all. Perhaps you'll be able to find a way to neutralize the sensation of reception within you?

Guest (his eyes light up): Oh, I've got it! You've always wanted to have me as your guest. So tomorrow, I will come here and behave in such a way that will make *you* feel like the receiver. I will still be the receiver, of course, eating all that you've prepared, but I will regard myself as the giver.

Act Two

The next day, in the same room, the host has prepared a fresh meal with exactly the same delicacies as the day before. He sits at the table and the guest enters, wearing an unfamiliar, somewhat secretive expression on his face.

Host   (smiling brightly, unaware of the change): I've been waiting for you. I'm so happy to see you. Do sit down.

The guest sits at the table and politely smells the food.

Guest (looking at the food): All this is for me?

Host: But of course! Only for you! I would be delighted if you were willing to receive all that from me.

Guest: Thanks, but I don't really want it all that much.

Host: Well, that's not true! You do want it and I know that for a fact! Why won't you have it?

Guest: I can't take all this from you. It makes me feel uneasy.

Host: What do you mean, uneasy? I want so much for you to have all this! Who do you think I've prepared this for? It would give me so much pleasure if you were to eat it all.

Guest: Perhaps you're right, but I don't want to eat all this food.

Host: But you're not just receiving a meal; you're also doing me a favor by sitting at my table enjoying what I have prepared. I've prepared all of it not for you, but because I enjoy your receiving it from me.
That's why your consent to eat would be doing me a favor. You'd be receiving all that *for me*! You wouldn't be taking, but rather, *giving* me great joy. In fact, it would not be you who would receive from my meal, but rather I who would be getting great joy from you. You'd be the one giving to me, and not the other way around.

The Host imploringly slides the fragrant plate in front of his reluctant guest. The Guest pushes it away. The Host again slides it near his Guest, and again he's turned down. The Host sighs, his whole appearance revealing how much he wants his Guest to accept the food. The Guest now takes the attitude of the giver who's doing the Host a favor.

Host: I implore you! Please, make me happy.

The guest starts to eat, then pauses to think. Then he starts again, and again he pauses. Each time the guest pauses, the host encourages him to continue. Only after some persuasion does the guest continue.
The host keeps placing new delicacies in front of his guest, each time begging him to please him by accepting them.

Guest: If I can be sure that I'm eating because it gives you pleasure, and not because *I* want it, then you've become the receiver and I've become the giver of pleasure. But for that to be so, I must be sure that I'm eating for your sake alone, and not for mine.

Host: But of course you're eating only for me. After all, you sat at the table and wouldn't taste a thing until I proved to you that you're not just eating, but rather rendering me great joy. You've come here to give me pleasure.

Guest: But if I were to accept something I did not initially desire, I would not enjoy receiving it, and you would not enjoy watching me willingly accept your offering. So it turns out that you can receive pleasure only to the extent that I enjoy your offering.

Host: I know exactly how much you like this food and how much of each dish you can eat. Therefore, I've prepared these five courses. After all, I know your desire for this and that dish and not for any other thing in your life.
Knowing how much you enjoy them evokes the

sensation of your pleasure in me. It also pleases me that you enjoy my dishes. I have no doubt that the pleasure I receive from you is genuine.

Guest: How can I be sure that I am enjoying these dishes only because you want me to, and because you've prepared all this for me? How can I be sure that I shouldn't turn you down because by receiving from you I will actually be giving you joy?

Host: Quite simple! Because you totally refused my offers until you were sure that you were doing it for my pleasure. Then you accepted. After each bite you take, you will feel you're eating for my pleasure, and you will sense the joy you bring to me.

Guest: I can get rid of the shame and take pride in giving you pleasure if I think, each time I receive, that I'm receiving it for you. .

Host: So eat it all! You want it all, and thus you'll be giving me every bit of pleasure you can!

Guest (eating with pleasure and finishing every last dish, but afterwards, realizing he is still not satisfied): So now I've eaten it all and enjoyed it. There is no more food to enjoy. My pleasure has gone because I'm not hungry anymore. I can't bring any of us any joy right now. So what do I do next?

Host: I don't know. You've given me great pleasure by receiving from me. What else can I do for you, so that you'll enjoy again and again? How can you want to eat again, if you've eaten it all? Where will you get a new appetite?

Guest: True, my desire to enjoy has turned into a desire to bestow joy upon you, and if now I can't enjoy, how can I bring you pleasure? After all, I can't create within me an appetite for another five-course meal!

Host: I have not prepared any more than you desired. I've done everything I can to please you. Your problem is: "How can I not stop wanting more, while I receive more and more."

Guest: But if the pleasure doesn't satisfy my hunger, I can't feel it as pleasure. The sensation of pleasure comes when I satisfy my needs. If I weren't hungry, I couldn't enjoy the food and hence could not have bestowed joy upon you. What can I do to remain in constant want, and constantly render you joy by showing you my pleasure?

Host: For that, you need a different source of want and a different means of satisfaction. By using your hunger to receive both food and the joy from eating it, you extinguish them both.

Guest: I've got it! The problem is that I prevented myself from feeling joy if I felt you would benefit from it. I refused to such an extent that, although the whole meal was set before me, I couldn't accept it because of my shame in receiving it. That shame was so intense that I was willing to starve, if only to avoid feeling the shame of being the recipient.

Host: But then, once you were convinced that you weren't receiving for yourself, you began to receive for my sake. Because of that, you enjoyed both the food and the pleasure you were giving me. That's why eating the food should be in accordance with your will. After all, without pleasure from the food, what pleasure could you render me?

Guest: But it's not enough to receive for you, knowing that you enjoy doing this for me. If my pleasure comes from your joy, then the source of my pleasure is not the food, but you! I have to feel *your* joy.

Host: That should be easy, since I'm totally open about it.

Guest: Yes, but what does my pleasure depend on? It depends on you, the one I'm giving pleasure to. That means that my pleasure depends on how strongly I wish to bestow joy upon you; that is, to the extent that I sense your greatness.

Host: So what can I do?

Guest: If I knew more of you, if I had a more intimate knowledge of you, if you really were great, then your greatness and almightiness would have been revealed to me. Then I would have enjoyed both giving you pleasure, being aware of who was receiving it. Then, my pleasure would have been proportional to the disclosing of your greatness.

Host: Is it up to me?

Guest: Look, if I give, it's important for me to know how much I am giving and to whom. If it is to beloved ones, such as my children, then I am willing to give to the extent of my love for them. This gives me joy. But if someone off the street comes to my house, I will give that person something because I can empathize with being in need, and hope that when I'm in dire need, someone will help me.

Host: This principle is what lies beneath the whole concept of social welfare. People realized that if there were no mutual assistance, they would all suffer. That is, they would themselves suffer when they became the needy ones. Egoism forces people to give, but it is not true giving. It is simply a way of assuring one's survival.

Guest: I really don't think this kind of giving is genuine. All our "generosity" is nothing more than a way for us to receive pleasure by satisfying ourselves and those we love.

Host: So how can I give you pleasure that goes beyond the pleasure found in your food?

Guest: That is not up to you, but to me. If the person coming to my house were not a common person, but a very important personality, I would receive greater pleasure in giving to that person than to an ordinary person. That means that my pleasure depends not on the food, but on who prepared it!

Host: So what can I do to make you respect me more?

Guest: Because I receive for your benefit, not mine, the more respect I have for you, the more pleasure I will get knowing to whom I'm giving it.

Host: So how can I deepen your esteem of me?

Guest: Tell me about yourself, show me who you are! Then I could get pleasure not merely from receiving the food, but also from knowing who is giving it to me, knowing with whom I have a relationship. The smallest portion of food I receive from a great figure will give me a much greater amount of pleasure. You see, the pleasure will grow in proportion to how great I consider you to be.

Host: That means that for the pleasure to become great, I must open myself up and you must develop a likeness of me in you.

Guest: Exactly! That is what creates a new hunger in me—the desire to give to you grows in proportion to your greatness. It is not because I want to escape the sensation of shame, because the shame won't let me satisfy my hunger

Host: That way you begin to sense not the hunger, but my greatness and your desire to render me pleasure. So are you saying that you wish not to fulfill my appetite, but to bask in my greatness and your desire to please me?

Guest: And what's wrong with that? I can receive pleasure from the food many times more than the food itself can actually give, because I add to the hunger a second desire: a will to bestow upon you.

Host: That, too, I must fulfill.

Guest: No. The will to do this—and its fulfillment—I will create in myself. For that I need only to know you. Reveal yourself to me and I will create within me a craving to bestow upon you. I will also receive pleasure from the giving, and not from the elimination of shame.

Host: What will you gain from knowing me, aside from the fact that your pleasure will increase?

Guest (clearly hinting that that's the point of it all): There's another major benefit. If I create in me a new will, apart from the inherent hunger, I can become the master of that will. I can always increase it, always fill it with pleasure, and always bestow it upon you by receiving pleasure.

Host: Won't you lose that will when it is filled, just as you lost your hunger?

Guest: No, because I can always create within me a greater impression of you. I can always create new desires to bestow upon you, and by receiving from you I will carry out these desires. That process can go on indefinitely.

Host: What does it depend on?

Guest: It depends on constantly discovering new virtues in you and sensing your greatness.

Host: That means that, for constant self-indulgence—that even when receiving selfish pleasure the hunger will not cease but rather increase by that reception—a creation of a new hunger must be formed: the will to feel the giver.

Guest: Yes, in addition to receiving pleasure (the delicacies), the receiver will develop a sense of the giver's greatness. The discovery of the host and the delicacies therefore becomes the same. In other words, the pleasure itself creates an awareness of the giver. The giver, the food and the attributes of the giver are one and the same.

Host: It turns out that what you initially wanted, subconsciously, was for the giver to be revealed. For you this is, in fact, a filling up and nothing else.

Guest: In the beginning I didn't even understand that this was what I wanted. I only saw the food and thought that that was what I wanted.

Host: I did it on purpose, so that gradually you would develop your own independent will that you would supposedly create yourself, so that you would fill it by yourself. You would be taking the place of both guest and host simultaneously.

Guest: Why is it all built like that?

Host: For the purpose of bringing you to completeness. So that you will want each thing in totality and will attain maximum fulfillment. So that you can enjoy each desire to the fullest and so that the pleasure would be unbounded.

Guest: So why didn't I know about it to begin with? All I saw around me were objects I desired, without suspecting that what I really wanted all that time was you.

Host: It's specifically done so that while you might be in a situation in which you weren't feeling me. You would come to me by yourself and would create that inner will on your own.

Guest (bewildered): But if I can create that will within me, where are you in the picture?

Host: It is I who created the simple egotistical will in you to begin with, and I continue to develop it by constantly surrounding you with new objects of delight.

Guest: But what is it all for?

Host: For the purpose of convincing you that chasing pleasure will never satisfy you completely.

Guest: I can see that: The minute I get what I want, the pleasure is instantly gone, and again I long for something, either bigger or altogether different.

Thus, I'm on a constant pleasure hunt, but never quite attain it; the minute I get my hands on it, it slips away.

Host: And that is precisely why you should develop your sense of self and become aware of the futility of this type of existence.

Guest: But if you were to develop in me the picture of how things really are, I would understand the meaning and purpose of all that was taking place!

Host: That picture will be revealed only after you are totally convinced of the purposelessness of your egoistical existence, and become aware that a new form of conduct is required. You need to know your roots and the meaning of your life.

Guest: But that process lasts thousands of years. When does it end?

Host: Nothing is created needlessly. All that exists is there for the sole purpose of revealing to creations a different form of existence. That process is slow because every little desire needs to appear and be recognized as unworthy of use in its preliminary form.

Guest: And are there many such desires?

Host: A great many, and in direct proportion to the pleasure you will receive in the future. But the pleasure from receiving the food doesn't change. You can't eat more than one lunch a day. The capacity of your stomach will not change. Therefore, the amount that comes from me and is received by you doesn't change.

But when you dine at my table in order to please *me*, that very thought creates in you a new will to eat and a new pleasure, apart from the pleasure for the food. That pleasure is measured in size and power, or in quantity and quality, according to the amount of pleasure you get from dining at my table in order to please me.

Guest: So how do I increase my desire to receive pleasure for your sake?

Host: That depends on your appreciation of, and respect for me. It depends on how great you consider me to be.

Guest: So how can I increase my appreciation of you?

Host: For that you simply need to know more about me—to see me in every action that I make, to observe and be convinced of how great I really am, and to be convinced that I am almighty, merciful and kind.

Guest: Then show yourself!

Host: If your request stems from a desire to bestow upon me, I will reveal myself. But if it stems from a desire to please yourself by seeing me, I will not only refrain from disclosing myself to you, but I will hide myself ever deeper.

Guest: Why? Is it not the same for you whichever way I receive from you? After all, you want me to enjoy. Why hide from me?

Host: If I disclose myself entirely, you will receive so much pleasure from the eternity, almightiness and wholeness of me, that you will not be able to accept that pleasure for my sake. That thought will not even cross your mind and you will later feel ashamed again. Besides, because the pleasure will be perpetual, it will, as we've seen before, eliminate your want, and again you'll be left drained of will.

Guest (finally realizing): So that's the reason that you hide from me, in order to help me! And I thought that it was because you didn't want me to know you.

Host: My greatest wish is that you'll see me and be near me. But what can I do if then you'll not be able to sense pleasure? Wouldn't that be the same as dying?

Guest: But if I am unaware of you, then how can I make any progress? It all depends on how much you show yourself to me.

Host: Indeed, only the feeling of my presence creates in you the ability to grow and to receive. Without that sense, you just swallow everything up and immediately stop sensing any pleasure. That's why, when I appear before you, you feel shame, the sensation of one who gives, and a will to receive the same attributes as the giver.

Guest: So reveal yourself to me as soon as possible.

Host: I will, but only to the extent that you will benefit from it, although I'd always like to show myself to you. After all, I hid myself on purpose to create conditions of free choice for you. In this way, you can be free to act and choose how to think independently of my presence. There will be no pressure on the part of the host.

Guest: So how do you reveal yourself to me?

Host: I do it slowly and gradually. Each degree of disclosure is called a "World," from the most hidden degree to the most exposed.

The End.

From here it follows that our main objective is to elevate the importance of the Creator in our own eyes, i.e., to acquire faith in His greatness and might. We must do this because this is our only possible means of escaping from the prison of personal egoism and entering into the Higher Worlds.

As mentioned earlier, we can experience extreme difficulty when we decide to follow the path of faith and to abandon all concern for the self. We then feel isolated from the whole world, suspended in nothingness, without the support of common sense, reason or prior experience to support us.

It is also as if we have abandoned our own environment, family, and friends for the sake of being united with the Creator. These sensations arise when we lack faith in the Creator, when we cannot sense Him, or His Presence, or His Rule over all creation. At these times, we can feel an absence of the object of faith.

However, once we begin to sense the Creator's Presence, we are ready to submit fully to His power and to follow the Creator blindly, always prepared to nullify ourselves completely to Him, disparaging our own intellect almost instinctively. For this reason, the most important problem confronting us is how to perceive the Presence of the Creator.

Therefore, whenever such doubts arise, it is worthwhile to dedicate all our energy and thoughts for the sake of the Creator. We must immediately aspire to cling to the Creator with every fiber of our being. This feeling about the Creator is called "faith."

The process can be accelerated if we make this an important objective. The more important it is to us, the faster we can achieve faith; i.e., our awareness of the Creator.

Furthermore, the more importance we assign to perceiving the Creator, the stronger the perception will be, until it becomes part of our being. Luck (*mazal* in Hebrew) is a special manner of Providence that we cannot influence in any way. But it is dictated from Above that we, as individuals, are responsible for trying to change our own nature . Afterwards, the Creator will evaluate our efforts in this direction, and eventually He will alter our nature, as well as elevate us above our world.

Therefore, before we make any efforts, we should realize that we cannot expect the Upper Forces, luck, or some other special treatment from Above to intervene on our behalf. Rather, we must begin by fully recognizing that if we ourselves do not take action, we will not arrive at what we desire.

However, once we complete a task, or engage in study, or exert any other effort, we should reach the following conclusion:

Everything that we have achieved as a result of our efforts would have come about anyway, even without exerting any effort, since the result has been predetermined by the Creator.

Thus, if we yearn to comprehend true Providence, we must early on try in every undertaking to assimilate these contradictions in ourselves.

For instance, in the morning we should start our daily routine of study and work, leaving behind all thoughts of the Creator's Divine Rule over the world and over its inhabitants. Each of us must work as if the final result depended only on us.

But at the end of the day, under no circumstances should we allow ourselves to imagine that what we have achieved is the result of our own efforts. We must realize that even if we stayed in bed all day, we would still arrive at the same result, because that result has been predetermined by the Creator.

Therefore, one who wishes to live a life of truth must, on the one hand, obey the laws of society and of nature just like everyone else, but on the other hand, must also believe in the Creator's absolute rule over the world.

All of our deeds can be divided into good, neutral or evil. Our task is to elevate our neutral deeds to the level of good ones.

We can accomplish this by being aware that, even as we are performing the deeds, ultimately, the Will of the Creator shall rule. For example, when we are ill, while we are aware that a cure is completely in the hands of the Creator, we should take the medication prescribed by an established physician and believe that the doctor's skill will help us overcome our condition. But when, after taking the medicine in strict accordance with the doctor's orders, we recover, we must believe that we would have recovered anyway because it was in the Creator's Plan.

Therefore, instead of thanking the doctor, we must thank the Creator. In this way, we are converting a neutral act into a spiritual one, and by repeating this procedure in regard to all our neutral acts, we can gradually "spiritualize" all of our thoughts.

The examples and explanations given above are important because they may actually become serious stumbling blocks that can impede our spiritual elevation. The problem sometimes escalates because we think we understand the principles of Divine Rule. We will concentrate our energies, artificially, on strengthening our belief in the Omnipresence of the Creator, instead of working hard on ourselves.

Often, in order to demonstrate our faith in the Creator, or simply out of laziness, we assume that we need not work on ourselves, since all is in the Creator's power. Or, we may close our eyes and rely on blind faith alone, at the same time eluding vital questions about real faith.

However, by avoiding answering these questions, we rob ourselves of the possibility of spiritual progress. It is said of our world, "Thou shall earn thy bread by the sweat of thy brow." Yet, once we have earned something, it is hard for us to admit that the outcome did not result from our hard work or abilities, but was instead the work of the Creator.

We must strive by the sweat of our brow to strengthen our faith in the Creator's absolute rule.

But in order to grow and experience new spiritual sensations, we must make an effort to understand and accept the contradictory nature of Divine Rule (which only appears contradictory due to our blindness).

Only then will we know exactly what is required of us and can grow to experience new spiritual sensations.

4

Nullifying Our Personal Interests

Prior to creation, the Creator alone existed. The process of creation begins when the Creator singles out a certain part of Himself in order to endow it, in the future, with certain different characteristics. By endowing this part with a sense of its own self, the Creator essentially "ejects" it from Himself.

This endowed part constitutes our "I." The distance of the endowed part from the Creator is the disparity in characteristics between the Creator and this part; it is perceived as "concealment of the Creator." Since this part cannot sense the Creator, there is a void between it and Him, generated by the part's egoistic characteristics.

If the Creator wants to bring the separated part closer to Himself, then the dark void between the Creator and the part will bestow a sense of hopelessness on the part. If, on the other hand, the Creator does not want to draw the part closer to Himself, then the void is not felt at all. It is merely the distance between the part and the Creator that is not perceived. The Creator Himself is not sensed by the part, which, at most, can only imagine how it feels to perceive Him.

The dark void, which is perceived by the part, is experienced as our normal suffering, caused either by materialistic difficulties, or ailments, or family troubles.

However, just as the Creator built the surrounding environment of the part, He is also able to influence it.

How and for what purpose does He do this? To show us that, to save ourselves from suffering, we must rid ourselves of all egoism, the Creator brings us to a state of such unbearable misery through our environment, children, work, debts, illnesses, or family troubles, that life seems to become a burden beyond all endurance.

We perceive that this miserable condition comes about as a result of our ambitions and our attempts to attain things. Then, a singular desire awakens in us—the desire not to want anything. In other words, we no longer have any personal interests, since they bring us only suffering.

Consequently, we have no other choice but to beg the Creator to save us from egoism. This forces us to strive to overcome all of our problems, which brings us further suffering.

For this reason, Rabbi Ashlag writes in his "Introduction to Talmud Esser Sefirot" (Paragraph 2), "But if you listen with your heart to one very famous question, I am sure that all your doubts as to whether you should study Kabbalah will vanish without a trace."

This is so because this question, coming straight from one's heart rather than from one's intelligence or knowledge, is a question about many things: the meaning of our lives; the meaning of our suffering (which is many times greater than our pleasure); the difficulties of life, which often make death seem an easy deliverance. And finally, the fact that there is no end to the whirlpool of pain until we depart from this life, worn out and devastated.

Who benefits from this, or more precisely, whom do we benefit? What else should we expect from this life? Although each of us is subconsciously bothered by this question of the meaning of our lives, sometimes it hits us unexpectedly, driving us insane, rendering us incapable of doing anything, shattering our minds, plunging us into a dark chasm of hopelessness and reflecting back to us our own insignificance.

In response, we choose to go on drifting with the stream of life, without pondering the question too deeply. This is a question no one even wants to think about. Nonetheless, the question remains before us with all its strength and bitterness.

Occasionally, we blunder into it, and it pierces our minds and knocks us flat. We continue to trick ourselves by drifting unthinkingly through the stream of life, as before. But the Creator imparts such sensations to us so we will gradually realize that all our misfortunes, and all our anguish, arise from the fact that we have a personal, vested interest in the outcome of our actions.

It is our egoism, our nature and essence, that makes us act for the sake of "our own good." And, since our desires are never fulfilled, we will continue to suffer.

However, if we were to nullify all our personal interests in everything, we would immediately break the chains of our bodies and would experience our world free of pain and distress.

The method to break free from the slavery of egoism can be found in Kabbalah.

The Creator purposely placed our world, with all its misery, between Himself and us. He did this to help us realize that we must get rid of egoism, since it is the cause of all our suffering. To remove suffering and to sense the Creator, the Source of all pleasure, is only possible if we sincerely desire to rid ourselves of all egoism.

In the spiritual worlds, desires are tantamount to actions, since genuine and sincere desires immediately lead to performing them. In general, the Creator brings us to a firm and final resolution to rid ourselves of all personal interests in any situation in life.

He does this by making us suffer so greatly, we will have only one desire—to stop the suffering. This is possible only if we have absolutely no personal or selfish interest in the outcome of any daily matters that arise in our lives.

But where, then, is our free will? Where is the freedom of choice to decide which road to take, or what to choose in life? The Creator pushes us to choose a certain solution by placing us amidst such misery that death seems preferable to life.

Yet, He does not give us the necessary strength to end our miserable existence and thus escape the suffering. Rather, the Creator suddenly gives us a glimpse of the only solution, which comes like a ray of sunshine through heavy clouds.

The solution is not in death, nor is it in escaping from our lives. It is in freeing ourselves from having a personal interest in the outcome of the mundane. This is the only solution that can bring us peace and rest from unbearable suffering.

There is no freedom of choice in this process; we are forced into this in order to escape our suffering. Free will is when we attempt to advance further by fortifying ourselves, choosing to focus all our actions on the Creator alone. We have learned that living for our own sake brings nothing but suffering. The constant process of correcting ourselves and controlling our thoughts is called "the process of refining."

The feelings of suffering caused by egoistic interests should be so acute that we should be prepared to "live on a bite of bread and a sip of water, and to sleep on the bare ground." Thus, we should be prepared to do anything necessary to rid ourselves of egoism and personal interests.

Once we reach the condition described above and feel comfortable in it, we can enter the spiritual realm known as "The World to Come" (*Olam HaBa*). Thus, suffering can lead us to decide that renouncing egoism would be beneficial to us. As a result of our efforts, by constantly remembering past suffering, and by upholding and strengthening this resolution in our hearts, we can reach a state where the aim of all our actions would be to benefit the Creator.

As to ourselves, apart from bare necessities, we would be afraid even to think of personal benefit and pleasure, for fear of once again experiencing the unbearable suffering brought about by personal interest.

If we have managed to oust all selfish thoughts from our minds, even thoughts about the most essential things, we are said to have reached the final stage in forsaking our own needs.

In our normal lives, we have become used to not thinking at all about ourselves, our interpersonal relationships, our families, our work, in all of the deeds we perform in this world. Outwardly, we will appear no different from anyone else in our surroundings. But within our bodies, because habit becomes second nature, nothing will remain of our personal interests.

From this point on, we can pass to the next stage of our spiritual lives and can begin to enjoy pleasing the Creator. However, this delight is no longer for us, but only for the Creator, for we have "killed" all need for personal pleasure.

For this reason, the new pleasure is infinite in time and unfathomable in magnitude, for it is not limited by our personal needs. Only at this point can we see how kind and magnificent the Creator is, for having given us the opportunity to attain the extraordinary bliss of uniting with Him in eternal love.

Let Kabbalah Be Your Guide

In order for us to reach this goal of creation, there are two successive stages in a person's path. The first entails suffering and ordeals until a person frees self from egoism. But once we have passed that first stage and gotten rid of all personal desires, once we are able to direct all thought to the Creator, then we may begin a new life, one full of spiritual joy and eternal tranquility, as originally conceived by the Will of the Creator at the beginning of creation.

We need not follow a path of complete self-denial to the extent of being satisfied with a slice of bread, a sip of water and a rest on bare earth as if to accustom our bodies to renouncing egoism. Instead of forcibly suppressing our physical desires, we have been given Kabbalah, the Light of Kabbalah, which can help each of us get rid of egoism, the root of all misfortune.

The Light of Kabbalah possesses a certain force that enables us to transcend the desires of one's body. But the spiritual force contained in Kabbalah can affect us only if we believe that it will help us, and that it is necessary in order to survive, rather than perish while experiencing unbearable suffering. It will help us only if we believe that studying Kabbalah will lead us to our goal and help us obtain the anticipated reward: freedom from selfish desire.

Those of us who feel this as a vital goal are constantly seeking ways to liberate ourselves. While studying Kabbalah, we are seeking direction as to how to break out of our prisons of self-interest. We can determine the depth of our faith in Kabbalah by our impetus to study and search.

If our thoughts are constantly occupied by the search for freedom from egoism, it can be said that we have complete faith. This is possible only if we truly feel that failing to find an escape from our condition is worse than dying, because the suffering caused by personal interest is truly immeasurable.

Only if we truly seek relief with determination will the Light of the Kabbalah help us. Only then will we be given the spiritual strength that will enable us to pull ourselves out of our own egos. And only then will we be truly free.

On the other hand, for those who feel no such urgent necessity, or no necessity at all, the Light of the Kabbalah turns into darkness. As a result, the more they study, the deeper they sink into their egoism, for they do not use Kabbalah for its sole true purpose.

When we begin learning Kabbalah and open one of the books by Rashbi, Ari, Rabbi Yehuda Ashlag or Rabbi Baruch Ashlag, our goal should be to receive a reward from the Creator—the power of faith—allowing us to succeed in finding the way to change ourselves. We should acquire confidence that even in our egoistic situation, we can still receive such a gift from Above, for to have faith is to have a bridge to an opposite state of being.

And even if we have not yet undergone all of the suffering that would force us to give up all our personal interests in life, nonetheless Kabbalah will help us; instead of suffering, we will receive another way to navigate our paths.

5

The Purpose of Studying Kabbalah

The Light that emanates from the writings of the great Kabbalists will help us overcome two challenges: our stubbornness and our tendency to forget the suffering caused by our willfulness. Prayer is the pathway to all correction, which the Creator will see in our hearts.

When we engage fully in prayer, we will attain whatever relief we seek; whatever correction we require.

But in order to achieve correction, we must give ourselves over completely to this effort—in body, mind and spirit. True prayer and the response to it relief, come only on the condition that one has engaged one's utmost effort, giving oneself entirely over to this effort, both quantitatively and, most importantly, qualitatively.

It is only by learning Kabbalah properly, however, that we can learn how to eradicate our egos and thus achieve personal redemption. Our yearning for relief must be so strong that we commit to our studies completely, unable to be diverted for a moment from the search for ourselves in the wisdom of Kabbalah.

However, if we have not yet been cornered by suffering, like the frightened beast in his cage, and still yearn for pleasure in the deepest corners of our hearts, then we will not realize that egoism still lives within us. Egoism is the enemy we must vanquish.

Until we do so, we will not be able to reach through our anguish and make a total effort to find in Kabbalah the

ATTAINING THE WORLDS BEYOND

strength and the way to escape the confines of our own egoism. Freedom will not be ours until we vanquish the ego that lives within.

However, although we may be filled with determination for this sole purpose when we begin studying, our enthusiasm may inadvertently escape us during the course of our studies. As mentioned before, our desires determine our thoughts, and our minds act as supporting instruments. Our minds merely seeks the means to fulfill the will and desires of our hearts.

What is the difference between studying Kabbalah and other systems? The answer is simple: it is only by studying Kabbalah that we can find the strength to liberate ourselves from the chains of egoism.

While studying Kabbalah, we are able to examine at first hand descriptions of the Creator's acts, His characteristics, our own characteristics, and their disparity from those of the spirit. Kabbalah tells us of the Creator's goal for His creation, and of the ways we may correct our egos.

We may see the Light of the Kabbalah, the spiritual force that helps us defeat egoism, only when we study Kabbalah. The other elements of these teachings merely draw us, against our will, into a discussion of material actions and legalistic matters.

Some may study Kabbalah merely to expand their knowledge; if so, they will be able to approach it only as a direct narrative. They will not be able to extract the Light of the Kabbalah from its pages. Only those who study Kabbalah for self-improvement will receive this benefit.

Kabbalah is a study of the system of our spiritual roots. This system emanates from Above. We may study it in accordance with strict laws which, when merged, point toward a single supreme purpose: "the Revelation of the

Creator's greatness, so that His greatness may be comprehended by the creations in this world."

Kabbalah, the perception of the Creator, consists of two
parts: the written work of the Kabbalists, who have
already perceived the Creator; and the body of knowledge
that is perceived only by those who have acquired the
spiritual vessels and the altruistic yearnings into which
they can receive spiritual sensations, or the perceptions of
the Creator.

If, after reaching a spiritual elevation, we sink to impure
desires, then the good desires that we had during our
spiritual elevation will join with the impure desires. The
accumulation of impure desires gradually decreases and
continues to do so until we are able to remain permanently in
the elevated state of solely pure desires.

Once we have completed our work and revealed to
ourselves all of our desires, we will receive a Light from
Above so immense that it forever brings us out of the shell of
our world to dwell permanently in the spiritual world. Yet,
those around us will not even be aware of this fact.

The "right line" denotes a condition in which the Creator is
always correct in our eyes; we will justify the Creator's
supervision in everything. That state is called "faith." From
our earliest attempts at spiritual development and elevation,
we must try to act as if we have already attained complete
faith in the Creator.

We should imagine that we can already feel, with all our
essence, that the Creator rules the world with utmost
benevolence, and that the whole world receives only goodness from Him. Yet, after examining our own situations, we
may see that we are still deprived of all that we desire.
Looking around, we may see the entire world suffering, each
person in his or her own way.

Despite this, we must tell ourselves that what we are seeing is a distorted image of the world, as seen through the magnifying glass of our own egoism, and that the true picture of the world will be revealed to us only when we reach a state of complete altruism. Only then will we see that the Creator rules over the world with this purpose: to lead His creations to perfect enjoyment.

In such a state, when our faith in the Creator's absolute goodness prevails over what we see and feel, we are experiencing a state called "faith above reason."

6

Spiritual Progress

Just as we are incapable of correctly assessing our own true condition, neither can we discern whether we are in a stage of spiritual ascent or descent. For although we may feel we are in a spiritual downturn, in fact it might be the Will of the Creator, showing us our true state. This demonstrates that without self-indulgence, we are incapable of functioning and are immediately given to despair. Even depression and anger may result because our bodies are not receiving enough pleasure from such an existence.

But, in fact, this lack represents a spiritual ascent, for at that moment we are closer to the truth than before, when we were happy in this world. It is said that "one who increases knowledge also increases sorrow." Conversely, a feeling that one is experiencing spiritual ascent may simply be a misinterpreted state of self-indulgence and complacency.

Only one who already perceives the Creator and His Divine Providence over all creations can correctly determine one's spiritual condition. Based on the above, it is easy to understand that the farther we advance along the path of self-improvement in an effort to correct our egoism, and the more effort we make to improve ourselves and to study, the more we grow to understand our own characteristics.

With each attempt, with each passing day, with each turn, we will become more and more disillusioned with our own abilities to achieve anything. The more we despair in our attempts, the greater grow our grievances toward the Creator.

We then demand to be taken out of that black abyss, that dungeon of physical desire in which we find ourselves.

In this manner, events progress until, having exhausted our own potential, and having done everything that is in our own power, we recognize that we are unable to help ourselves. We must turn to the Creator, who places these obstacles in our path to compel us to turn to Him for help and to arouse in us a desire to establish a bond with Him.

But for this to happen, our pleas must come from the depths of our hearts. This is not possible to achieve until we have exhausted all possibilities and realize that we are helpless.

Only a plea coming from the depths of our whole being, one that has become our only wish—for we have understood that only a miracle from Above can save us from our greatest enemy, our own egos—will be answered by the Creator. He will then replace the egoistic heart with a spiritual one, replacing "a heart of stone with a heart of flesh."

Until the Creator rectifies our condition, the further we progress, the worse we begin to feel about ourselves.

In truth, we were always this way, but to a certain extent, having grasped the attributes of the spiritual worlds, we have begun to feel how hostile are our personal wishes to entering those worlds.

However, despite feeling tired and hopeless, we can still regain control over our own bodies. Then, having thought carefully and concluded that there is seemingly no way out of our state, we may understand the true cause of such emotions, and force ourselves to feel buoyant and optimistic.

By doing so, we attest to our trust in the fairness of the management of the world, and in the Creator's kindness, and in His Rule over the world. Then, by doing so, we will become spiritually fit to receive the Light of the Creator, because we are basing our entire perspective of our surroundings on our faith, elevating faith above reason.

There is no moment more precious in the life of the seeker who is spiritually advancing than when one realizes that all powers have been exhausted, all efforts have been made, and the goal has still not been achieved. For only at such an instant can one sincerely appeal to the Creator from the bottom of one's heart, because it is now clear that one's own efforts will be no help at all.

But before recognizing defeat, the seeker is still certain that no other help will be required to achieve the desired objective. Still unable to beg for help sincerely enough, the seeker falls prey to the deceptive voice of the ego, which urges that, rather than ask for help, an intensified effort should be made to accomplish the objective.

Finally, the seeker will realize that, in the struggle against the ego, the ego is the stronger of the two combatants, and that help is needed to overcome this enemy. Only then does one realize one's insignificance and inability to conquer the ego, and become ready to bow to the Creator and implore Him for help.

Not until the seeker arrives at this lowly state, however, does it become clear that only fervent prayers to the Creator can elevate the seeker from the depths of his or her own nature.

Faith: Believing in the Oneness
of the Creator

Faith in the Oneness of the Creator implies that we see the entire world, including ourselves, as vessels in the Creator's hands. And conversely, if we think ourselves capable of influencing events, it reveals that we believe in the presence of many different powers in the world, rather than only in the Will of the One Creator.

Therefore, by destroying our egos, we can bring ourselves into accord with the true condition of the world, where nothing exists but the Creator's Will. Until then, however, we will not have the merit to act as those who believe in the Oneness of the Creator, and thus, our spiritual progress remains idle.

The only way we can become convinced of the Oneness of the Creator is by working hard on ourselves, and by cultivating appropriate aspirations in ourselves. Only after achieving absolute unity with the Creator in all our perceptions, having risen to the highest level of the worlds, can we understand His Oneness. Only then can we proceed to act in accordance with this accurate view of reality.

Before achieving this condition, we must act in accordance with the level that we are on, and not the level about which we fantasize and dream. In order to genuinely improve on our present level, we must combine confidence in our own powers at the start of the work, with the belief that what we achieve as a result of our own labors would have happened anyway.

We must realize that the entire universe develops according to the Creator's Plan, and according to His idea of creation. We may say that all goes according to the Creator, but only after we have put forth our best efforts.

It is beyond human comprehension to understand the essence of such spiritual qualities as total altruism and love.

This is simply because human beings cannot comprehend how such feelings can exist at all, as everyone seemingly requires an incentive to perform any act.

In fact, without personal gain, people aren't prepared to extend themselves. That is why a quality such as altruism can only be imparted to us from Above, and only those who have experienced it can understand it. But if this quality is awarded to us from heaven, why then, should we try so hard to attain it? Won't our labors fail to yield any results by themselves, until the Creator helps us and consigns to us new qualities and new natures?

The fact is, we must pray from below and request these changes. We must, express a strong desire for the Creator to change our qualities, for only if the desire is really and truly strong will the Creator grant it. We must also put great effort into making this desire strong enough for the Creator to grant it.

While we are trying to accomplish this goal, we will gradually realize that we have neither the desire nor the ability to achieve it on our own. Then we will have a real demand of the Creator: to free us from the constraints of our old qualities and to grant us a new characteristic—a soul.

But that cannot possibly happen unless we first attempt to apply all our powers and abilities to change by ourselves. It is only after we have become convinced that these efforts bring no result and cry for help, from the depths of our hearts, that the Creator will answer us.

We can utter this cry for help to change our qualities only after we have found that neither our desires nor a single limb of our bodies agrees to this change of nature to the extent that we will unconditionally hand ourselves over to the Creator. In fact, we are equal in our desires to remain a slave to our nature, and to become a slave to altruism.

Only after we realize that there is no hope of our bodies ever agreeing to such a change can we appeal to the Creator for help from the bottom of our hearts. Only then will the Creator accept our plea and respond to it by replacing all of our egoistic qualities with their opposite, altruistic ones, so that we may draw closer to Him.

If we consider that we must work unwillingly in this world, then what is the result of our efforts at the end of our days? What is the point of our efforts in this world? When we consider these questions, we will conclude that working to change ourselves is not as difficult as we might have thought.

And when we have achieved change, our changed qualities will have revealed to us great pleasures as a result of our inner efforts. The pleasure arises when we see what we are working for.

Therefore, we see our efforts not as troublesome, but as bringing joy. The greater our efforts, the happier we are to receive these new qualities, since we immediately feel a great and everlasting reward for each of them we now possess.

Even in our world, we can see how excitement and exaltation make it easier for us to expend strong efforts. If we feel great respect for someone, and that person is the most exalted person in the world in our eyes, then everything we do for someone so worthy of our esteem will be done with joy and gratitude—simply to have the opportunity to serve such a person.

The greatest effort will seem a pleasure. Just as we may love to dance or exercise, our exertion is not considered as work, but rather, pleasure. For this reason, one who feels and recognizes the greatness of the Creator feels joy at the opportunity to please Him.

Thus, what at first seemed to be slavery actually turns into a freedom full of pleasures. Consequently, if our spiritual aspirations come to us with difficulty, and if we must make a formidable effort to attain the spiritual, this should indicate to us that the Creator is not yet great enough in our eyes or our perception, and that our attention is being drawn to other goals than attaining the spiritual.

As long as we pursue these other goals, we will receive no support from the Creator and will only be moving farther and farther away from our primary goal.

But even when striving toward the Creator, we will not receive His spiritual support immediately.

For if we received immediate inspiration and joy from our efforts, then our egos would certainly rejoice, and we would continue to make the effort only because of the resulting pleasure.

However, we would have lost the opportunity to transcend our egoistic natures and rise to pure altruism. Ideally, we should only be interested in the pleasures derived from spiritual self-improvement, which are greater than any others.

7

Our Perceptions

When someone performs a particular kind of work, that person gradually develops a special insight concerning the objects and language surrounding that work. Therefore, there is nothing in the world that we cannot begin to experience as a result of habit, even without prior understanding of the particular object.

We are, however, operating under a vital limitation to our perception and understanding: we see ourselves as separate from objects we perceive.

There is the one who perceives and there is the perceived— the object that is perceived by the person. Similarly, there exists the person who comprehends, and separately, the object of comprehension.

A certain contact between the perceiver and the object of perception is necessary for perception to occur: it is a bond, something that unites them both, something that they have in common during the perception. We can grasp all that surrounds us only through our perception. What we perceive is considered to be truthful and reliable information.

However, because we are incapable of seeing all that surrounds us objectively, we assume that the pictures our senses create for us are true. Yet, we do not know what the universe is like beyond our senses, or what it would appear to be like for beings with a different set of senses than our own. This is because we acquire our sense of reality from how we perceive our environment; we assume that our senses are accurate and we accept as true the picture of reality that we perceive through them.

If we proceed from the assumption that nothing exists in the universe but the Creator and His creations, we can say that our pictures and perceptions are the means by which the Creator appears to our consciousness. At every stage of spiritual elevation, this picture grows closer and closer to the true one. Finally, at the last stage of elevation, we can perceive the Creator and nothing but the Creator.

Therefore, all the worlds, as well as everything that we believe to exist outside of us, in fact exist only in relation to us. That is, they exist in relation to one who perceives reality in this particular manner.

If we do not perceive the Creator or the Creator's domain over us at the present moment, then it can be said that we remain "in darkness."

Nevertheless, we cannot determine an absence of sun in the universe because our perceptions are subjective. Only we construe reality in this manner.

However, if we realize that our negation of the Creator and Divine Rule are purely subjective and prone to change, then we can still begin our spiritual elevation by an effort of will and with the help of various texts and teachers. Moreover, once we begin our spiritual ascent, we may realize that the Creator made the condition of darkness for the sole purpose of compelling us to develop a need for His help, and in order to draw us closer to Him.

Indeed, the Creator made such conditions specifically for those individuals whom He desires to draw closer to Him. Thus, it is important to realize that the elevation of an individual from the state of darkness brings delight to the Creator, since the greater the darkness from which a person has emerged, the clearer the recognition of the Creator's greatness, and the greater the appreciation of one's new spiritual state.

But even while perceiving the darkness, being blind to the Creator's Rule and lacking faith in Him, by using our willpower, we can try to find a way out of the darkness with the help of a book or a teacher, until we can perceive at least a tiny ray of Light, a weak perception of the Creator.

Then, by making this ray of Light stronger and stronger by cultivating constant thoughts of the Creator, we can escape the darkness and enter into the Light. Going even further, if we realize that these states of darkness are necessary for spiritual advancement, and are even desirable, and sent to us by the Creator Himself, then we will welcome them.

We will recognize that the Creator has offered us the gift of perceiving shadows, or the incomplete darkness, so that we may seek the Source of the Light.

However, if we do not use the opportunity to cross into the Light, then the Creator will conceal Himself from us completely.

Absolute darkness will prevail, bringing with it a sensation of the absence of the Creator and His Rule. Then, we will no longer understand how and why spiritual goals were ever entertained, and how reality and personal reason could have been ignored.

This complete darkness will continue until the Creator again shines upon us a tiny ray of Light.

8

Structure of Spirituality

A person's desires are called "vessels," and these can hold spiritual Light, or pleasure. However, in their essence, one's desires must be similar to the qualities of the spiritual Light. Otherwise the Light cannot enter them, according to the Law of the Equivalence of Form of Spiritual Objects.

The activity of spiritual objects—whether close, or distant, or merging and unifying—is always based on the principle of the similarity of properties.

The Creator will bestow upon a person that which the person wants—to return to the Creator.

Therefore, a person's heart, or vessel, will be filled with the perception of the Creator to the same degree that egoism has been ejected. This is in accordance with the Law of the Equivalence of Qualities Between the Light and the Vessel.

We can, in fact, begin our spiritual ascent from any condition that we are in. We must simply realize that of all possible conditions, ranging from the highest to the lowest, the Creator has chosen this particular one as the best situation for us to start on the path of spiritual advancement.

Therefore, there can be no other frame of mind, mood, or external circumstances better suited or more beneficial to our progress than our present circumstances, however hopeless or dismal they may seem. Realizing this, we can rejoice in the opportunity to appeal to the Creator for help and to thank Him, even if we are in the most wretched of situations.

Something is considered "spiritual" if it is eternal and will not disappear from the universe, even upon reaching the ultimate goal. On the other hand, egoism (all the original inborn desires and the essence of a human being) is considered to be merely material because once corrected, it disappears.

Our essence remains until the end of correction, when only the form is changed. If our desires are corrected and become altruistic, then even our negative inborn qualities will enable us to comprehend the Creator.

The existence of a spiritual place is not related to any actual space. All those who reach this state after correcting their spiritual qualities can see and perceive the same things.

The ladder of the Creator has 125 levels. These levels are divided evenly between five spiritual worlds. These worlds are:

The World of Adam Kadmon

The World of Atzilut

The World of Beria

The World of Yetzira

The World of Assiya.

Each level provides a different perception of the Creator, depending on each level's particular properties. Therefore, those who have acquired the properties of a specific level see Kabbalah and the Creator in a completely new way. Everyone who attains a particular level of the spiritual world receives the same perception as everyone else on the same level.

When the Kabbalists said, "Thus said Abraham to Isaac," it indicated that the Kabbalists were situated on the same level as Abraham. Thus, the Kabbalists understood how

Abraham responded to Isaac, since in their spiritual state they were like Abraham.

In his lifetime, the Kabbalist Rabbi Yehuda Ashlag reached all 125 levels. From this exalted place, he dictated the Kabbalah, which we are now able to enjoy in this generation. From this level, he wrote his commentary to the Zohar, the master text of Kabbalah.

Each of the 125 levels exists objectively; all those who perceive each of them see the same things, just as all those who inhabit our world see the same surroundings if they are in the same place.

As soon as we attain the smallest altruistic desire, we can embark on a path of spiritual ascensions and descents. At one moment, we are ready to nullify ourselves completely before the Creator, but the next moment we will not give it a single thought. Suddenly, the idea of spiritual elevation becomes absolutely alien to us and is thrust from our minds.

This is much like the way a mother teaches her child to walk. She holds it by the hand so that it feels her support, and then she suddenly withdraws, letting go of it. When the child feels totally abandoned and lacking all support, it is compelled to take a step toward the mother. Only in this way can it learn to walk independently.

Thus, though it may seem to us as if the Creator has suddenly abandoned us, in fact He is waiting for us to take a step on our own.

It is said that the Upper World is in a state of complete rest. The word "rest," in the spiritual world, implies no changes in desire.

However, the desire to bestow good never changes. All acts and movements, in both our inner emotional (egoistic) world and in the spiritual (altruistic) world, are involved in replacing a former desire with a new one.

If no such change has taken place, then nothing new has happened and no movement forward has occurred. This applies even if the original, constant desire may in itself be very vivid and very intense, giving us no peace.

But if that desire is invariable and consistent, then there is no movement.

Therefore, when it is said that the Upper Light is in a state of absolute rest, this means that the Will of the Creator to benefit us is unwavering and constant.

We exist in the Sea of Light. But that point in us which we call our "I" is encased in a shell of egoism. In this state, we are incapable of enjoying the Light and are merely floating.

False Pleasures

The pleasures of our world as seen by society can be divided into several types: status symbols (wealth, fame), natural (family), criminal (pleasures experienced at the expense of others' lives), illegal (pleasures experienced at the expense of others' property), amorous (romantic pleasures), and more. All of these are understood by society, even though some of them are condemned and punished.

But there is a certain type of pleasure, unacceptable in any type of society, that always evokes protest. It causes enormous funds to be spent on attempts to combat it, even though the damage it causes society is, perhaps, the least significant.

For example, drug addicts are, as a rule, unpretentious people who are deeply absorbed in their inner sensations. Why, then, do we not allow our fellow human beings to engage in pleasures that pose only a small threat to society?

Why not just give them a chance to enjoy their unassuming, peaceful pleasures, which don't harm others, unlike criminal, illegal and other pleasures?

The answer is that false pleasures divert us from our true goals. They cause us to forget ourselves, and propel us to spend all our lives chasing them as if we were dazed.

Is it then true that all objects that attract us are false pleasures? Instead of seeking true pleasure and turning to spiritual things, we seek satisfaction in forever changing fashions, in improving our lifestyles, and in manufacturing new articles.

It is as if we were in a race to perpetuate attractive bearers of new pleasures, lest we feel life will not give us sufficient enjoyment.

As soon as we attain what we have been striving for, we must immediately set the next goal, because what we have attained soon loses its attraction.

Yet, without hope for new pleasures, without seeking and chasing them, we seemingly have no incentive to live. Therefore, can't it be said that all of our fashions and our lifestyles, all that we constantly pursue, are but another kind of drug?

What is the difference between a drug addict's pleasure and the pleasure derived from the mundane and the material? Why does the Creator, the Divine Supervisor, oppose the pleasures derived from drugs? Why does He cause us to pass anti-drug legislation in this world? Why do we not extend the same approach to all other material pleasures derived from the common objects of this world?

Drugs are prohibited in our world precisely because they allow us to escape reality. They make us incapable of facing the blows and beauty of life, which are caused by the absence of egoistic pleasures. These blows are, in fact, a means of reforming us, since only a small part of the population turns to religion and to Kabbalah in order to change.

Paradoxically, we turn to the Creator in times of hardship, when we are shaken by grief. It is odd that we do not turn away from the Creator during the hard times, since it was He Who sent us our suffering.

Drugs are a source of false pleasure and are therefore prohibited. Those who fall under the influence of drugs are under an illusion of pleasure that bars them from finding the path to true spiritual pleasure. For this reason, drugs are subconsciously seen by society as the most dangerous addiction, although they present no immediate hazard to other people.

9

A Plea for Help

The only thing that the Creator created in us is our egoism. If we can nullify the effects of our egoism, then we will once again perceive only the Creator, and the egoistic element will no longer exist.

When working on ourselves, we should try to cultivate both a sense of our own inferiority in relation to the Creator, and a sense of pride in the fact that as human beings we are the center of creation. We are accorded this position if we fulfill the purpose of all creation; otherwise, we are no more than animals.

As a result of experiencing these two contradictory states, we will develop two responses toward the Creator. The first is a plea for help. The second is an expression of gratitude for the chance to be elevated spiritually.

The principal means by which we can progress spiritually is by pleading for help from the Creator and asking Him to increase our yearning for spiritual development. This request for the gift of strength will help us overcome our fears of the future. Furthermore, by opposing inclinations of our egos, we should increase our faith in the greatness, the power, and the Oneness of the Creator.

Therefore, we must plead with our Creator to give us the ability to suppress our continuous urges to act in accordance with our own reason. Some of us will begin to dwell on various intentions during our prayers (*kavanot*), pleas or even certain actions.

However, the Creator does not listen to the words that we utter, but instead reads the feelings in our hearts.

Therefore, it is senseless to spend energy on uttering beautiful phrases that have no inner, heartfelt meaning, or to read obscure symbols or *kavanot* from Kabbalistic prayer books. The only thing required of us is to strive toward the Creator with our whole being, to understand the essence of our desires, and to ask the Creator to alter them. Most important, we should never stop communicating with the Creator!

In Memory of the Kabbalist, Rabbi Baruch Ashlag

The Creator acts upon us by using various elements that make up our world. The events we experience are actually messages from the Creator. If we respond correctly to Divine action, we will clearly grasp what the Creator expects of us, and we will feel Him.

Not only does the Creator act upon us through the people around us, but He uses everything that exists in our world. The structure of our world is such that the Creator can influence us and draw us nearer to the goal of creation.

We rarely feel the Presence of the Creator in the daily situations we need to face. This is because our attributes place us opposite the Creator and make it impossible for us to feel Him. As soon as we acquire attributes similar to those of the Creator, we will begin to feel Him proportionately.

Therefore, when hardships befall us, we need to ask ourselves, "Why is this happening to me?" and "Why is the Creator doing this to me?" Punishments, as such, do not exist, although many are mentioned in the Bible (which includes the Five Books of Moses, the Writings and the Prophets).

There are only "incentives" that force us to progress towards our selfish desires. Our awareness of things is only an ancillary mechanism that helps us properly understand what we feel.

Whenever we picture our lives, we should think of a gigantic classroom with the omniscient Creator acting as a teacher and lavishing on us the knowledge we are prepared to receive. This progressively awakens in our newborn spiritual sensory organs the feeling of the Creator.

The Creator has made a ladder for our ascension. It is a moving ladder. This ladder appeared in Jacob's dream and was described by Baal HaSulam Rabbi Yehuda Ashlag and his son, Baruch Ashlag.

Often, we turn our backs on the source of knowledge symbolized by this ladder, and only through great effort will we manage to turn around and start moving towards the Creator. This is why He sends us teachers, books, and study companions.

Students who follow the teachings of Kabbalah live in the physical world, but are overburdened by their selfishness. This is why they cannot properly understand the sages who are physically close to them, but who also evolve in the spiritual worlds.

Those who can leave aside reason and opinions, and follow the ways of writers of authentic books of wisdom, will be able to bond unconsciously with the spiritual. It is because we do not see or feel the Creator in our world that we cannot selfishly surrender our consciousness to Him.

The thoughts of teachers or masters can penetrate their students and induce faith in them. This corresponds with the teacher's spiritual *AHaP*: *Auzen* (Ear), *Hotem* (Nose), *Peh* (Mouth), representing the vessels of reception, coming down to the *GE* (*Galgalta ve Einayim*), representing the vessels of bestowal of the level below (i.e., the student's level).

Rising to the level of the master's *AHaP* means bonding with the master's wisdom and thoughts. Likewise, if students delve into the *AHaP* of a text of wisdom, they rise temporarily and the spiritual is revealed to them.

Whenever we read the works of such Kabbalists as the Baal HaSulam, Shimon Bar Yochai, we bond directly with them through the Surrounding Light. We are then enlightened, and our vessels of reception purified.

It is important when reading to bear in mind the stature of the author, whether alive or dead. We can always bond with the author through our feelings as we study the work.

There are many paths leading to the Creator, and He uses many means to act upon us. Any difficulty or obstacle on the student's path, in particular the death of a master, may be considered an opportunity for transformation at an individual level.

10

Counteracting the Desire for Self-Gratification

Our sense of hearing is called "faith," because if we wish to accept what we hear as true, we must believe what we have heard. Eyesight is called "knowledge," for we do not have to take anything on trust, but can see for ourselves. However, until we have received altruistic qualities from Above, we are unable to see, since whatever we see, we perceive with our egoistic senses.

This makes it all the more difficult for us to break away from egoism. Therefore, at first we must walk blindly, while conquering what our egos tell us to do. Then, having acquired faith, we will start acquiring higher knowledge.

In order to replace our egoism with altruism, and our reason with faith, we must truly appreciate the greatness and grandeur of the spiritual, as compared to our pitiful, material, temporary existence. We must realize how insignificant it is to serve ourselves compared to serving the Creator.

We must also see how much more beneficial and enjoyable it is to please the Creator than to please our insignificant egos (our bodies). The ego, in fact, can never be satisfied and can show appreciation only by awarding us fleeting pleasure.

When we compare the human body to the Creator, we must decide for whose sake we should work, whose slave we should become. There is no other alternative. The more we understand our own insignificance, the easier it will be for us to choose the Creator.

There are four aspects of a desire to receive: *inanimate, organic, animate and speaking*.

The aspect of *inanimate* nature represents completeness. The sense of perfection originates in the Surrounding Light coming from afar, and this distant Light shines on those of our world, even though the qualities of this world are opposite to those of the Creator.

In the same way, one who is spiritually inanimate maintains one's existence as is. This individual has the same desires as others who are similar. This person is incapable and unwilling to make any spiritual effort of his own.

Just as the *organic* world is built upon the foundation of inanimate nature, the spiritual world also requires a prior inanimate base. A person has no other choice but to begin with the inanimate level.

However, those who wish to ascend from the spiritually inanimate level must find a new reason to replace what previously motivated them to commit their actions: force of habit, upbringing, and environment.

A person who wants to grow further, to come alive spiritually, to make spiritual strides independently, refuses to blindly follow others, but moves forward irrespective of the opinion of others, or the habits or education of society.

This decision to stop performing mechanical acts gives rise to the root of a new, *organic* spiritual state. Just as a seed must first decompose in the soil in order to grow, so, too, must a person cease to feel any spiritual life among the inanimate masses. Instead, an inanimate life should be perceived as death. This sensation will in itself constitute a prayer for change.

In order to become *organic* and capable of individual spiritual growth, we must perform several kinds of work on ourselves, starting with "tilling" the inanimate soil. Spiritual progress can be made only by counteracting our desires for self-gratification.

Therefore, if we aspire to advance toward the Creator, we must regularly check our own desires and decide which pleasures we can accept. Since the Creator wishes to please His creations, we must accept certain pleasures.

However, we must exclude all pleasures that are not for the sake of the Creator. In the language of Kabbalah, this can be described in the following way: Our willpower, a screen located in the mind (*Peh de Rosh*), calculates the amount of pleasure that we can experience in order to bring joy to the Creator, and in accordance with our exact amount of love for Him. We can experience precisely this amount. However, any other amount of pleasure we experience that is not meant for the sake of the Creator is not out of fear of upsetting the Creator.

Thus, our actions should be determined by our desire to please the Creator, rather than by our desire to advance closer to Him, or out of fear of being distanced from Him. The latter two are considered to be egoistic aspirations, as compared to selfless unconditional love.

The desire to please the Creator or the fear of upsetting Him represent altruistic yearnings. We experience strong emotions such as joy, grief, pleasure and fear with our whole bodies, rather than with some part of them. If we wish to check our desires, we must determine if every part of our bodies agrees with our thoughts.

For example, when praying, we must make sure that all of our thoughts, desires, and body organs are in agreement with what we are saying. We must also be aware of whether we are simply uttering words automatically, without paying attention to their meaning.

A "mechanical reading" occurs when we wish to avoid the discomfort from a conflict between our bodies and the meaning of prayer. It can also arise from a lack of understanding of how prayer can be of benefit when derived from mechanically uttered pleas from the prayer book.

It is worthwhile to ask our hearts what they want to pray for.

A prayer is not what our lips say mechanically, but what the whole body and reason desire.

Thus it is said that "a prayer is the work of the heart," meaning that the heart is in absolute agreement with what the lips are saying.

Only if we work with the entire body will we receive a response from it, signifying that not a single organ desires to rid itself of egoism or to ask the Creator for help in this endeavor. Only then will we be able to direct a sincere prayer to the Creator, asking for redemption from our spiritual exile.

We must strive to make the *reason* for an act correspond to the actual mechanical act of carrying out the Creator's Will. Just as the body acts as a robot, carrying out the Creator's Will without understanding the reason for it, or without seeing any immediate benefit from it, so must the reason for observing His Will be "because such is the Will of the Creator."

There is an easy way to check the motivation behind an individual's act. If it is "for the sake of the Creator," then a person's body is incapable of making even the slightest movement. Yet, if it is for one's own benefit in this or the world to come, then the more one thinks of one's reward, the more energy is expended for taking action.

All the above makes it clear that it is our motivation (*kavana*) that determines the quality of our acts. An increase in the number of our acts does not necessarily improve their quality. All that happens occurs under the influence of upper spiritual forces. And we, down here in our world, have been observing the cause-and-effect relationship of spiritual forces for centuries.

A person who can see the consequences of events in advance, and therefore predict and avert undesirable consequences, is called a "Kabbalist." Our world is the world of consequential manifestations of the spiritual forces, whereas the actual arena of interaction between these forces is situated above and beyond our perceptions.

Only a Kabbalist has the ability to foresee events before they manifest themselves in this world, and possibly even prevent their manifestation.

However, since all these events are sent in order to allow us to correct ourselves, and since we need this correction in order to reach the ultimate goal of creation, no one can help us in this endeavor but ourselves.

The Creator does not send us suffering, but rather sends the means we need to accelerate our spiritual progress. A Kabbalist is not a wizard who performs miracles, but is one whose mission is to help people in general, to assist us in elevating our consciousness to the level necessary to initiate the process of self-correction.

Finally, the Kabbalist is there to help people individually if they desire it.

We have no power whatsoever over our hearts, no matter how strong or intelligent or capable we might be. Therefore, all we can do is mechanically perform good deeds and implore the Creator to replace our hearts with new ones. (The word "heart" usually denotes all of our desires).

All that is required of us as individuals is to have one great desire, rather than numerous desires. The desire that an individual perceives in the heart is a prayer. Thus, a great, wholehearted desire leaves no room for any others.

We can create this great desire in our hearts only by persistent, continuous efforts. In the process, we must overcome numerous obstacles. We must proceed even though we clearly realize that we are far from our goal, and that our study of Kabbalah is for our personal benefit and not for the sake of the Creator.

The obstacles to be overcome include: the body's arguments that it is weak; the conflict between spiritual and egoistic efforts; the belief that, when the time is right, the Creator will bring the desired result, just as He brought a person to this particular state, and the theory that one must test one's achievements, as should all work be tested.

They also include the belief that things have worsened since study of Kabbalah began; the belief that others' studies are going more successfully than one's own and thus ad infinitum—complaints, reproaches, accusations, coming both from one's own body and from one's family.

Only by overcoming these difficulties will a person develop a true desire for spirituality. There is but one way we can overcome these obstacles: by "knocking out" egoism as Kabbalah prescribes.

We can either ignore the ego's demands, or reply: "I am going ahead without any explanations or tests, for those could only be based on egoism, which I must leave behind. And since I do not yet have any other senses, I cannot listen to you, but only to those great sages who have already entered the Higher Worlds and know how a person should act. And if my heart is becoming even more selfish, it means that I have made progress and thus deserve to have a little more of my true egoism revealed to me from heaven."

In response, the Creator will reveal Himself to us, so that we will feel His greatness and will involuntarily become His slaves. At that point, we will no longer experience any temptations of the body. This process signifies the replacement of the "stone" heart, which is aware only of itself, with a "flesh" one that is aware of others.

11

Inner Motion and Development

In this world, we advance physically by using our organs of motion—the legs. Once we have moved forward, we then use our organs of acquisition—the hands.

In contrast, spiritual organs are opposite to ours: we can ascend the stairs only if we have consciously rejected all support of reason. In addition, we can attain the purpose of creation only by opening our hands and giving, rather than taking.

The purpose of creation is to bestow pleasure upon us. Why, then, does the Creator lead us to this goal by such a painful path? Let us try to find the answer.

First, the Creator has, in His perfection, created human beings.

One attribute of ultimate perfection is the state of rest, for movement is induced either by a lack of something, or by an attempt to reach that which is considered desirable.

Human beings also like to rest, and will only sacrifice it when they are lacking something vital, such as food or warmth, etc.

The more they suffer from the lack of what they want, the readier they are to make greater and greater efforts in order to obtain it. Therefore, if the Creator makes people suffer from the lack of the spiritual, they will be compelled to make an effort to reach it.

Once they have attained the spiritual, which is the purpose of creation, people will experience the pleasure that the Creator prepared for them. For this reason, those who wish to advance spiritually do not consider the suffering the ego brings as punishment, but only as evidence of the Creator's good Will to help them.

Therefore, they view their suffering as a blessing, rather than a curse. Only after having achieved the spiritual will they understand what it really is and what pleasures are found in it. Until then, they will only suffer from the lack of it.

The difference between the material and the spiritual is that our lack of material pleasures causes us to suffer, while our lack of spiritual pleasures does not. Therefore, in order to bring us spiritual pleasures, the Creator imparts to us a sense of suffering from our lack of spiritual sensations.

On the other hand, when experiencing material pleasures, we will never reach the complete, infinite fulfillment that is present even in the smallest of spiritual pleasures. As soon as we begin to acquire a taste for the spiritual, there is a danger that we might receive pleasure from perceiving the spiritual as an egoistic desire, and will consequently move further away from the spiritual.

The reason for such a turn of events is that we begin to pursue the spiritual after we find much greater pleasure in this pursuit than we had previously experienced in our entire distasteful lives. We now see that we no longer have a need for faith—the basis of all spirituality—for it has become clear that pursuing the spiritual is worth doing for our own benefit. But the Creator uses this approach only with beginners, in order to attract and then correct them.

Each of us feels that we know better than anyone else what we should do and what is good for us. This feeling stems from the fact that in an egoistic state, we perceive only the self and nothing else. Therefore, we see ourselves as the most wise, since only we know what we desire at each moment of our lives.

The Creator rules our world in strict accordance with the material laws of nature. Therefore, it is impossible to get around these laws or to counteract them: if we jump off the cliff, we will fall to our death; if we are deprived of oxygen, we will suffocate, and so on.

The Creator has confirmed such laws of nature in order to make us understand that survival requires effort and caution. In the spiritual world, where we cannot foresee the consequences of events and do not know the laws of survival, we must at the very outset understand the principal law. This law cannot be evaded, just as the laws of nature in our world cannot be evaded.

The principal law states that we cannot be guided by sensations of pleasure, since it is not pleasure, but altruism, that determines whether a spiritual life is beneficial or harmful:

Light—that which emanates from the Creator and is perceived by us as immense pleasure. Comprehending the pleasure or perceiving the Creator (which is, actually, one and the same, for it is not Him we perceive but the Light reaching us) is the purpose of creation.

Faith—the power that gives an individual confidence in the possibility of attaining a spiritual life, coming alive after being spiritually dead. The more clearly we realize that we are spiritually dead, the more strongly we feel a need for faith.

Prayer—effort made by an individual, particularly in the heart, to perceive the Creator and implore Him to grant the individual confidence in the possibility of attaining a spiritual life.

Any work, any exertion of effort, and any praying is possible only if the Creator is concealed from human beings. A genuine prayer asks the Creator to grant one the strength to counter egoism with closed eyes—without the Creator revealing Himself to the person, since this is the highest reward. Our level of spirituality is defined by our willingness to proceed selflessly.

When we gain confidence in our own altruistic strength, we can gradually begin to experience pleasure for the sake of the Creator, for by so doing we are pleasing the Creator. Since it is the Creator's Will to bestow pleasure on us, this congruity of wishes brings the Giver and the receiver closer together.

Apart from the pleasure we receive by perceiving the Light of the Creator, we also experience infinite pleasure from perceiving the Creator's stature, that is, from our union with the Ultimate Perfection. Attaining this pleasure is the purpose of creation.

Since egoism—our desire to receive—is our essence, it predominates on all levels of nature, from the atomic-molecular to the hormonal, animal, and higher levels.

Egoism extends all the way up to the highest systems of human reasoning and the subconscious, including our altruistic desires. It is so powerful that we are incapable of deliberately opposing it in any situation.

Therefore, if we want to escape the power of the ego, we must fight it. We must act contrary to the desires of our bodies and our reason in everything relating to our advance toward the spiritual, even if we cannot see any benefit to ourselves.

Otherwise, we will never transcend the limits of our world. In Kabbalah, this principle of work is known as, "Force him until he says 'I want.'"

Once the Creator helps us by imparting to us His Own Nature, our bodies will themselves want to function in the spiritual realm. This condition is called "the return" (teshuvah).

The transformation of our egoistic essence into an altruistic essence happens as follows: In His wisdom, the Creator generated a desire for self-gratification and implanted it in human beings. This desire represents egoism, a black point in one's essence. It is black as a result of the contraction of Light (tzimtzum), which took place when the Light of the Creator departed from it.

The correction of the egoistic essence takes place with the aid of a screen (masach), which transforms egoism into altruism. We are incapable of understanding how such a miraculous transformation can take place until we experience it ourselves. It seems incredible to us that the general law of nature would change so that we were suddenly able to act where previously we could not.

In the end, we will discover that our actions have remained the same as before, and that there is nothing we can give to the Creator, since the Creator is perfect and His only desire is to fill us with His perfection.

In return for the immense pleasure that we receive from the Creator, we are incapable of giving anything back to Him except the thought that, although we continue to perform the same acts as before, now we are performing them because doing so pleases the Creator, rather than us.

But even this thought is not for the Creator, but for us. This allows us to receive unbounded pleasures without being ashamed of getting something for nothing. We may become more like the Creator by becoming altruists. When we do so, we are able to receive infinitely and experience pleasure, since altruism is not for the self.

Although we can force ourselves to commit a specific physical act, we cannot change our desires at will, because we cannot do anything that is not for the self. Kabbalists say that a prayer without the right motivation is like a body without a soul, for actions pertain to the body and thoughts to the soul.

If we have not yet corrected our thoughts (soul), for the sake of which we perform an action (body), then the action itself can be said to be spiritually dead. Everything is comprised of both the general and the particular. The general, the spiritually dead (*domem*), demonstrates that for most people, there can only be a general movement, but not a particular spiritual movement, for they have no inner need for it.

Therefore, there is no particular, individual growth, but only general growth in accordance with the general Providence from Above. For this reason, the masses always perceive themselves to be right and perfect.

Being spiritually *organic* (*tzomeach*) means that individuals possess a unique degree of inner movement and development. At this point, a person becomes known as Man, or Adam, as written in the Bible: "Adam—a tree in a field." Since spiritual growth requires moving forward, and movement can only be caused when one senses a shortage of something, Man is constantly aware of those shortcomings that compel him to seek ways of growing.

If Man stops at any level of spiritual development, then he is pushed down in his perceptions. This is intended to urge him to move, rather than to stand still.

If, subsequently, he rises again, it is to a higher level than before.

As a result, one either ascends or descends, but one cannot stand still, for this state is not characteristic of Man. Only those belonging to the masses stand still and cannot fall off their levels; thus, they never experience falling down.

Let us mentally divide space with a horizontal line. Above the line is the spiritual world. Below the line is the egoistic world. Those who prefer to act contrary to their reason can exist above the line.

These individuals reject earthly reason, even if it gives them an opportunity to know and to see everything. They prefer to proceed with their eyes closed, by means of faith, and to pursue the spiritual (altruism instead of egoism).

Every spiritual level is defined by the measure of altruism present within it. We occupy the spiritual level that corresponds to our spiritual qualities. Those of us who are above the line are able to perceive the Creator. The higher above the line we are, the stronger the ability to perceive.

Higher or lower positioning is determined by the screen within each of us. This screen reflects the direct egoistic pleasure that can be derived from the Light of the Creator. The Light above the line is called "*Torah*." The screen, or the line separating our world from the spiritual one, is called a "barrier" (*machsom*).

Those who pass this barrier never again descend spiritually to the level of our world. Below the line is the realm of egoism, while above the line is the realm of altruism.

Advancing toward Altruistic Pleasure

Atzilut is the world of complete perception of, and unification with, the Creator. An individual gradually rises to the world of *Atzilut*, acquiring altruistic qualities. When one has reached this world, having fully acquired the ability to "give," even standing on its lowest step, one starts "receiving for the sake of the Creator."

We do not destroy our desire to experience pleasure, but rather alter our essence by changing the reason for which we are seeking the pleasure. By gradually replacing egoism with altruism, we can rise accordingly until we receive everything to which we are entitled, in accordance with the root of our soul (*shoresh neshama*), which originally was a part of the last level (*malchut*) of the world *Atzilut*.

As a result of corrections we make to ourselves, our souls will rise to a state of complete unification with the Creator, and in the process we will receive 620 times more Light than what our souls possessed prior to entering the human corporeal body.

All the Light, the entire pleasure that the Creator wants to impart to His creations, is known as the "common soul" of all the creations (*Shechina*). The Light allotted to each of us (the soul of each of us) is part of that common soul. Each of us should receive this part as we correct our desires.

We can perceive the Creator (one's own soul) only after we have corrected our desire for pleasure.

This desire is known as the "vessel of the soul" (*kli*). That is, the soul consists of the vessel and the Light, which comes from the Creator.

When we have totally replaced the egoistic vessel with an altruistic one, then this vessel will merge completely with the Light, for it has acquired its characteristics.

Thus, we can become equal to the Creator and absolutely merge with His qualities, experiencing everything that exists in the Light and fills it.

There are no words to describe this state. For this reason, it is said that the sum total of all pleasures in this world is but a spark from the infinite fire of the joy that the soul experiences during its unification with the Creator.

We can ascend on the spiritual ladder only in accordance with the law of the middle line (*kav emtzai*). This principle can be briefly described as: "One who is happy with what one has is considered rich."

We should be content with as much as we understand of what we study in Kabbalah. Most important, we must realize that, by learning Kabbalah, we begin doing good deeds before the Creator. When we carry out His Will, we will feel as if we have carried it out to the utmost.

This sensation will award us immense happiness, and we will feel as if we have received the greatest gift in the world. We have this feeling because we are placing the Creator as King of the Universe, far above ourselves. Therefore, we are happy to have been singled out from among billions by the Creator Who, through books and teachers, informs us of what He wants from us.

This spiritual state is known as "the longing to give" (*hafetz hesed*). In it, a person's qualities can coincide with the qualities of the spiritual object, known as *Bina*. But this state does not represent human perfection, for we do not use our reason during such a process of self-correction.

Thus, we are still considered to be "poor in knowledge" (*ani be da'at*), because we are not aware of the correlation between our actions and their spiritual consequences. In other words, we act without knowing what we are doing, guided only by faith.

In order to commit spiritual acts consciously, we must invest a lot of effort into realizing that our thoughts need to be "for the sake of the Creator." At this point, we may begin to feel that we are not ascending spiritually. Yet, in truth, every time we observe something, it becomes evident that we are farther than ever from possessing the appropriate intention—

to please the Creator to the same extent as the Creator desires to please us.

However, we must not criticize our state further than the level that allows us to remain content with perfection. This state is called "the middle line" (*kav emtzai*). As we gradually build up our knowledge with the left line (*kav smol*), we then can achieve total perfection.

Once again, let us analyze the work that takes place in the middle line. We must begin our spiritual ascent by being in accordance with the right line, which represents a sense of perfection in the spiritual, happiness with our lot, and our desire to carry out the Will of the Creator selflessly and sincerely.

We must ask, "How much pleasure do we derive from our spiritual quest?" We consider any amount sufficient, because we are convinced that the Creator controls everything in the world, and whatever we feel during our spiritual quest, it must be so desired by the Creator.

Whatever our condition may be, it must ensue from the Creator. Thus, the mere realization of Divine Rule and spiritual perfection is sufficient to make us happy, to give us a sense of our own perfection, and to induce us to thank the Creator.

But this state lacks the left line, in which we check our own condition (*heshbon nefesh*). This inner task is opposite to the work done in the right line, where the main focus is on glorifying the spiritual and the Creator, irrespective of oneself or of one's own condition.

When we begin checking how serious our attitude is toward the spiritual, and how close we are to perfection, it becomes obvious that we are still immersed in petty egoism and cannot lift a finger for the sake of others or the Creator.

Having discovered the evil in ourselves, we must strive to oust that evil, and must apply our utmost efforts to this task.

We must also pray to the Creator for help as soon as it is clear that we are unable to transform ourselves without assistance. Thus, there become two opposite lines in a person. Alongside the right line, we feel that all is in the power of the Creator and, therefore, all is perfect. So we do not wish for anything and are, therefore, happy.

By the left line, we feel no interest in the spiritual; we have no sense of spiritual progress, and we sense that we are still encased in the shell of our ego, just as before. Furthermore, we do not ask the Creator for help to escape from this state. Having discovered the evil within, we decide to dispense with our common sense because it tries to dissuade us from our efforts to pursue the hopeless task of correcting our egoism.

At the same time, we should continue to thank the Creator for our present state, sincerely believing that this state is truly the perfect state. We should also continue to be just as happy as we were prior to checking our state.

If we can manage to follow this, we will advance along the middle line. Thus, it is crucial to avoid becoming too critical of ourselves by excessively following the left line.

It is also important to remain in the content state of the middle line. Only then will we be able to enter the spiritual realm with "both feet," so to speak.

There are two levels of human development: animal and human being. (These are not to be confused with the four levels of desires). As we can observe in animal nature, an animal continues to live in the same state as it was born. It does not develop. The qualities that were accorded to an animal on the day of its birth are sufficient for the entire duration of its existence.

The same can be said of a person who rests on this level of development—one who remains the same as during one's upbringing. All changes that take place in the life of such a person are quantitative in nature.

However, this cannot be said of the "human being" type. In this state, a person is born as an egoist. At some point, this person will discover that egoism rules, and in response, aspires to correct this flaw. If a person truly wishes to earn the Revelation of the Creator, then the following must be so:

1. This must be the person's strongest desire, so that no other desires exist. In addition, this desire must be permanent, for the Creator is eternal and His Will to bestow good is constant. Thus, one who wishes to come closer to the Creator must resemble the Creator in this quality as well, i.e., all desires must be constant. They cannot change depending on circumstances.

2. One must acquire altruistic desires, and devote all thoughts and desires to the Creator. This level is called *hesed* or *katnut*. Eventually, one will come to earn the Light of Faith, which will bestow the gift of confidence upon the person.

3. One must earn the complete and perfect knowledge of the Creator. The consequences of one's actions are determined by one's spiritual level. However, there will be no difference between the spiritual levels if the Light of the Creator shines upon an individual. Since the Creator bestows the vessel and the Light of the soul simultaneously upon the recipient, the person perceives the received knowledge to be perfect. Usually, we are in total accord with our bodies; the body dictates its desires to us, and repays us for our labors by letting us experience pleasure. Pleasure, in itself, is spiritual, but in our world it must be connected to some material carrier

(e.g., food, sex, music) to enable us to experience it. Even though within ourselves we feel pure pleasure, we are incapable of detaching it completely from its carrier.

Different people enjoy different things and different types of pleasure carriers. But pleasure, in itself, is spiritual, even though we experience it in our brains as an effect of electrical impulses. Theoretically, it is possible to fully simulate a wide range of pleasures by applying electrical impulses to the brain. Since we are accustomed to receiving various pleasures in the form of their material carriers, this pure pleasure will recreate the images of various carriers in a person's memory, so that the mind will create music, the taste of food, and so on.

The above makes it clear that we and our bodies service each other. Therefore, when our bodies agree to work, they expect to be rewarded with some form of pleasure.

Escaping from disagreeable sensations can also be considered a kind of pleasure. Any correlation between the work performed and the pleasure received (reward) is a definite indication that the person has performed an egoistic act.

On the other hand, if a person feels that the body is resisting and is asking, "Why work?" it means that the body does not foresee a greater degree of pleasure in the future than it already possesses now. At the least, there is enough increase in pleasure to overcome the propensity to remain in a state of rest. Thus, it does not see any benefit in altering its state.

But if a person decides to abandon the considerations of the body and elects to concentrate on improving the condition of the soul, then the body will refuse to make even the slightest move unless there is the prospect of some personal benefit. The individual will be unable to force the body to work.

Thus, only one solution will be open—to appeal to the Creator for help in moving forward. The Creator does not replace a person's body, nor alter one's nature. He doesn't make miracles to change the fundamental laws of nature.

However, in response to a true prayer, the Creator gives a person a soul—the power to act on the principles of truth.

When we receive egoistic pleasures, it implies that someone else will not be happy while this is occurring.

This is because egoistic pleasures center not only on what we have, but also on what others do not have, since all pleasures are comparative and relative.

For this reason, it is impossible to build a fair society on the basis of reasonable egoism. The erroneous nature of such utopias has been proven throughout history, particularly in ancient communities, in the former USSR and in other attempts to build socialism.

It is impossible to satisfy each and every member of an egoistic society because individuals always compare themselves with another. This is best seen in small settlements.

Thus, the Creator, Who is always willing to award everyone boundless pleasure, set down one condition—that this pleasure should not be limited by the desires of the body. Pleasure would be received only in the desires that are independent from the desires of the body. These are known as "altruistic" (*ashpa'ah*).

Kabbalah is a sequence of spiritual roots proceeding from one another in accordance with immutable laws, merging and pointing toward their single common purpose—"the comprehension of the Creator's greatness and wisdom by the creations of this world."

Kabbalistic language is closely related to spiritual objects and their acts. Thus, it can only be studied while examining the process of creation. Kabbalah touches upon certain issues, which are then revealed to those seeking spiritual perception. There is no concept of time, but only of a cause-and-effect chain, where every effect becomes, in its turn, the cause of the next effect—the creation of a new act or object.

In principle, what we take for time, even in our world, is actually our perception of inner cause-and-effect processes. Even science maintains that time, as well as space, are relative concepts. A place, or space, is a desire for pleasure. An action is either the receiving of pleasure or its rejection.

"In the beginning," that is, prior to the creation, nothing existed but the Creator. He cannot be denoted by any other name, for any name implies a certain perception of the object. But the only thing that we perceive in Him is the fact that He created us. Thus, we can only address Him as our Creator, Maker, etc.

The Creator transmits Light. The Light represents His desire to generate a creation and endow this creation with a sense of being pleased by Him. Only this single quality of the Light that issues from the Creator gives us a basis by which we can judge Him.

To be more precise, the perception of the Light does not permit us to make judgments about the Creator alone, but only about the perceptions that He wants to inspire in us. For this reason, we refer to Him as we would to Someone Who wants to please us.

This pleasure is not derived from the Light alone, but is produced in us by the effect of the Light on our "organs of spiritual sensations." Similarly, a piece of meat does not, in itself, contain the pleasure that one feels when one tastes it.

Only by coming in contact with the sensory organs can an object produce in us related sensations of pleasure.

Any act, either spiritual or physical, consists of both a thought and an action that embodies the thought.

The thought of the Creator is to bestow pleasure on His creations. Consequently, He awards us pleasure.

This act is called "giving for the sake of giving." It is called a simple act because its purpose corresponds to its direction.

The creation was generated to be egoistic in nature, meaning that we have no other goal but to attain pleasure. We can either engage in receiving or in giving as part of the pursuit of what we desire, but our ultimate goal always remains to receive, even if we also give something physically to another.

If the act is characterized by the same direction as the goal, that is, if the result of an action is to receive, and the result of the goal is to receive, then such an action is referred to as "a simple act." If, on the other hand, the direction is to give but the purpose is to receive, then the act is referred to as "a complex act," because its purpose and its direction diverge in their intentions.

We are incapable of imagining the desires and the realms of our desires' effects beyond space. Therefore, we can only imagine the Creator as a spiritual Force that fills a space. The Kabbalists say that the Creator originally designed human beings with the ability to engage only in simple acts; however, we have since complicated the original design.

The higher we ascend on the spiritual ladder, the simpler the laws of creation become, as the basic, fundamental categories are simple, not complex.

But because we fail to perceive the Source of creation, and instead see only its remote consequences, we view the laws of

ATTAINING THE WORLDS BEYOND

creation in our world as being comprised of conditions and limitations, and thus complicated.

Since authentic Kabbalistic books contain hidden Light, which emanates from the authors in the course of writing their books, it is vital to have the right intention while studying such works; namely, the will to perceive the Creator. It is also very important, while studying, to pray to receive the spiritual intellect and understanding that the author possessed. In this way, we may forge a bond with, and can address, the author.

Thus, it is also essential to refrain from reading the works of other authors, especially those who also deal with the spiritual worlds. The reason for this is that these authors may influence the reader, as well. If we wish to acquire spiritual knowledge, we must establish a special daily routine and shield ourselves from extraneous influences, irrelevant news, and harmful books.

We must also avoid contact with other people, except when it becomes necessary for work or for study, without deliberately shunning them, but keeping our thoughts continuously in check. When necessary, we can think of our work. The rest of the time we should devote to contemplating the purpose of life.

Attaining the purpose of life depends more on the quality of the effort made than on the quantity: one person can pore over the books for days on end, and another can only devote an hour a day to one's studies, due to the demands of work and family.

Any effort can be measured only in relation to one's free time, and by determining how much one suffers because of a lack of time to devote to the spiritual. The result is directly proportional to the intensity of the person's intentions:

discovering is the objective of devoting one's time to study and self-correction.

There are two methods of feeding a child. One method is by force. It brings the child no pleasure, but still provides the nourishment necessary for growing and building up strength. In Kabbalah, this kind of spiritual nurturing of a person is known as "on account of the Higher One."

However, the "child" may wish to grow spiritually by taking spiritual nourishment independently. This may occur after having developed an appetite for it (realizing the necessity or experienced the pleasure from the Light). Then, not only does one grow spiritually, but one also enjoys the process of living, that is, of developing spiritual perception.

An acute sensation produced in us by the awareness of good and evil is known in Kabbalah as "the process of nurturing": just as a mother raises her infant to her breast and gives it food, so a Kabbalist is given the Light contained at an Upper Spiritual Level so that one clearly sees and feels the gulf between good and evil.

And then, just as the mother takes the infant away from her breast, so a Kabbalist loses the bond with the Higher Source, as well as the clear distinction between good and evil. This process is designed to induce a person to pray to the Creator to acquire the same capabilities for perceiving (*kelim*) the good and evil as are possessed by the Higher Source.

We receive both egoism and altruism from Above. The difference is in the fact that human beings receive egoistic desires upon birth, while one must persistently ask for altruistic desires.

First, we must reach a state in which we want "to please the Creator," the same way as the Creator pleases us, irrespective of our egoistic desires (ascending the levels of the worlds *BYA*). Then, we should determine what will please the Creator.

Consequently, we will see that we can only please the Creator by experiencing pleasure. This is called "receiving for the sake of the Creator," and denotes the level of the world (*Atzilut*).

Attaining the different degrees of intensity of the desire to give selflessly to the Creator is called "the steps of the worlds *BYA*" (*Beria, Yetzira, Assiya*). Acquiring the power to receive pleasure from the Creator for His sake is known as "reaching the level of the world" (*Atzilut*).

Beit midrash is the place where we learn to demand (*lidrosh*) spiritual strength of the Creator and the spiritual strength. There we also learn to demand the perception of the goal of creation, as well as the perception of the Creator. Since we (our bodies, our egoism) strive naturally toward all that is larger and stronger than ourselves, we must pray for the Creator to reveal Himself to us and let us see our own insignificance, as compared to His greatness. Then, we will strive toward Him naturally, as toward the greatest and the strongest.

What matters most for us is the importance of our pursuits. For instance, rich people may work hard simply to make others envy them. But if wealth were no longer important, they would not be envied anymore, and thus, they would have no more incentive to work.

Therefore, the most important thing is to realize the importance of perceiving the Creator. There will never come a time when an individual will be able to reach the spiritual realm without any efforts, for these efforts are the vessels for the Light.

Before the Kabbalist Ari introduced his corrections in this world, it had been somewhat easier to attain the spiritual.

However, after Ari opened the way to comprehend the spiritual, it became much harder to give up the pleasures of this world.

Prior to Ari, the spiritual ways were closed, and there was no actual readiness from Above to confer the Light on creations. Ari slightly opened the source of the Light. This made it harder for people to battle their egoism; in fact, the egoism became stronger and more sophisticated.

This can be schematically illustrated by the following example. Let us suppose that prior to Ari's time, one could obtain 100 units of comprehension. Each effort amounting to 1 unit would yield 1 unit of perception. Today, after the corrections were introduced into the world by Ari, one can obtain 100 units of perception for just 1 unit of effort, but it is incomparably harder to carry out this 1 unit of effort.

Rabbi Yehuda Ashlag (Baal HaSulam) has introduced such corrections into the world that now an individual cannot deceive oneself, thinking that one is perfect, but must follow the path of faith above knowledge. Though the path has become somewhat clearer, this generation is incapable of making the required quantity and quality of effort, the way the previous generations could. This, despite the fact that the perception of individual shortcomings is clearer than before.

But this generation does not elevate the spiritual to the level it deserves, that is, above the material, the way previous generations did, when the majority of people were willing to do anything for the sake of spiritual ascent.

A significant correction was introduced into the world by the Kabbalist Baal Shem-Tov. Even the masses could feel a slight increase in the amount of the spiritual in the world. For a while, those who desired it found it even easier to reach the spiritual.

In order to select worthy students for his Kabbalistic group, Baal Shem-Tov instituted *Admorut*—a division of Jewish society into sections, with each section having a Kabbalist as its own spiritual leader. These leaders (*Admorim*) selected individuals whom they deemed to be worthy of studying Kabbalah in their *Heder* (room) classes. Here they engaged in raising the next generation of Kabbalists and leaders of the people.

But the effect of the correction introduced by Baal Shem-Tov has passed, so not all leaders of our generation are Kabbalists and are able to perceive the Creator. After the departure of Baal Sulam, our world has been in a state of spiritual degradation, which always precedes an approaching elevation.

Perceiving ourselves as beings that were created means perceiving ourselves as being separate from the Creator. Since our egoistic nature causes us to instinctively withdraw from anything that causes us suffering, the Creator uses this to lead us to the good. He removes pleasure from the material world that surrounds us and awards us pleasure only through altruistic acts. This is the path of suffering.

12

Eradicating Egoism

The path of Kabbalah is different from other paths. Even though there are pleasures in our world, we can break away from egoism by having faith (above reason) in the purpose of creation. In this way, we may go beyond listening to what our bodies and our reason tell us.

When we do so, we start experiencing love for the Creator, as well as feeling His love for us. This is the path of peace and joy, and of faith in the fact that the long way is, in fact, the short way without suffering. When we are not capable of receiving the Light into the self—the Inner Light (*Ohr Pnimi*)—our spiritual development will take place only under the influence of the Surrounding Light (*Ohr Makif*).

This path of spiritual development is called "the natural way" or "the way of suffering" (*Derech B'ito*). This is the path of all humanity.

Another alternative for our spiritual development is to establish a personal bond with the Creator, characterized by the work in three lines. This way is called "the way of Kabbalah" (*Derech Kabbalah, Derech Ahishena*). It is much shorter than the way of suffering.

Thus, the Kabbalists say that an individual who wishes to go directly toward the Creator shortens the time of correction. Although it is difficult to have faith if suffering does not force us to do so, it is very important for us to believe that the results of our work depend only on our efforts.

That is, we should believe in the Divine Rule by reward and punishment. The Creator rewards an individual by awarding good thoughts and desires. We should obtain faith from fellow students and from books.

However, once we have attained faith—the perception of the Creator—we must convince ourselves that it was given to us by the Creator. The Upper Spiritual Power may be a medicine of life if it provides strength and the will to work. However, it is considered poison if we believe that all is determined from Above and nothing depends on our efforts.

The principal effort should be the preservation of the lofty aspirations given to us from Above. First, we are sent spiritual sensations from Above. Then, we are elevated, followed by a time of hard work, and of constant effort to remain on that particular spiritual level by our own strength. We should concentrate on appreciating the value of our spiritual elevation.

As soon as we begin to disregard what we have acquired, or derive self-gratification from it, we begin to lose the attained spiritual level. All that falls under the power of egoism is situated in the central point of creation (*Nekuda Emtzait*).

Everything that does not wish to gratify the self is placed above that point. Thus, it is said that the line that represents the descent of the Light (*Kav*) makes contact (thus imperceptibly reviving the creation) and does not make contact (does not fill the creation with the Creator's Light) with the central point.

It is said that one who aspires to advance spiritually is helped by being given a soul—a part of the Creator—the Light. As a result, one begins to feel like a part of the Creator! How does the Light of the Creator generate the desire to derive joy from Him?

For example, in our world, if a person were given unexpected honors, which were then taken away, that person would crave the familiar pleasures derived from those honors. The desire to get back the taken pleasure is known as a "vessel" (Kli). The Light gradually makes the vessel grow in order to fill it with pleasure (from the Light).

Abraham asked the Creator: "How can I be sure that You will save my descendants? How can I be sure that my children will be able to break away from egoism with the help of Kabbalah? Why give them the Light if they have no yearning for it?"

The Creator answered that they would be given a sensation of enslavement by their egoism, and so, for contrast, they would be given a sensation of the Light. In attempting to overcome our desires, we need to recognize that our bodies do not understand the dimensions of time, and thus do not perceive the past or the future, but only the present.

For instance, if it is crucial to exert an effort for five minutes in order to be able to rest afterwards, the body will still resist putting forth that effort because it is unable to grasp the benefit that will follow shortly.

Even when we remember the pleasure we previously attained after hard work, our bodies will still withhold the necessary strength to complete the task. This can be similar to a case where a person gets paid for work prior to its completion, and does not truly want to put forth a good effort to finish the job.

Therefore, it is important not to delay the struggle against the body, but instead to use every opportunity at a given moment to counter the body with loftier thoughts.

Since we are all 100% egoists, we will never voluntarily wish to form a bond with the Creator. Only when we are convinced that this bond will bring a certain benefit will we desire connection.

Thus, we can conclude that simply seeing our own evil and understanding that only the Creator can send help is still insufficient impetus to seek help from the Creator. Only by realizing that coming closer to the Creator, and forming a bond with Him, will bring redemption will we have the incentive to seek help.

Kabbalah offers us its path, rather than the path of suffering. Time changes the conditions around us: two thousand years ago, only a precious few searched for a connection with the Creator, as in the time of Rabbi Shimon.

In the times of Ari and Ramchal, small groups were already engaged in the study of Kabbalah. In the times of Baal Shem-Tov, the number of groups grew to dozens.

Finally, in the times of Baal Sulam, the numbers increased even further. In our times, the barrier that separates the masses from Kabbalah has been obliterated altogether, and there is hardly any resistance to the teaching. If in the past only those of very strong character could attain the connection with the Creator, today beginners—and even children—can reach the same results simply by studying Kabbalah under the proper supervision.

We are unable to separate the good from the evil, just as we are unable to discern what is good for the self and what is detrimental. Only the Creator can help us in this respect by opening our eyes. Only then do we begin to see everything, which means "to choose life."

But until we come to realize our absolute necessity for the constant connection to the Creator, He will not open our eyes. In this way, He will induce us to ask for compassion.

Inside the internal sensations of the Kabbalist exists a part of the Higher Level, of the future state (*AHaP*). One who perceives a Higher Spiritual Level as an unattractive vacuum, rather than a state full of Light, does not receive from the Higher level.

Even though the Higher Level is full of Light, the lower level perceives the Higher only to the degree that the lower qualities permit one to do so. Since the present qualities are not sufficient to receive the Higher Light, the individual does not perceive it.

The concealment of the Creator causes each of us to put forth a tremendous effort to attain the level of existence customarily accepted by our society. We blindly move forward, guided by the quiet internal whispers of our egoism. Acting as the ego's blind tools, we rush to carry out its commands to avoid being punished through suffering, thus propelling us to accept the ego's will against our own will, and carry out its wishes without thinking twice.

Our egoism is rooted so deeply inside us that we have begun to accept it as a basic part of our nature, one that represents our true desires.

It penetrates all the cells of our bodies and forces us to evaluate all our perceptions in accordance with its desires. It also forces us to plan our actions in accordance with its design, thus increasing its benefit from our actions.

We do not even imagine that we can shed the influence of egoism, and cleanse ourselves of it. But it *is* possible to expel the egoistic cloud that takes the form of our body, penetrates us, and garbs itself with our flesh. Once we have been left without these desires, the Creator will accord us His altruistic aspirations.

As long as the egoistic presence remains within us, however, we are unable to imagine any benefit that would make us want to eradicate it. Moreover, altruistic thoughts and desires appear to us as unacceptable, silly, not serious, and certainly unable to form the basis of our society, much less that of the universe.

But this takes place only because our thoughts and desires remain under the influence of egoism. In order to be objective about our own condition, we must attempt to consider egoism as something outside of our essence, as an enemy who tries to pass itself off as a friend.

We must try to see egoism as something foreign to us, which was placed in us by the Will of the Creator. Such actions are considered to be our attempts to recognize the evil that stems from the ego. But this is possible only to the extent that we can sense the Creator's existence and perceive His Light, since everything is understood merely in relation to other objects, by the perception of opposites.

Thus, rather than concentrating all our energy on the search for the evil within us, we should make the utmost effort to perceive the Light of the Creator. All creations, with the exception of human beings, operate according to the laws of altruism.

Only human beings and the world surrounding us (our world, *Olam Hazeh*) are created with the opposite, egoistic qualities. If by chance we got a glimpse of the Creator and of all the spiritual worlds, we would immediately understand how minute our world is in comparison to the spiritual worlds. Therefore, the egoistic laws of nature operate only in a tiny, pea-sized world.

Why, then, did the Creator conceal Himself, after placing us deliberately in a world that is full of darkness, insecurity and sadness? When the Creator was creating us, His goal was to bestow on us an eternal existence together with Him.

However, we must reach this state by our own means, in order not to feel ashamed for having unjustly acquired eternal pleasure. Thus, the Creator generated a world that was opposite to Him in nature, and that epitomized the one quality opposite to His Essence: the desire to gratify oneself, or egoism.

Therefore, He endowed us with this quality. As soon as a human being is influenced by this quality, that human is born into this world, and immediately stops perceiving the Creator. The concealment of the Creator exists in order to give us the illusion that we possess free will to choose between our world and the world of the Creator—the Upper World.

If, despite our egoism, we were able to see the Creator, naturally we would prefer His world over ours, since the first contains all pleasure and no suffering.

However, freedom of choice and free will can only exist in the absence of our perception of the Creator while He is in concealment. But if, from the moment of birth, we are so strongly dominated by the ego that we cannot distinguish between the self and the ego, how can we choose to be free of the ego's influence?

Also, what choice can there truly be if our world is full of suffering and death, whereas the world of the Creator is full of pleasure and immortality? What is left for human beings to choose?

In order to allow us to have free will, the Creator gave us two options:

1. At times, He reveals Himself to one of us to enable that person to see His grandeur and Providence and, as a result, to experience calmness.

2. He gave us Kabbalah—the study of which (assuming that one truly wants to come out of the present state and perceive the Creator) brings forth a hidden, surrounding, spiritual Light (*Ohr Makif*). The process of our connecting with the Creator, starting from the

lowest level (where we live) and extending to the highest level (where the Creator dwells) can be compared to climbing the steps of a spiritual ladder.

All the steps of this ladder exist in the spiritual worlds. The Creator resides on the highest step, whereas the lowest step comes down to our world. Human beings are situated below the lowest spiritual step, since our initial egoistic level is not connected with the first spiritual state, which is completely altruistic.

We can perceive an Upper Spiritual Level when our qualities and those of the spiritual state coincide. Then, our degree of perception will be proportional to the degree of congruence between our qualities and those of the spiritual.

We can perceive the Upper Level because all the spiritual steps are arranged sequentially from lowest to highest. Moreover, the subsequent states overlap with one another; the lower half of the higher state is situated within the upper half of the lower state (*AHaP* of *Upper* falls into *GE* of *Lower*).

Thus, the lowest part of our Upper State is always present within us, but is usually not felt by us. The Upper State above us is referred to as "the Creator" because it functions as the Creator for us.

It gives birth to us and it gives us life and guidance. Since we do not have a perception of this Higher State, we often insist that the Creator does not exist.

But if we are in a state in which we clearly see the Creator's Upper Domain over all the creations in this world, then we lose the possibility to choose freely.

We can see only One Truth, only One Force, and only One Will that operates in everything and in everyone.

Since the Will of the Creator is to grant each human being a free will, then the concealment of the Creator from His creations is necessary. Only if He is hidden can we argue that we can aspire *of our free will* to attach ourselves to the Creator—to act for His sake, without any trace of self-interest.

The entire process of self-correction is possible only when the Creator is concealed from us. As soon as He reveals Himself to us we immediately become His servants and fall into the control of His thought, grandeur and power.

At that point, it is impossible to determine what our true thoughts are. Thus, in order to allow us to act freely, the Creator has to conceal Himself.

On the other hand, to give us a chance to break free from the blind slavery of egoism, the Creator must reveal Himself. This is so because a human being obeys only two forces in this world: the force of egoism—the body—and the force of the Creator—altruism.

It follows, then, that alternating the two states is necessary. These states are the concealment of the Creator from us when we perceive only ourselves and the egoistic forces governing us, and the Revelation of the Creator when we feel the power of the spiritual forces.

In order for one who is still under the influence of egoism to perceive the closest Upper Object (the Creator), the Creator must equalize some of His qualities with those of the lower being—the person seeking a connection with the Creator.

He will endow some of His altruistic qualities with egoistic attributes, and can then come into balance with the person seeing connection with Him.

The Upper Part elevates the *Malchut-Midat hadin* to the level of His *Galgalta ve Eynaim*. As a result, His *AHaP* acquires egoistic qualities. In this manner, His *AHaP* "descends" to the lower part (the spiritual level of the seeker) and comes into a state of equivalence with the qualities of the lower part.

Initially the lower part was not able to perceive the Upper Spiritual State. However, because the Creator hid His highest altruistic qualities behind egoistic ones, He was able to descend to the level of the person so that the person was able to perceive Him.

Because we perceive higher qualities as being egoistic, we are unable to truly grasp their essence. It appears that there is nothing positive in the spiritual that may bring pleasure, inspiration, confidence, or tranquility.

It is precisely at this point that we have an opportunity to exercise our willpower. We may, instead, declare that the absence of pleasure and taste in the spiritual and in Kabbalah is because of the Creator's deliberate concealment for our own sake. Because we do not yet possess the necessary spiritual qualities, it is therefore impossible for us to perceive the Upper spiritual pleasures; rather, all our earthly desires are governed by egoism.

It is crucial for beginners to understand that they are given depression and distress in order to overcome them.

They may direct their pleas for relief to the Creator, they may study, or they may do good deeds. The fact that such people do not experience pleasure or vitality from spiritual aspirations is directed from Above.

This gives them the free will to conclude that their lack of pleasure comes from a lack of appropriate altruistic qualities in themselves. Hence, the Upper One must hide His true qualities from them.

Therefore, we must remember that the first stage of perceiving the spiritual is the feeling of spiritual deprivation. If the lower part is capable of realizing that the Upper One is concealing Himself because of their incongruity of qualities, and if that lower part asks for help to correct its own egoism by raising a prayer (*Ma'N*), then the Upper Part partially reveals Himself (lifts His *AHaP*) and displays His true qualities, which prior to this moment, were disguised beneath egoism.

As a result, spiritual pleasure also becomes apparent. Thus, the lower part begins to experience the grandeur and the spiritual pleasure felt by the Higher Being, Who possesses spiritual altruistic qualities.

Because the Upper Part elevated His altruistic qualities in the eyes of the individual, He thus elevated the individual to the middle of His State (He lifted *GE* of the lower together with His own *AHaP*).

This spiritual state is known as a person's "lesser spiritual level" (*Katnut*). The Upper Part, in a way, elevates the lower part to His own spiritual level by revealing both His grandeur and the grandeur of altruistic qualities. By seeing the magnificence of the spiritual and comparing it to the material, we may spiritually rise above our world.

When we perceive the spiritual, regardless of our will, our egoistic qualities are changed into altruistic ones, that is, into the qualities of the Creator. In order to allow the lower part to take complete possession of the higher first level, the Upper Part wholly reveals Himself and all His qualities to that lower part; meaning He reveals his Grandeur, makes *Gadlut*.

At this point, the person perceives the Upper Part as the One and Only Absolute Sovereign of everything in the universe. At the same time, the lower part grasps the highest knowledge of the purpose of creation and of the Upper's dominion.

It becomes clear to the lower part that there is no other way to conduct oneself than in the way prescribed by Kabbalah. Thus, the lower part's reason now requires proper action. As a result of this clear awareness of the Creator, one must deal with the contradiction between faith and knowledge, between the right and the left lines.

Now, having acquired altruistic qualities (*Katnut*), the lower part prefers to proceed only by means of faith in the strength of the Creator. This serves as an indication of the seeker's sincere desire to come closer to the Creator.

However, the Creator's Revelation of His grandeur (*Gadlut*) now obstructs one from advancing by faith. Consequently, the individual must willingly dispense with the acquired knowledge.

When one pleads to proceed blindly, relying only on one's faith in the magnificence of the Creator, rather than by realizing His power and grandeur, and only by using reason in proportion to one's faith, the Creator is compelled to limit His disclosure. When such an action compels the Creator to diminish His disclosure of His general dominion, His omnipotence, and His Light (*Ohr Hochma*), this is called "the screen of *hirik*."

Through this screen, we are able to diminish the revelation of the Upper reason (the left line) to the point at which this revelation can be balanced with faith, the right line. The correct correlation between faith and knowledge is called a "spiritual balance," or the middle line.

We, as individuals, determine the state we desire to be in. Once the correct correlation of faith and knowledge is in place, we can then attain perfection. This is known as "the middle line."

The part of revealed knowledge (the left line) that we can use in proportion to our faith (the right line), by proceeding by faith above reason (the middle line), is added onto those spiritual qualities that we possessed before, in the state of *Katnut*. The newly acquired spiritual level is known as *Gadlut*, meaning big and complete.

After the first complete spiritual level has been attained, we will become equal in qualities to the very first (the lowest) state of the spiritual ladder. As was mentioned earlier, all the states, or steps of the ladder, overlap with each other.

Having reached the first level, we may discover the presence of a higher level within us. Using the same principle as when advancing to the first level, we can proceed step by step to the goal of creation—complete unification with the Creator on the highest level.

An essential part of our spiritual ascent is a special process that requires that, on discovering a greater evil within us, we ask the Creator to grant us the strength to overcome that evil. We then receive strength in the form of a greater spiritual Light.

This continues until we actually reach the original level and size of our souls: at that point, our egoism is completely corrected and filled with Light.

The Search for the Creator

When we are distracted by outside thoughts, we feel that thoughts obstruct us from ascertaining the spiritual, because our strength and minds are wasted on extraneous concerns, while our hearts become filled with petty desires. At times like this, we lose faith in the fact that only Kabbalah contains the true life.

Once we overcome this condition, we come out of our state and move into the Light, receiving a higher Light that helps us ascend further. In this manner, our extraneous thoughts work to help us in our spiritual advancement.

We can overcome obstacles only with the help of the Creator. We can only work on something if we perceive some personal benefit in the task. However, our bodies, hearts and intellects do not understand what benefits can result from altruism.

Therefore, as soon as we try to make even the slightest altruistic move, we lose all strength of the mind, heart and body. We are left with nothing else but to turn to the Creator and ask Him for help. In this way, unwillingly and without any free choice, we advance toward the Creator until we merge with Him completely.

We should not complain of having been born insufficiently smart, strong or courageous, or lacking qualities that others possess.

If we do not advance on the right path, what difference does it make if we are endowed with the best abilities and potential?

It may be that a talented person can become a great scientist, but without a connection with the Creator, this person's purpose will not be achieved, and will fail just as the majority of people do.

It is crucial to attain the level of a righteous person; only then can we use all of our potential for the right tasks, rather than squander our strength in vain. Even the weakest and most trivial abilities given to us by the Creator should be used for the sake of the loftiest goals.

If we are in a state of spiritual descent, it is useless to try to convince us to cheer up, or to subject us to listening to the learned wisdom of others. Nothing that others will say can help us. The stories of what other people lived through and their advice will not enliven us when depressed, because we have lost all faith in everything, including the achievements of others.

However, we must repeat to ourselves what we used to say and feel when in a state of spiritual exhilaration and full of life, as opposed to being spiritually dead as at present. If we remember our own goals and spiritual progress, then we can grow to regain our good spirits.

By remembering that at some point we had faith and advanced in life by means of faith above reason, we can help ourselves emerge from the state of spiritual death. For this reason, we should always rely on our own recollections and experiences. Only these will motivate us to forsake the state of depression.

The task of one who has reached a certain spiritual level is to make a selection from the myriad of pleasures that arise, immediately discarding all those pleasures that cannot be balanced by faith, since they are not fit for use. In Kabbalah, that part of pleasure that a person receives for the sake of the Creator, for the sole purpose of strengthening one's faith, is considered "food."

On the other hand, the other part that one is unable to receive is considered "refuse." If a person is incapable of distinguishing between the two and wants to devour the entire portion (in Kabbalistic terms, "to become drunk from the excess of pleasure"), then that person loses everything and is left with nothing. In Kabbalah, such a person is known as a "pauper."

All of us are "prescribed" in what we can and cannot do. If we decide to ignore the "prescription," then we are punished.

If we are unaware of the pain and suffering that may result from breaking the law, then we are bound to break the law, since as a result we will receive pleasure. Consequently, we will receive the punishment as well, in order that we realize that in the future we should not act in this particular manner.

For example, there exists a law that one is not permitted to steal money. But if a person possesses a strong pull toward money and knows where the money can be stolen, the crime will be committed. This is so even if there is no doubt that a theft will be followed by a punishment; the potential thief will still be incapable of realizing the full extent of the suffering that will follow the transgression.

Therefore, the person will decide that the pleasure from acquiring the money will exceed the suffering from the punishment that will follow. But when the suffering actually arrives, the thief then realizes that the suffering far exceeds expectations, and is certainly greater than the pleasure procured by the theft. At that point, the thief becomes ready to follow the law.

Once a person becomes free, a warning is given that the punishment for the next transgression will be much greater. This is done so that one does not forget the suffering that was experienced.

Thus, when the desire to steal arises again, one is reminded of both past suffering and the warning that the next punishment will be much more severe than the previous. This provides some incentive to hold oneself back from engaging in theft.

From the above example, and from many others that surround us every day, we can see that suffering directs a person to a path that otherwise would not be chosen if one were to follow the ego. It is always easier to steal than to earn, to rest than to think or to work, and to receive pleasure rather than suffer.

A person who decides to learn Kabbalah should know that it is for one's own good. In other words, a person should realize that the ego will benefit from such actions. None of us can take upon ourselves the burden of work that is completely selfless, that does not yield money, honor, pleasures, or hope for a better future.

Moreover, we are incapable of engaging in work that does not yield any results or any fruits; that does not bestow anything upon another; that does not result in any benefit being conferred upon another, or that appears to produce only senseless efforts in empty space.

It is natural that our egoistic reason and bodies are not prepared for such a task, because they have been designed by the Creator to receive pleasure.

We are forced to feel and act "altruistically" because of the suffering we receive in our daily lives, the complete loss of any delight or desire in life, and our strong conviction that we are incapable of receiving even the smallest pleasure from our surroundings.

Thus, we try altruism in the hopes that we will find redemption on this new path. Although this new approach to life cannot be considered to be ultimate altruism, since the goal of our actions is personal well being and salvation, this approach nevertheless approximates altruism.

It allows us to proceed gradually to the desired state, under the influence of the Light that is concealed in our actions. By behaving altruistically, but still benefiting because we are giving in order to receive, we begin to perceive the Light (pleasure) that is concealed in our actions. The nature of this Light is such that it corrects us.

We can observe similar events in nature. For instance, it can rain extensively, but not in the places where the rain would yield the greatest benefit. Thus, the rain may fall in the desert, where it produces little effect, rather than in the fields, where even the slightest precipitation can give rise to a variety of crops.

Similarly, a person can be engaged in the constant reading of spiritual texts, but the fruits, the spiritual understanding of the Creator that should result from these efforts, may be elusive. On the other hand, it is possible that by investing a much smaller effort in studying the right portions of Kabbalah, one may reap a greater harvest from one's efforts.

The same can be applied to the study of Kabbalah. If the entire process of studying is dedicated to the search for the Creator, rather than to the mere accumulation of knowledge, then the whole life-bearing effect of Kabbalah is rendered in the proper place.

But if the person is studying only to receive greater knowledge or, even worse, to display and take pride in the intellect, even Kabbalah will not yield the right results. In this case, it can, however, reveal the proper goal of studying, and thus help focus efforts in the right direction.

This process of correcting the direction of one's thought occurs while one constantly studies Kabbalah, since every human being's task is to steer thoughts and deeds in the right direction. By doing so, they will commune uniquely with the goal of creation. This is especially important while studying Kabbalah, since there is no stronger means of coming closer to the spiritual.

In the Bible, Egypt symbolizes the supremacy of our egoism (it is thus known as *Mitzraim*, from the words *mitz-ra*, the concentration of evil). *Amalek* represents the tribe that waged war against *Yisrael* (derived from *yisra*, straight, and *el*-Creator, that is, those who want to steer themselves directly to the Creator).

Amalek personifies our egoism, which under no circumstances wants to permit a person to become free of its power. Egoism is displayed (attacks) only in the desires of a person who attempts to depart from the Egyptian captivity (egoism). Even if one is situated at the very beginning of one's path, *Amalek* will immediately bar that individual's passage.

A sudden increase in perceiving one's egoism is sent only to those who are distinguished and chosen by the Creator.

Only those who are selected in order to attain a higher understanding of the Creator are sent the *Amalek*. This is intended to invoke in these people a real need for the Creator, rather than a mere need to improve their personal qualities, or simply to "become good people."

An individual, so chosen, begins to experience great difficulties in the realm of self-improvement. The desire to study, which was so strong in the past, suddenly wanes. The body becomes heavy when faced with actions it must take. The struggle with the body (the intellect, our "I") focuses on the body's desire to understand who the Creator is, where the body should go and why, and whether the body will benefit from each of the efforts.

Otherwise, without any benefit, neither the mind nor the body will have any energy or motivation to do something. And in this they are correct, since it is silly to carry out actions without knowing, in advance, the outcome. There is no way to transcend the limitations of our human nature and enter into the spiritual meta-world, other than by acquiring the intellect and the desires common to that meta-world.

These desires are opposite in nature to those of our world, since everything that we perceive and sense, and everything that creates the picture of "our world," is the product of our egoistic intellects and our egoistic hearts. Thus, only through the process of replacing the existing notions with opposite notions (faith replacing reason, and "giving" replacing "taking"), can we enter the spiritual world.

But since we only possess those tools that we were originally created with, intellect and egoism, and since our intellect works only for the benefit of our egoism, we cannot produce the different tools of reason and perception internally. These must be obtained from the outside, from the Creator.

For this reason, the Creator draws us to Himself, showing us in the process that we are unable to alter ourselves without His help. Even though the body refuses it, we must search for, and foster, a bond with the Creator, because only this bond will facilitate our spiritual redemption.

We should not ask the Creator for the ability to see and experience miracles, falsely believing that this experience will help us overcome the self and bring an appreciation of the grandeur of the spiritual, rather than simply being overtaken by blind faith.

Kabbalah warns against such thinking when it tells the story of exodus from Egypt: When *Amalek* attacked the people, Moses defeated them only by raising up his hands and asking for the power of faith.

In the process of spiritual ascent, we constantly acquire a higher reason that increases with each attained level.

As a result, we must constantly increase the power of our faith, so that it is always greater than the power of the intellect; otherwise, we may once again come under the influence of egoism.

This process continues until we are clinging only to the Creator. In the final stage we attain the ultimate understanding, the utmost reception of Light (*Ohr Hochma*) without any gradations. It is described as "the Light that was created in the first day of creation, in which (light) the first man saw from one end of the world to another end;" and in Kabbalah, it is said: "at the beginning of creation, everything was engulfed in the highest Light."

In other words, when the Light shines on all, without distinguishing the levels, then everything becomes clear. There is no beginning or end to this Light, there are no shades, and everything is absolutely comprehensible.

13

The Way of Kabbalah

The way of Kabbalah is a long, difficult period of reevaluating one's goals in life, of reassessing the self, clearly defining the direction of one's desires, truthfully assessing the motivating forces of one's actions, attempting to overcome the desires of the body and the demands of reason, as well as completely grasping the power of one's egoism. The way of Kabbalah is, at the same time, a hard, prolonged period of suffering to search to satisfy one's desires; it is a period of disappointment that one is unable to find a genuine "focus" of one's aspirations; it is the time of realizing that the only escape from the ultimate source of suffering (egoism) is the shift to altruistic thoughts, which will exclude any thoughts about the self, and will gradually lead to thoughts about the Creator. The latter will, in turn, bring about such pleasant feelings of serenity that one will not want to think about anything else.

Only after we have passed through all the stages of initial spiritual development—the way of Kabbalah—do we begin to perceive the Upper Light—the Light of Kabbalah—which shines more and more strongly upon us as we ascend the steps of the spiritual ladder that lead to our ultimate merging with the Creator.

Thus, our entire path is comprised of two parts: the way of Kabbalah and the Light of Kabbalah.

The way of Kabbalah is a period of preparing for new thoughts and desires, during which we experience feelings of suffering. But once we move over this bridge that leads to the dwelling of the Creator, we enter the world of spirituality, the Kingdom of Light. At this point, we reach the final goal of creation—the ultimate perception of the Creator.

The generation of the flood is called "a period of work of the heart," whereas the generation of building the Babylonian Tower is regarded as "the period of working with one's intellect." Each of us strives to satisfy every desire from the first moment of life up to the very last moment.

The difference between us is in the object from which we want to receive pleasure, whereas the pleasure itself is always spiritual. Only the outer shell creates the illusion of a material nature of pleasure. For this reason, subconsciously, we strive to change the outer "garments" of pleasure, hoping to receive pleasure in the pure form of the bare Light of the Creator.

However, since the difference between us is in our aspirations to different outer casings of pleasure, we judge people in accordance with the different names of these casings. Those casings, or "garments" of pleasure assumed to be "normal" are widely accepted, such as the love for children, for food, for warmth, etc. Other "garments" are much less acceptable, such as drugs, murder, or theft, so we must conceal our aspirations for these kinds of pleasure.

However, all of humanity accepts that within certain set boundaries, egoism can be utilized without any shame. Moreover, the acceptable boundaries within which egoism can be used constantly vary, as does the fashion that dictates which boundaries are better.

Each of us, in the course of our lives and under the influence of age, meaning under the general Providence of the Creator from Above—nature, also changes the "garments" we use to satisfy our need for pleasure.

Even from one individual to another, the change from one casing to the next is dramatic. For instance, a girl receives pleasure from a doll, but is not able to receive pleasure by caring for a real baby. On the other hand, her mother cannot receive any pleasure from a doll, just as she is unable to convince her daughter to find joy in taking care of a real child.

From the girl's point of view, formed in accordance with her own perceptions, her mother works very hard looking after a real baby, and gets no pleasure from it. In the girl's mind, no pleasure can be derived from a real child because it is not a doll. She is convinced that her mother will be compensated for her hard toil in the world to come, whereas the girl desires to receive pleasure in this world, and, thus, opts to play with the doll.

A child thinks in this manner, and one is not going to disagree with her because she is not of the age when she can derive pleasure from the real objects in this world. Therefore, she derives it from toys—from illusory, unreal objects.

All of us, being godly creations, only aspire to pleasure that emanates from the Creator. All of us can have a desire only for Him, and we all perceive life only in this aspiration. In this, we are no different from our souls prior to their descent into this world, when they garbed themselves with our bodies.

Nor are we different from our souls after they passed all the cycles of life, and finally returned to the Creator.

We are created so that we desire to be gratified by the Light that emanates from Him, and this cannot be changed, nor should it be changed!

All that is required of us is that we change the outer "garments" of our pleasure and that we replace the doll with the real baby, and thus attain real pleasure! A human being is like a child during feeding time, wishing to receive only what is desired. We humans will exert a certain effort if convinced that pleasure will follow as a result of the effort.

But if we want to engage in self-improvement and study Kabbalah, then the body immediately poses the question: Why is this necessary?

There are four answers to this question:

1. In order to spite others. This is the worst of all possible reasons because it aims to cause suffering to another.

2. In order to receive a good position, honor, and money; to find a promising match for oneself. This goal is better than the first because it will bring something useful to others. This is regarded as "working for others," since other people will compensate the person expending the effort.

3. In order to let only the Creator know about one's studies and efforts to improve oneself, but to keep it secret from others, thus avoiding being honored by others. Only a reward from the Creator is desired. This is regarded as working for the Creator, because one awaits the reward only from the Creator.

4. In order that the Creator will accept all the fruits of one's labors, while the laborer expects no reward in return. And only in this case will egoism pose the question: "What will you get for this?" There is no reasonable answer that can be given to oneself, so the solution is to proceed contrary to one's reason and feelings; that is, above one's reason and feelings.

In this manner, one's entire task comes down to a single effort to separate reason and feelings from the process of critically evaluating one's own state. Consequently, one places complete trust in the Creator.

All personal efforts should involve concentrating all thoughts and feelings on the Creator and on the grandeur of spiritual life. But should the inner voice of reason challenge one, advancing arguments for refocusing on the issues of daily life, that person should answer. "All that is required is indeed being fulfilled."

At the same time, every thought and desire should be for the benefit of the Creator. Moreover, one must refuse to accept the whole criticism of this inner voice, even when one finds oneself as if suspended in midair, without any concrete rational and mental foundation. Such a state is known as being "above reason and feelings" (lema'la me ada'at).

The greater the pleasure received from a certain possession, the more valuable one considers that possession. The more one values something, the more one fears losing it.

How can a person arrive at the realization of the importance of the spiritual without having experienced spirituality? This realization comes to one precisely while in the state of a spiritual vacuum, when one is troubled by the lack of even the smallest perception of the grandeur of the spiritual. That is, one feels far removed from the Creator, and unable to change oneself.

The efforts of one in such a state, regarded as one's "daily work," give rise to the importance of attaining spiritual perception, known as the Sabbath. This is a time when one no longer needs (and is actually forbidden) to work on oneself, but is only obligated to observe the Sabbath, so as not to lose this gift of the Creator.

If an individual has a personal stake in something, then that person can no longer objectively judge anything connected to it. For this reason, if one person attempts to tell another person directly that certain behavior is wrong, it is unlikely that the person will agree with these insights, since the behavior in question is convenient, and thus one is convinced that one is acting properly.

However, if that person agrees to behave in accordance with instructions from others, time will reveal that the truth lies not in one's past actions and thoughts, but in the behavior that is suggested at present.

Since the goal of the Creator is to benefit His creations (meaning us, since everything else is created by Him only for auxiliary purposes), then until a person discerns the quintessence of receiving pleasure and stops seeing deficiencies in quality, level, etc., that person still has not attained the goal of creation.

But in order to receive pleasure, which is the goal of creation, one must first undertake the correction of one's own desire to be gratified. One must be gratified simply because the Creator desires this.

We need not worry about receiving pleasure, since as soon as this correction is made, we will immediately feel the pleasure. Thus, we should concentrate on the task of correcting our *desire* to receive pleasure—our vessel.

This can be likened to the process of acquiring an apartment. We should not worry about how to get it. The concern should be how to pay for it, and how to earn the money needed for it. As soon as the financial aspect is arranged, we will own the apartment.

Therefore, all the efforts should be concentrated on the money, not on the apartment. The same can be applied to perceiving the spiritual. All efforts should be directed towards creating the conditions necessary to receive the Light, not on the Light itself. When we focus on cultivating altruistic thoughts and desires in ourselves; then we will feel the spiritual pleasure immediately.

The benefit of the progress of humanity, despite the fact that humanity appears to err constantly and never seems to learn from its own mistakes, is in the process of amassing suffering, which takes place in the eternal soul, as opposed to the temporal bodies. In this respect, not a single act of suffering is lost. It will eventually lead, in some cycle of life in this world, to realizing the necessity for turning to spiritual elevation in search of salvation from suffering.

It is correct to denote the Higher Spiritual Worlds as "anti-worlds" in relation to us, since in our world all the laws of nature are built on the basis of egoism, on striving to grab and to understand.

In contrast, the nature of the Higher Worlds is absolute altruism—the striving to give and to have faith. The foundations of the spiritual and the material natures are so diametrically opposed that there is no similarity between them.

Thus, all our attempts to imagine what takes place in the other world will not yield any result. Only by converting desires of the heart from "to grab" into "to give," and changing the desires of the intellect from "to understand" into "to believe" contrary to reason, will we receive the spiritual perceptions.

Both desires are connected to each other, even though the desire to grab is found in the heart and the desire to understand is found in the brain. This is because the foundation of both is egoism.

Kabbalah explains that the birth of the spiritual object is initiated when "the father takes the mother outside" in order to give birth to a son; the perfection "displaces" reason from analyzing the surroundings in order to receive a new, higher reason that will be independent of any desires, and, therefore, truly objective.

Mere faith in the Creator is not sufficient. This faith has to exist for the *sake* of the Creator, rather than for an individual's personal benefit. A prayer is regarded as turning to the

Creator in order to arouse a desire in Him to help the seeker, through prayer, attain a feeling of reverence for, and the grandeur of, the Creator.

It is only such turning towards Him that makes the Creator react by elevating the praying person to the Highest World, and by revealing to this person His whole grandeur. In this way, one can receive the strength to rise above one's own nature.

Only by receiving the Light of the Creator, which provides sufficient strength to overcome one's own egoistic nature, does a person have the sensation of having reached eternity and certainty.

Nothing can now change in the person. In fact, there can be no return to egoism, but instead, there will be eternal existence in the spiritual world. For this reason, such a person will perceive the present and the future as equal, thus producing the feeling of having attained eternity.

The Desire To Receive Pleasure

Since the Creator always remains in the state of absolute rest, we, as His creations, also strive to attain the state of rest in order to reach that which is desired. The Creator has created two forces for the sake of our development: the force that pushes us from behind—the suffering that forces us to escape from the unbearable state we are in; and the force of attraction, which draws us by the pleasures anticipated ahead.

But only the combination of these two forces, rather than each one of them separately, can advance us. Therefore, under no circumstances should we complain that the Creator has endowed us with laziness, thus implying that it is the fault of the Creator that it is so difficult for us to start advancing.

On the contrary, the fact that we are lazy means we do not impulsively and thoughtlessly follow every little temptation in life, but instead evaluate whether the object of temptation is worth the effort needed to follow it. And we do not attempt to escape suffering immediately. First, we attempt to assess the purpose of any suffering we have received, and learn how to avoid it in the future, as suffering coerces us into action and motion, which we are trying to resist.

In all situations in life, we would prefer to use our entire egos. However, people around us prevent us from acting in this manner. The rules of social conduct are built on everyone's tacit agreement to use egoism in a manner that causes others minimal damage.

This arrangement results from the fact that we expect to receive maximum benefit from any social contact that we engage in. For instance, the seller would prefer to receive money without parting with the object of sale. On the other hand, the buyer would like to receive the goods for free. An employer dreams of free laborers, while the laborers want to get paid without working.

Our desires can be measured only by the degree of suffering resulting from the absence of the desired. The greater the suffering from a lack of the desired, the greater the desire for that object.

It is said: "The Creator desires to dwell in lowly creations." Our goal in life, as well as the purpose of creation, is to create in ourselves the right conditions for the Divine to dwell within us.

Idol worship (*avoda zara*) is the adherence to the egoistic desires of the body. In contrast, spiritual work (*avodat*

Hashem, avodat haKodesh) follows from the adherence to altruistic desires or goals, if desires do not yet exist.

"Spiritual attachment" results when the qualities of two spiritual objects are completely similar. "Spiritual love" is the feeling of complete attachment of two opposite qualities: a human being and the Creator. If human beings do not have the desire to regain the power to return to rule their own desires, then they have attained true love of the Creator, rather than a mere subordination to Him.

The congruence of qualities implies that just as the Creator experiences joy from having a positive influence on His creations, so human beings experience joy from recognizing that it is possible to give something back to the Creator.

The return, *teshuva*, implies our return, while living in this world, to the spiritual state of existence at the time our souls were created, that is, to the state of the first Adam prior to his Fall.

We have two sources of action and two beginnings: the intellect and the heart, the thought and the desire. Both should undergo a transformation from their egoistic foundation into an altruistic one.

All our pleasures are experienced through the heart. Therefore, if we can refuse any earthly, or selfish, pleasure, then we deserve to receive the real pleasures from Above, because we no longer use our egoism.

On the other hand, the intellect does not receive pleasure from understanding what it is doing. If we can engage in a particular action from sheer faith, rather than from our own understanding, and can proceed contrary to the arguments of reason (go "above reason"), then we have eliminated egoism in the mind and can follow the Creator's reason, rather than our own understanding.

The Light of the Creator permeates all creations, including our world, even though we do not feel it.

This Light is called "the Light that invigorates the creation." It is due to this Light that the creations and the worlds exist. Without it, all life would cease, and the material dimension of the world would disappear.

This life-giving Light displays its effect in various material "garbs" of the objects and in different phenomena of our world that take place before our eyes. Everything that surrounds us, including ourselves and the crudest of the creations, is nothing else but the Light of the Creator.

We perceive it as many objects, since we respond to the outer shells, to the garb of the Light. In reality, it is the one and only Force that acts within each one of the creations—the Light of the Creator.

The majority of people do not perceive the Light of the Creator, but only the external garb. There are the people who perceive the Light of the Creator, but only in Kabbalah.

But there are also those who see the Light of the Creator in everything that surrounds them. This latter group perceives everything surrounding us as the Divine Light, which emanates from the Creator and fills everything with Itself.

The Creator decided to place a human being in this world so that the human being would rise spiritually from the depth of the original state to the level of the Creator, and thus become like the Creator. For this reason the Creator created the quality of egoism—the desire to receive pleasure.

In the beginning of creation, the Light (pleasure) filled the entire created expanse (egoism). It also completely filled all kinds of desires to receive pleasure. These were created as part of the conceived egoism.

Then, the Creator restricted the progression of Light and concealed it. In place of the Light, which existed in the creation, in the desire to receive pleasure, and in egoism, there came pain, emptiness, darkness, sorrow, and everything else imaginable when pleasure is absent.

In order to maintain in one a minimal desire to live, and to prevent suicide from lack of pleasure, the Creator endowed human beings with the desire to be gratified with a small portion of Light (*ner dakik*). This is enclosed in different objects of our world to which we aspire.

Therefore, subconsciously and automatically, we persist in the constant pursuit of the Light of the Creator, and are slaves to this natural aspiration. We must believe that the concealment of the Creator, and the feeling of hopelessness that results from the lack of pleasure, are purposely given to us by the Creator for our benefit.

If the Light of the Creator filled our egoism, we would lose the opportunity to exercise our free will, and no longer be able to act freely and independently. Instead, we would become slaves to the pleasure that fills us.

Only when separated from the Light of the Creator do we experience His concealment, causing us to perceive ourselves as entirely independent, self-sufficient beings. This allows us to make decisions with regard to our actions. But even this kind of independence demonstrates itself only in certain circumstances, because despite the fact that the Creator concealed Himself from us, we still possess egoism, which directs all of our thoughts and feelings.

Therefore, true freedom will arise only when: 1. An individual does not experience the bestowal of the Creator, and 2. An individual can act independently from the desires of the body.

An opportunity to exercise our free will exists only in the earthly life, which is precisely why we exist here.

Every individual must believe that there is nothing else in the world but the Creator.

One perceives in one's "I" a certain degree of independence only because the Creator endowed our perception with egoism. However, if we were to rid ourselves of this quality, we would once again become part of the Creator.

We must believe that the Creator is concealed only because we cannot perceive Him, and that this concealment was designed only for our benefit. Thus, until we are ready to face the truth, we must believe that the truth is very different from the way we perceive it.

The truth can only be grasped gradually and only to the degree that we have been able to attain perfection. Hence, any spiritual work is possible only as long as the pleasure of the spiritual realm is concealed from us. Only then will we be able to say that our loathing towards the spiritual was purposely sent by the Creator, and that, in fact, nothing is more perfect than the spiritual.

If, contrary to feelings of gloom, depression and emptiness, and contrary to the arguments of reason, we can search for the perception of the Creator and proceed above our own reason in accordance with the principle of "faith above reason," then the Creator will reveal Himself to us, since in all states of being, we await that revelation.

A true desire to perceive the Creator is born in us in the manner described above, and this constitutes a necessary condition for the Revelation of the Creator. The power of faith in the ability to perceive the Creator is measured by the depth of our spiritual fall, from which we can call out to the Creator.

However, we must understand that without proper preparation to perceive the Creator, we will unwillingly gain egoistic pleasure from experiencing such unworldly phenomenon. Thus, we must ask the Creator: 1. For preparation for the experience of higher pleasure. 2. For the necessary strength to retain faith above reason, even after the Revelation of the Creator.

There are two kinds of obstacles deriving from the impure forces (*klipot*) that operate in us: restraint (*ahizat klipot*) and drawing nourishment (*yenikat klipot*). When we experience no pleasure from learning or from self-improvement, and advance with great difficulty, then the *klipa* demonstrates to us various shortcomings of the spiritual existence.

As a result, we feel that there is no value in the spiritual. Thus, the *klipa* receives an opportunity to hold us back from our studies, since we see no greatness in the spiritual. Such a state is known as "the Revelation of the Creator in ashes" (*shchinta be afra*).

But if, with the power of the will, we persist in advancing, then we begin to receive the taste of working on ourselves. At that point, the *klipa* begins to feed off our spiritual accomplishments. It wants to appropriate everything that we have earned from our efforts (the pleasure from the spiritual).

The *klipa* achieves this goal by instilling in us the desire to continue to work. However, the motivation behind this work is personal pleasure, rather than the fact that this work is desired by the Creator. If we acquiesce to this tendency, then the entire pleasure is surrendered to one's ego. This is known as "the drawing nourishment" of the *klipot*. In such a case, we must ask the Creator for help in withstanding the temptation of harmful thoughts.

In conclusion, at first we must ask the Creator to provide pleasure from Kabbalah, and then we must implore Him that this pleasure should not be absorbed by egoism. The protestations of the body against the spiritual work, which brings no pleasure for the body and gives no assurance that a reward will follow in the future, is known as "a mean tongue."

In order to escape the temptation, we must pretend to be blind and deaf to the calls of the body, as well as to imagine that the Upper Light exists, but is invisible. Only then will the Creator open our eyes and ears to be able to perceive His Light, and be able to hear what the Creator is telling only to us.

The efforts that we allot to every task of perceiving the spiritual gradually add up to a sufficient quantity to form the vessel (*kli*) or the garment (*levush*) needed to receive the Light of the Creator—our spiritual souls.

14

Revelation and Concealment

There is nothing else in the world except the Light (the Creator) and that which was created by the Light (the person, who remains inside this Light). A person can perceive this Light when there is a correspondence between the qualities of the human being and those of the Creator. If the qualities do not correspond, then the person will be unable to perceive the Light—the Creator.

At first, we are placed in the conditions of an explicit and complete domain of egoism, known as "our world." Only by means of our own efforts can we gradually bring up and cultivate within ourselves such a desire and necessity to perceive the Creator (create a vessel for the Light of the Creator) that we will begin to perceive Him.

Our efforts should focus on an attempt to correct ourselves with all the strength we possess until it is obvious that all efforts to attain the desired goal will be futile. Then, it is time to turn to the Creator with a prayer, asking for help in finding redemption from egoism and in uniting with Him.

This process can take months, and even years, if we undertake this effort under the guidance of a teacher-Kabbalist; or it can take several lives or reincarnations (*gilgulim*), if such efforts are undertaken on our own, by way of suffering.

Only the right efforts in the correct direction will produce the vessel of the soul, within which the Creator will reveal Himself to us. In Kabbalah, the reasons behind our actions are known as "the fathers," whereas the consequences of actions are known as "the sons" (the correct spiritual acts).

One is not born because of one's own will. Spiritually, one is forced to be born (to receive a soul—the Light of the Creator) by the Creator through suffering. But one has the capacity to be born independently by means of the Kabbalah.

One does not live because of one's own will. If one does not act (live) in accordance with one's egoistic will, then a true eternal spiritual existence will be the reward, which can actually be called "life."

One does not die because of one's will. If one does not want to die (spiritually) or to be in the state of spiritual death (without the soul; without the Light of the Creator) then one should not act in accordance with one's own will.

The work in the middle line of the soul begins with the work in the right line: since its use is prohibited (restriction, *tzimtzum*), the Light of Wisdom (*Ohr Hochma*) shows egoism as bad (*aviyut*); one feels that there is no worse act than to work for the sake of the self.

But the person still possesses neither the desire nor the strength to work for the sake of others, that is, to give. Therefore, there is a need for the left line, which gives us altruistic desires and strength.

The spiritual organs of perception, just like our five senses (sight, hearing, smell, taste, and touch), operate in accordance with a particular set goal. The effect of the Light of Wisdom causes us to realize that there is no personal benefit in using the five senses; that is, there is no point in working for our egoism.

In the absence of the desire to gratify ourselves, which normally induces the five senses to operate, we experience a complete lack of energy to perform any act, leading to lethargy and inaction. At this stage, we have not realized that the goal of our efforts can be the "giving," that is, our actions can be altruistic.

For this reason, we need the influence of another spiritual quality, known as the "red light," the left line (*"malchut memuteket be Bina"*). This second quality is required to convince our desires to agree to work altruistically (qualities of *Bina*). Once we receive the spiritual energy and the altruistic motion has begun, we begin to act with a combination of the qualities both from the right and the left lines.

As a result, we receive the Light of the Creator into our new desires (the middle line), and thus continue receiving pleasure from the perfection. If we are ready to receive the powers of faith and altruism, then eventually we will be able to receive the highest reason.

The principle of rejecting self-gratification, which was adopted by one of the world's major religions, and the principle of attaining pleasure, which was chosen by another, both stem from the impure (egoistic) forces (*klipot*) of the right and the left lines of the spiritual ascent. Thus, where Kabbalah discusses the subject of placing limitations on oneself, it implies a preliminary stage of working on the self: making an attempt to reject the idea of self-gratification using one's own willpower.

The roots of all different types of faith, of all spiritual tendencies, of all groups, and of all religious philosophies can be traced to the various *klipot*. These surround the left and the right spiritual pure lines, which are sustained through the process of seizing-grasping (*ahiza*) or through drawing nourishment (*yenika*).

But the goal of any task is to attain the middle line, to rise to the infinite that has no end or boundary, thus attaining the perception of the Creator, unlimited by particular human qualities.

In spiritual vocabulary, a desire is regarded as a "place." The absence of desire is considered to be "the absence of a place." This is similar to a situation when a person declares that no place exists in the stomach for food, since there is no more desire to eat.

A spiritual place, or the desire of an individual to perceive the Creator, is known as "the vessel" (*kli*) of the soul, or *Shechina*. This vessel receives the Light of the Creator or the Revelation of the Creator, also known as "the soul" of the person. The Creator Himself is known as the *Shochen*.

Since all our desires are permeated with our egoism (desire to receive), the Light of the Creator is concealed. As egoism is gradually ejected from our desires, a greater place becomes available. An uncorrected desire is known as "egoism." A corrected desire is called "Israel."

Once a "place" is vacated as a result of a corrected desire, the Light of the Creator is revealed, but the Creator still continues to operate in a manner concealed from us. After we have corrected and purified our desires (places, vessels), we perceive the process of the Revelation of the Creator as the appearance of the Light. In reality, however, no motion takes place, but rather, as in the process of developing a negative, the Light gradually appears in our perception.

Since we do not perceive the Light itself, but only its effect on our vessel, we address the Creator by the name associated with His Revelation: *Shechina*. However, we can only determine His Essence by the sensations and feelings that He invokes in us. For this reason, the Revelation of the Creator is known as *Shechina*.

If the Creator conceals Himself, then it said that "the *Shechina* is in exile"; or that "the Creator is hidden." But if an individual has earned the Revelation of the Creator, then it is known as "the return from the exile."

The varying degree to which the Creator reveals Himself to us is called "the soul" (*neshama*).

As soon as we are able to correct at least one of our desires into an altruistic one, we receive an immediate perception of the Creator.

Thus, it is said that the human soul is part of the Creator.

Once we reach the final stage of correction, the Creator will fill all our desires, that is, He will reveal Himself to the ultimate degree to which He planned to reveal Himself in His creations. All our desires were designed for this ultimate purpose at the very beginning of creation.

Shechina is the root and sum of all individual souls. Each soul is a part of the general Revelation of the Creator. When the Creator reveals Himself, He is expressing His desire to please His creations. This is the understanding of those who attain the perception of the Creator.

We are unable to answer the question of what caused the Creator to wish to create us in order to please, because this question deals with the process that took place prior to the creation. We can only comprehend those things that can be revealed to us, that is, those things that developed after the creation.

The initial stage from which we begin to comprehend the creation is the perception of pleasure that emanates from the Creator. For this reason, the goal of creation—"the desire of the Creator to please"—refers only to those creations that already perceive Him.

All the questions that concern issues beyond this level are above our ability to understand them. We must always remember that all human understanding and knowledge are derived solely from personal perception.

The only thing that we are comprised of is our desire to be pleased.

All our physical and mental potential, all our capabilities, and all our progress are for the sole purpose of letting us receive pleasure from various objects, which we continue to invent, find, and consider necessary, fashionable, or acceptable. This is done for the sole objective of being able to constantly receive pleasure.

We cannot complain about the unlimited forms of the desire to receive pleasure. It was sufficient for the Creator to generate but a single desire in order to induce human beings to feel like independent (desiring) beings, able to behave independently on the basis of a single instinct—that of maximizing our personal pleasure.

This process takes place with the aid of all our faculties: intellectual, subconscious, physical, ethical, and many others. It also includes all levels of memory, ranging from the molecular and biological to the highest levels of our intellect.

Here is a simple example: a man loves money, but is willing to give up his entire fortune to a mugger when threatened with death. In this manner, he exchanges one pleasure source (money) for an even greater pleasure (staying alive).

We are incapable of performing an act unless we are sure that, as a result of this act, we will be in a more advantageous position. It is irrelevant how the benefit will be conferred. What is crucial is that the resulting level of pleasure will exceed the initial level. Only then will we act.

What, then, is the difference between the pleasure received from egoism (from getting) and the pleasure received from altruism (from giving)? The significant difference is in the fact that, when we receive pleasure from egoism, our feeling of pleasure is invariably accompanied by a feeling of shame. But if we receive for the sake of the giver, then we have no feelings of shame and our pleasure is absolute.

The original spiritual being, known as "the common soul" or "the first man" was unable to undergo such a transformation of thought when it received the tremendous pleasure from the Creator. Therefore, it was divided into 600,000 parts (souls).

Every part, every soul, receives a small portion of the burden of egoism, which it must correct. When all the parts are corrected, they will once again unite to form "a common corrected soul." When such a state is reached, the corrective process known as *gmar tikkun* will be completed.

For example, in our world a person can refrain from stealing a small amount of money because it represents an insignificant amount of pleasure. The fear of punishment, combined with feelings of shame, prevails over the desire to steal.

However, if the amount is sufficiently great, then the pull toward gratification is much stronger than the ability to withstand it. In this way, the Creator generated the conditions for freedom of choice that we require to overcome our egoism.

He divided the soul into a multitude of parts, and then separated every part into many successive stages of corrective phases (where each phase compels the part to garb into a human body). He then broke every state of a human being into a number of ascents and descents required for the quest to alter one's nature.

If we feel love for the Creator, we must immediately attempt to adjoin in ourselves feelings of fear as well, in order to be sure that our feeling of love is not egoistic. Only if both fear and love are present is our aspiration to come closer to the Creator in perfect form.

Those who experience a yearning for spiritual perception, but do not perceive the Creator, are filled with spiritual confusion and panic. Though given the desire to grasp the Creator from Above, such individuals are not ready to take the independent step forward toward the desired end.

Instead, they choose to wait to be sent a very strong desire from Above. This will serve as a thrust forward. It will permit these individuals to realize that every feeling and circumstance is filled with the Creator's desire to attract their attention to Him, and to prompt them to move closer to Him. Then it is possible to detect the Creator's address.

It is for this reason that each of us sees the world in a very personal way and uniquely interprets all that takes place around us. The rule that "there are as many points of view as there are people" underscores the fact that each of us is unique. By paying attention to our own feelings, we can begin a dialogue with the Creator according to the principle that "every person is a shadow of the Creator."

Just as the shadow moves with the motion of the individual, and all the motions of the shadow just repeat the motions of an individual, similarly, our inner motions—our desires, aspirations, perceptions, spiritual essence, and outlook on life—repeat the motions (the desires) of the Creator.

Thus, if a person suddenly experiences a desire to perceive the Creator, that person must immediately recognize that this desire did not result from any particular actions, but rather from the fact that the

Creator took a step forward toward this person, creating a pull and an attraction to Him.

At the beginning of the path, the Creator uses every appropriate opportunity to communicate with us by arousing in us both a longing and anguish for the spiritual perceptions. But every time the Creator grants us a pull toward the spiritual, He expects an equal reaction from our side.

Therefore, if we understand that the vigor with which we yearn to perceive the Creator is just as strong as the vigor with which the Creator wants to bring us closer to Himself, we should try to develop and strengthen in ourselves these feelings. In this way, we can advance toward the Creator until we can finally cleave to Him in all desires and qualities.

But when we are still at the beginning of the path, we neither sense nor understand the Creator. After making a number of unsuccessful attempts to advance towards Him, it suddenly appears to us that while we want to draw close to the Creator, He disregards us.

In response, instead of increasing our yearning to the degree required to attach ourselves to the Creator, we begin in our hearts to blame Him for ignoring us. We become angry and completely forget that the Creator wants us, to exactly the same extent, and for this reason gave us such yearnings toward Him.

As long as we lack complete faith in the oneness of the Creator, we will inevitably repeat our mistakes time after time, until the Creator makes us realize that all of our desire for Him comes from the Creator Himself, and that He will accept all the efforts we require, and will help us by revealing Himself to us by showing us the full true picture of the worlds and of Himself.

We can only attach ourselves to the Creator by joyfully directing all of our yearnings, and this is called "with all of the heart." This even includes those desires not required to be brought into an equivalence of form with the Creator.

If we can completely suppress all the egoistic desires unveiled in us before, while feeling happiness in our hearts, we establish conditions conducive to fill our hearts with the Light of the Creator.

The most important aspect of the task of self-improvement is reaching a point where we find a joy in actions that gratify the Creator, because all that is done for our sakes brings us away from the Creator. Therefore, all of our efforts must focus on achieving pleasantness in addressing the Creator, and towards acquiring sweetness in thoughts and feelings about Him.

When we feel empty, it is an appropriate time to search for the grandeur of the Creator and to find support in Him. The more lowly we feel about ourselves, and the greater we perceive the Creator, then to this degree we can rise after requesting that the Creator save us and alleviate the present situation.

The Creator brings about this elevation after revealing His greatness in order to offer the strength to move forward. In such a condition, we need the Creator and His help, since our reason is pulling in a completely different direction. Therefore, the feelings of emptiness are given precisely in order that we feel them, with the perception of the Creator's greatness, called "faith."

A righteous person is the one who, in all that is felt, be it bad or good, justifies the actions of the Creator, regardless of the feelings experienced by body, heart and reason. By justifying all sensations received from the Creator, it is as if one takes a step forward towards the Creator, called the "right" step.

Under no circumstances should we ignore our true state and feelings, regardless of how unpleasant they may be. Even if such difficult situations as these are required, nonetheless we should not try to annul them. By acting in this manner, we would take a "left" step forward.

Perfection in spiritual growth consists of the fact that we constantly advance forward, alternating the two aforementioned conditions.

An absolutely righteous person is the one who justifies all actions of the Creator, both towards self and towards all other creations.

An individual who has attained the possibility to perceive all sensations outside the limitations of egoistic wishes has already separated from them, and wants only to be happy in giving. In such a state, a person cannot experience spiritual downfalls, since every event is not evaluated from the position of personal gain.

Thus, anything that happens, happens for the good. However, since the goal of the Creator in the creation is not in this, but rather in that the created beings should benefit specifically in their own feelings—the achievement of the level of a righteous person—this is not the final state for man.

Therefore, after a person achieves the level of the righteous, it is time to begin gradually restoring the egoism that was destroyed upon achieving this level. That same egoistic desire that the righteous person returned to himself can be added to the desire to make the Creator happy, which was acquired through spiritual work.

Because of this, not only can one give pleasure, but this person can also receive pleasures in the returned egoistic desires, always with the intention to give happiness to the Creator. This situation can be compared to an altruist of this world who longs to do good for others, since these qualities were present at birth.

In fact, the altruist did not receive them from the Creator as a reward for work on the self. Indeed, it is as if the altruist wants nothing, since enjoyment from bestowing good on others fills the ego. The altruist is unable to act differently.

This is reminiscent of a situation where a person is a guest at a friend's house. The greater the guest's appetite and pleasure for what is offered, the more satisfaction is received by the host. This pleasure would not be received if the guest were not hungry.

But since the guest may feel shame at all the pleasure being received, he or she may decline further offerings. By declining often enough, the guest will begin to feel that when the offered delicacies are accepted, the host is receiving a favor. Then, all feelings of shame will vanish, and the guest will experience pleasure to the full extent.

In spiritual sensations, there is no self-deception, such as a pretense that a righteous person does not want to receive pleasure for one's own sake. In earning levels of right-eousness, one will, with the help of the Creator who replaces our egoistic nature with an altruistic one, truly refuse all egoistic pleasure and aspire only to benefit the Creator.

But when a righteous person realizes that the Creator receives pleasure only when His creations are delighted by the pleasures emanating from Him, pleasures that are not belittled or destroyed, that person is once again forced to turn to egoism. This time, however, there is a different goal: to experience pleasure for the sake of the Creator.

In the end, the Creator and the individual completely converge in their intentions and actions as each party attempts to gratify the other, and through this gains pleasure. There are no limits to perceiving pleasure in this manner.

On the contrary, the higher the experienced sensation of pleasure, the higher the spiritual level attained. There is also pleasure from the recognition of infinite strength, power and might without any concern for self.

Therefore, the level of a righteous person is not sufficient to fulfill the goal of the creation. Receiving pleasure from the Light emanating from the Creator is crucial for the correction of our intentions: "the reasons for which we seek pleasure."

The attainment of the level of the righteous only permits us to rid ourselves of the feelings of shame that we experience when we receive pleasures from the Creator. As much as egoism constitutes our nature in this world and altruism is considered to be a utopian notion, they are perceived as opposite by those who occupy the realm of the spiritual world.

The difficulties arise from the concealment of the Creator. We receive pleasures only when we fulfill our desires. But Kabbalah teaches that this is evil, and not good for us. We do not understand why this is so, since we can perceive no pleasure in suffering, and yet we must still believe that suffering is good for us. Thus, our every action or thought produces a multitude of deliberations.

Moreover, the closer we are to the entrance of the spiritual world (*machsom*), the more complex the situation becomes. Only one truth becomes evident: "There are many thoughts in the heart of a person, but only the advice of the Creator will be established."

The difference between a person who wants spiritual elevation (that is, to acquire spiritual characteristics like those of the Creator), and a person who fulfills His Will for a payment (as a result of the education received), is this: the latter has faith in rewards and punishment, and for this reason fulfills the Will of the Creator.

The Creator is like an employer who pays a salary; the person is like a worker who does not care about the employer, but rather the salary: reward and punishment in this world, or in the world to come. This gives the "employee" the strength to observe the commandments without asking the question, "Why am I fulfilling the Will of the Creator?" The answer is, because the employee believes in rewards.

However, one who seeks to carry out the Will of the Creator without receiving payment in exchange constantly asks, "Why am I doing this?" and "If this is the Will of the Creator, why does the Creator need this? He is perfect and complete, so what do our actions add to Him?"

It would appear that these questions are just for the person in question, who then would begin to wonder: "What do I gain from fulfilling the Will of the Creator?" Little by little the person comes to realize that the reward for fulfilling the Will of the Creator is one's own self-correction, until one receives from Above the *Neshama* (soul)—the Light of the Creator.

Kabbalah teaches that evil inclination (egoism) appears to sinners as a wisp of hair (a small obstacle), while to the righteous person it appears as a high mountain.

Kabbalah must be applied as if it were just referring to one person, in whom the characteristic thoughts and desires are called by various names of our world.

Therefore, under the categories of "sinners" and "the righteous" are described the states of one individual. Concealment refers not only to the concealment of the Creator, but also to the concealment of a person from oneself. We do not really know ourselves or our true characteristics. These are revealed to us only to the degree to which we are able to correct them. (In this matter, a person is comparable to a container of garbage: the more one searches within oneself, the greater is the stench perceived).

For this reason, the Creator shows those who are only at the beginning of the path, the sinners, that their egoism is not so formidable that it cannot be overcome. This is so they will not give up hope at the sight of work that is not appropriate to the task.

For those who are already on the path, the Creator reveals a greater measure of the evil (egoism) within them. This is done to a degree appropriate to the feeling of the importance of the correction, and the power of resistance to egoism that they have acquired.

Finally, to those who desire to be righteous, the Creator reveals the full magnitude of their egoism. Consequently, it appears to them as a high, unsurpassable mountain.

Thus, as a person progresses, the evil within is revealed more and more, in amounts that are correctable. Because of this, if a person suddenly becomes aware of something new within that is negative, this indicates that it is now possible to correct it. Rather than falling into despair, one should ask the Creator to correct it.

For example, when we begin to work on ourselves, we can only feel 10 grams of pleasure from all the pleasures of the world that surrounds us, and we are able to dispense with them. Afterwards, the Creator gives us a taste for 15 grams of pleasure.

In the beginning of our work, because of our additional taste for the pleasures, we feel ourselves more lowly (from the feeling of being drawn to things that did not previously attract us), and weaker (because of the difference between the strength of our attraction to the pleasures and the power of our own resistance to them).

However, in a situation like this, we must tell ourselves that since the Creator added 5 grams of pleasure to the taste of the pleasures we receive from the world around us, yet we are unable to correct ourselves, we must request strength from the Creator. But when we receive the strength to overcome 15 grams of pleasure, afterwards we receive an additional 5 grams of taste for the pleasure, and once again we feel that we are weaker and lowly, and this process continues.

Transforming Egoism to Altruism

One who wants to experience the true taste of life must pay special attention to the spiritual point found in one's heart. Everyone has a point in the heart. However, it does not generally show signs of life and does not illuminate, and because of this, we are not aware of it.

In such a situation it is called a "black point." This point is a seed of a soul. The characteristic of this point is altruistic, because it is a seed of the future vessel of the soul and its Light, a portion of the Creator.

However, in its initial state it is hidden from us, since we do not appreciate it, and for this reason this state is called "*Galut* (exile) of the *Shechina*" (the Divine Presence). Such a state of the soul is called a "point."

If we elevate the importance of that point above our own "I," above our heads, like the crowns above the letters, in this way we make it comparable to a crown on our heads, rather than dust at our feet. Then Light is emitted from the center into the body, and from this potential center it becomes the source of strength for our spiritual elevation.

Hence, instead of all our appeals for help from the Creator, our only prayer should focus on realizing the importance of perceiving the Creator as a means to our improvement for His sake.

The ability to perform acts of goodness (altruistic acts) is not a means, but a reward for a person who wishes to resemble the Creator.

The sequential order of the process by which a person shifts away from egoism and towards the spiritual world can be found in the Bible as the exodus from Egypt. The appearance of vessels of bestowal in a person is called "the exodus from Egypt."

However, altruistic desires (vessels of bestowal) mean that a person would rather follow the path of faith than the path of knowledge. To exit from egoism is only possible when we feel spirituality, perceive the Creator; and the Light of Wisdom splits the *yam suf* (Red Sea)in the middle. At this point, one passes over the boundary between two worlds.

In order to do this, the Creator performs a miracle. He gives us the Light of Wisdom (*Ohr Hochma*), despite the fact that we do not possess the appropriate vessel to receive the Light. With the help of this Light, we can break the barrier (*machsom*). Afterwards, when the miracle passes, those who have entered the spiritual world do not return to the level of our world.

In the next stage, we must acquire a vessel for receiving the Light of Wisdom, and this is accomplished on the difficult path of advancement in the spiritual desert until we merit receiving the Light of the Creator by ascending onto "Mount Sinai." In this state, we observe the commandments by virtue of faith above knowledge, when we place our own thoughts and wishes below the faith.

A so-called lesser state, *katnut*, that is, *Malchut* in this case, connotes only the center or *Keter* ("crown"). In such minimal presence, our evil egoistic dispositions cannot sway us because we have placed faith above knowledge and perception.

This is considered to be a lesser state because in it we do not take into account egoism, since we have no strength to counter it. This situation can be compared to a case in which we are unable to consume only a small amount of food, and refuse the entire portion altogether.

However, a bond with the Light of the Creator can only transpire if we are able to receive that Light into ourselves; that is, to work altruistically with our own egoism. As we transform our egoism into altruism, the altered vessel will be filled with the Light of the Creator.

That state of our spiritual vessel (of corrected egoism, *kli*) is called "the greater state, *gadlut*." *Malchut* descends from *Keter* to the level at which we can withstand the pull towards self-gratification and be able to receive, but not for the sake of our own pleasure.

To fully receive the Light of the Creator, to perceive the Creator to the full extent of one's ability, to completely cling to Him, is possible only by fully utilizing our egoism for the service of altruism. Such a state is known as "the end of the correction process," and is the goal of creation.

All our perceptions are strictly subjective, and the view of the world open to us depends entirely on our inner spiritual and physical states, our moods, etc. But in spiritual perception, sensations comprise reality itself, since we understand the present in accordance with our spiritual position.

Our world is considered to be our immediate sensation. The future world is that which will be felt in the next instant. There is no dimension of time, but only a change of sensations. If we perceive everything by faith above knowledge, then we live entirely in the future.

For example, in ordinary life, if we own a business, we systematically assess the outcome of our work and our profits. If we see that our expenses and efforts are not justified, that is, the profit is less than the investment, then we close down the business and open a new one, because the anticipated profit stands before our eyes.

Under no circumstance do we deceive ourselves, but clearly assess our benefits in the form of money, honors, fame, tranquility and so on—in whichever form we want our profit to be.

One might ask, why don't we sum up the general outcome of our lives, for instance, once a year, and consider for what purpose did we live and spend the year? Yet, if we deal even slightly with our spiritual development, then why do we need to ask ourselves about every single moment?

Our world is a world of falsehood.

As a result, our bodies do not want to face these questions because they cannot provide the answers. In truth, what can our answer be as the year comes to an end, or as the end of life itself approaches?

All is passed, the good and the bad, and what are we with? Why have we worked for the needs of our own bodies? There is no answer, because there is no reward for the life that passed. Because of this, the body does not permit us to ask these questions.

Spirituality, on the other hand, since it is true, and the spiritual reward is eternal, poses to us the question of our spiritual reward with the aim of arousing us to receive even greater benefits from our efforts. In this way, we will correct ourselves to a greater degree and will receive a greater eternal reward.

Why, then, does the Creator give us false preoccupations with life in this world? The process of creating a spiritual vessel is very complex and lengthy. We believe that we must experience the entire spectrum of worldly egoism, to experience it all, in all of its lowliness, and to taste all of its false pleasures, down to its lowest levels (of egoism).

During our work, as we approach the boundary between the physical and spiritual realms, we accumulate experiences until we reach the spiritual realm. This process of gaining experience does not occur in one single revolution of life in this world. All information is stored in our souls and exhibited at the appropriate moment.

But until then, the process of acquisition is hidden from us, and we only experience our present state. Since our entire essence centers on our desire to gain pleasure, the Creator gives "life," known as "falsity," to those who are not yet ready for spiritual ascent, so that they will have a source of strength in order to live.

There is a Light that brings the lessening of the desires vessel, and there is a Light that brings knowledge and pleasure. In essence, it is one and the same Light of the Creator, but we ourselves extract from the Light the particular quality we want to use for our spiritual aims.

"Abandon evil and do good." The first stage of the correction is called "the realization of evil," since as soon as we become convinced that egoism is our most dangerous and deadly enemy, we will hate it and abandon it. A situation like this has now become unbearable.

However, it is not necessary to run away from the evil, but just to feel what the evil really is, and afterwards we will instinctively separate from the harmful. Our realization of what is evil occurs precisely while under the influence of doing good acts—while observing the commandments and learning Kabbalah, because when we are under their positive influence, we begin to long for spiritual perfection and to sense what exactly is preventing us from experiencing a spiritual life.

The concealment of the Creator from us, which is experienced as suffering, questions about the Divine Providence, lack of confidence and trust in the Creator, and interfering thoughts—all of these are called "night." The Revelation of the Creator to us, which is experienced as pleasure, trust in Divine Supervision, a sense of being connected to the eternal, understanding of the Upper Sources of all the laws of nature—all of these are called "day."

While the Creator is still in a state of concealment, we must work towards acquiring faith in the fact that such a state is to our benefit, because in all states the Creator does only what is most useful and beneficial for us.

If we were ready to receive the Light of the Creator without harming ourselves, undoubtedly the Creator would reveal Himself to us.

But since we are unable to control pleasures that we already feel, the Creator does not give such immense pleasures as these from His Light, since we would immediately become a slave to them, and would never be able to escape from the chains of our egoism. For this reason, we would become even further distanced from the Creator.

Each new generation and its majority determine the value and beauty of things, objects, events and categories. Each generation rejects the norms of the previous one. Therefore, there are no absolute norms; rather, the majority in each group of people and each generation dictates its own norms, so that the rest can follow them.

For that reason, there always exist new trends and new role models to which one can aspire. Therefore, all that is dictated by the majority is considered to be beautiful, while those who uphold these values receive respect and honors. Consequently, one is willing to devote great effort in order to attain that on which the society places great value.

As a result, it is difficult to acquire spiritual qualities, since the majority does not hold this aim in high esteem as they do the current trends. In truth, is it so very important to perceive the spiritual? In fact, spirituality is exceedingly important.

Yet, if this is so, why does the Creator keep it hidden? The answer is, in order that we should not spoil it, He created a special "trick" called "concealment." This prevents all of the greatness of the spiritual world from being seen, since we cannot control feelings we have already felt, as explained above.

And since it is now hidden from us, we are only able to rely on faith concerning the immense importance of perceiving the Creator. However, according to the majority opinion, the value of spiritual appreciation amounts to zero; thus, it is loathed practically by everyone.

This process occurs despite the fact that clearly the standards of beauty, order of priorities, norms of behavior, and laws of society are determined by contemptible personalities who constantly change their principles, thus proving that they lack substance and that their norms are groundless and false.

15

Gradual Spiritual Correction

Faith above reason allows us to perceive our greatest enemy (the one who stands in our way of attaining goodness) precisely by reason. We can sense and perceive evil only to the degree that we believe in spiritual pleasure above reason. Objectively, there is nothing else but the Creator, but this realization occurs on the highest level of Kabbalistic perception.

Until that time, however, we perceive ourselves in this world as well. In the process of gaining perception, we come to understand what is: (1) the Creator (2) the First creation (3) creations (4) the pleasure that the Creator wishes to bestow upon His creations.

The entire progression, naturally, unfolds in accordance with the chain of "cause and effect," rather than in accordance with time. The Creator exists. The Creator wishes to bring forth a creation in order to gratify it. The Creator generates the desire to be delighted precisely by that pleasure (both in quantity and in appearance) that He wishes to give.

The first created being is called *Malchut*. The first perception of the Light of the Creator by the created being is known as the "World Without End." The term, "Without End" is used because in that state, Malchut received the Light of the Creator without limiting the amount of Light it received.

The created being gained much enjoyment from receiving the Light. However, while receiving enjoyment, it also sensed the Creator Himself—His desire to bestow. Since *Malchut* longed to be similar to Him, *Malchut* eventually rejected receiving the Light, and the Light then departed.

This action of *Malchut* is called "restriction" (the restriction of the reception of the Light—*tzimtzum*). The Creator has no lack, so *Malchut* cannot give to the Creator in the same way as the Creator gives to *Malchut*.

How can *Malchut* "give" to the Creator? By complying with the Creator's Will, which is to bestow good to the created beings, and receiving from the Creator, thus pleasing the Creator. This is considered "giving" on the part of the created being.

Malchut can only change the form in which it receives. This change can be achieved by adding to the act of receiving, the intention of pleasing the Creator.

The first stage required to reach this new form is the restriction—having the Light leave. The restricted *Malchut* later became divided into many, many parts—souls, in which each one separately must correct its egoism.

These small portions of *Malchut*, devoid of the Creator's Light, are then put in the condition and situation that we call "our world." After this, little by little, these portions abandon the desire to receive for themselves, and acquire the desire to bestow while still in "our world."

The force that aids the soul to depart from egoistic inclinations is known as the "salvaging" one, the Messiah. The levels of gradual spiritual correction are called the "spiritual worlds," while the inner gradations are known as *Sefirot*.

The aim of correction is the return to the original state, before the restriction, at which pleasure is received not for one's own sake, but for the sake of the Creator. Such a condition is known as "the end of correction."

All the thoughts and questions that arise in us about the goals of creation and the goal of one's efforts, such as, "Is it necessary?" and "in any case, the Creator will act according to His own plan and desires, why does He require anything of me?" etc., arise because they are sent directly by the Creator. So one more question occurs to us: "What for?"

If all the questions that arose in us concerning the creation strengthened us on our way to the spiritual, then the meaning of the questions would be clear. But in those who first embark on this journey, there are constant thoughts about the difficulties, the hopelessness and the disadvantages of this path.

There is no other force and desire other than the Creator, and all is created by Him to gain an understanding of the purpose of creation, including, of course, the "disruptive" questions, thoughts and forces that hinder our progress to Him.

The Creator put many obstacles on the path that He decided should be followed for spiritual elevation, precisely in order that we should fear not reaching our goal of perceiving the Creator's grandeur, instead remaining forever in our lowly state. This perception can convince our hearts to want altruism.

We must understand that only the Creator can open our eyes and our hearts so we can recognize the greatness of the spiritual. Disruptive questions arise specifically so we can feel this necessity.

One of the most fundamental questions that beginners ask can be phrased in the following manner: "If the Creator wanted, He would reveal Himself to me; and if He did so, then I (my body—egoism—my present dictator) immediately and automatically would agree to replace my egoistic acts with altruistic ones, and the Creator would become my dictator.

"I do not want the freedom to choose my own actions. I believe that the Creator is correct, that the best thing for me is not to think about my own gain. Only then will I truly deserve. But I cannot change myself. So let the Creator come and do that for me, since He created me in this manner, and only He can correct what He has done."

The Creator could certainly give one a desire and feeling for the spiritual, the so-called "awakening from Above." However, if the Creator did so, then we would never be able to escape the dictatorial rule of the egoistic desire to gratify ourselves, and then we would be forced to work for the sake of pleasure without a free choice.

Such work is not considered to be done for the sake of the Creator, but instead for the sake of receiving pleasure. The goal of the Creator is to induce us to choose the right path in life of our own free will, thus justifying His actions in creation. We can understand this only when we are completely free from egoism, regardless of personal pleasure.

For this reason, the Creator formed a condition essential to spiritual elevation: the acceptance of faith in Him and His fairness as our Supervisor. Given the above, our task amounts to the following:

1. To believe that there is a Ruler to the world

2. To recognize that, although for us faith may not be important, the Creator specifically chose this path for us

3. To believe that we must follow the path of "giving," and not the path of "receiving"

4. To believe, while working "for the sake of the Creator," that He accepts our work despite how it may look in our eyes.

5. To pass through, during the process of self-development, two categories of "faith above reason": a) proceeding with faith above reason because we have no other alternative; b) choosing to follow the path of faith above reason, even if we become sufficiently knowing so that we no longer need to rely on faith above reason.

6. To know that if work is done within the grounds of egoism, then the fruits of all success, which in our imagination we hope to reach, go towards our own pleasure. However, when a person loves the Creator, all benefits will be joyously handed over to Him, and all the fruits of his efforts to others.

7. To thank the Creator for the past, because on this depends the future, since one's degree of appreciation for the past, for which one thanks the Creator, is equal to one's appreciation for what is received from Above. We are then able to preserve and retain the help received from Above.

8. To carry out the primary work—which is mainly in advancing along the *right line*—with a feeling of completeness. The individual is happy even with a small connection that exists with spirituality.
   One is happy to have deserved to receive the desire and abilities to do even the slightest in the spiritual realm before the Creator.

9. To advance also in the left line. However, thirty minutes per day are sufficient in order to reflect on how much one prefers the love of the Creator over self-love.
   To the degree that the person recognizes any lacks, to this measure one is required to pray to the Creator about these feelings, that He should draw one closer on the true path that specifically combines the two lines.

In the work itself, we must concentrate our thoughts and desires in a specific order:

1. To learn the ways of the Creator and the secrets of Kabbalah, so that this knowledge can assist in fulfilling the Creator's Will. This is the individual's main goal.

2. To long to completely correct one's soul, and to return it to its root—the Creator.

3. To long to recognize the Creator, and to cling to Him with the recognition of His perfection.

The Creator is in a state of absolute rest, as is the person who achieves the goal of creation. It is clear that this state of rest can only be appreciated by someone who has previously been in conditions of movement, toil and work. Since what is being referred to here is "spiritual rest," clearly the intention is that the person's movement, toil and work is also spiritual in nature.

Spiritual work consists of striving to bring pleasure to the Creator.

All our work begins precisely when our body (desire to receive) opposes the work, which is without any self-benefit. This is because it (the body, egoism) does not understand the implications of altruistic work, and does not feel any reward in it.

Great efforts are required from us to withstand the justifiable (in principle) complaints of the body. For a long time, we torture ourselves in an effort to gain some understanding of the spiritual.

What do we receive in return? Do you know anyone who has excelled in this task? Is it possible that the Creator wants us to suffer in this manner?

Learn from your own experience. What have you achieved? In your present state of health, can you abuse yourself as you are doing? Think of yourself, your family, your growing children.

If the Creator so desires, He will continue to lead us further in the same manner that He has brought us to Kabbalah, since in everything only the Creator rules and leads! All these complaints and many other similar ones (often heard from relatives, who are also related to the concept of the body) are absolutely justified, but there are no answers to give them.

Indeed, answers are not needed, because if we desire to exit from the boundaries of our bodies, we simply must not accept these arguments, and not pay attention to them.

Instead, we should say to ourselves: "Our bodies are right, the arguments are logical, its complaints are true. However, I want to exit my body, or in other words, exit from its desires. Therefore, I will follow the path of faith, and not the path of common sense. Only in our world is my reasoning considered to be logical.

"However, in the spiritual world, even though I don't understand this, since I don't yet have spiritual vision or spiritual intellect, everything works according to a different law, which at the moment appears strange to me, since it is not founded on the basis of physical reality.

"All functions by the law of the omnipotence of the Creator and by the complete and voluntary surrender to Him, both in mind and in spirit, in complete faith in His help, contrary to the body's desire to receive and its protestations."

This work on ourselves is called "to bestow for the sake of bestowing;" that is, a purely altruistic act, represented by the right line. We give all, simply because we desire to give. The pleasure we receive from such work emanates from our resemblance to the Creator, since one only gives, like the Creator. This is called "the Light of faith or mercy," or *Ohr Hassadim*.

If one attempts to behave in this manner, then the Creator opens to this person the feeling of His infinite grandeur and power. Faith gives way to knowledge; the body begins to feel the importance of the Creator and is ready to do everything for His sake, because it has now perceived the importance of the Great One and His acquiescence to receive anything from us.

This is accepted as the attainment of pleasure. But in this case, we once again feel that progress with the body is being made. It is not the greatness of the Creator, but the pleasure and the degree of personal confidence in the work done for the sake of the Greatest One that determines our actions. Thus, once again we have fallen to the bosom of egoism and personal gain.

Our complete inability to perceive the Creator allows us to insist that we have undertaken all actions for His sake, both altruistically and spiritually. The Revelation by the Creator that is represented by the left line is known as "the knowledge of the Light of Wisdom."

Therefore, the Revelation of the Creator makes it necessary for us to apply strict restrictions on acquiring knowledge, management and perception of His grandeur. This balances the faith and the knowledge, the absence of perception and the delight in the Creator in a proportion that would ensure that we not fall prey to egoism again.

By adding a small portion of egoism to the original state, we can use that small portion and still proceed as if we had learned nothing, just as in the original state. By balancing the right line with a small amount of the left line, we create a middle line.

The part of the left line in the middle line determines the elevation of our spiritual level. The spiritual state itself is considered to be that of the "Greater One." The following progression leads up to the final and highest level, our merging with the Creator in our qualities and desires.

This occurs by the gradual, alternating increase of the right and then the left lines. The balancing of both lines takes place at each level of the spiritual ladder. In the state of the right line, we must be happy without any reason, but only from the thought that the Creator exists in our world. We do not require any other conditions for happiness.

Such a state is known as "being happy with what one has." If nothing can bring us out of this condition it is considered to be absolute. But if we begin to test our spiritual state, we will see that we do not in any way get closer to the Creator. Since we have also experienced the fact that we cannot correct ourselves, we ask the Creator for help. The Light of the Creator that helps us overcome the egoism of the body (desire to receive) is known as "the soul."

The most assured way to determine if an act is altruistic or egoistic is to see if we feel that we are ready to disregard any outcome, be it pleasure of payment, regardless of the immense drive to gratify ourselves as a result of our own work.

Only in this case, having received pleasure, can we still insist that we did it for the sake of the Creator, and not for ourselves.

The entire path of spiritual ascension is a gradual refusal to receive greater and greater pleasures: first, the pleasures of our world, and then from the real spiritual pleasures, in particular the perception of the Creator.

The Creator concealed Himself in order to allow us to gradually adjust to this task. Therefore, the concealment of the Creator should be viewed as an aspect of our correction and we should ask Him to reveal Himself to us, since as soon as we are able to perceive Him without any harm to ourselves, He will immediately reveal Himself.

If we could feel the pleasure of perceiving the Creator in our initial egoistic state, we would never gather enough strength to part with our egoism, to ask the Creator to grant us the willpower to withstand the pull of gratification. Like the night butterflies that rush toward the light that kills them, so we would perish in the flames of pleasure, but still would not be able to resist them.

Only those of us who have experienced the lack of strength in the face of great pleasure understand that we would not be capable of stopping ourselves from deriving pleasure if the enjoyment were greater than the power of our will and our recognition of evil.

The Creator hides from us specifically for our own good in order that we should not be overwhelmed by pleasures and in this way make it possible for us to go in the path of faith, and to acquire vessels of bestowal. If we want to do something that is not for our benefit, then immediately our bodies (egoism) demand an exact accounting as to whether it is worthwhile to do this.

For without a goal, without the reward of pleasure, we are not capable of working, and seek all different kinds of shortcomings, spiritual desires and defects in our spiritual goal or aims. Our bodies first ask, "For what purpose do we need to be involved in this?"

In this situation, the body is called "the evil inclination." In the stage after this, it disturbs us from accomplishing what we have planned. In this situation it is called "satan" (in Hebrew *satan* is derived from the verb *listot*, which means to veer) because it wants to cause us to veer from the path.

After this, it kills our spirituality by taking away all of the feelings of spirituality from our learning and our involvement in Kabbalah, and specifically gives pleasures dressed in the garments of this world—in this situation, it is called "the angel of death."

There is only one answer to all grievances of the body: "I proceed forward despite what you say to me, on the strength of faith, because so the Creator requires."

This condition of the Creator is known as "the law of the worlds beyond." We do not have the strength to hold ourselves back from receiving pleasure unless we first convince ourselves that it is harmful to us. That is to say, we set our minds against our hearts.

However, even in this case, it will take no more than a simple calculation of what is for our good: immediate pleasure and subsequent suffering, or avoiding the pleasure and remaining in our current situation. Whenever we reject pleasure, we must give our bodies an exact account why it is not worthwhile for us to derive pleasure from that which came to us.

Thus, we can answer our bodies in the same language that the body understands: either in the language of pleasure, that it is worthwhile to get rid of foolish and occasional pleasures now for the sake of pleasures in the afterworld, or in the language of suffering, to say that it is not worthwhile to have pleasure now, but afterwards endure the suffering of hell. In this manner, we must build the line of defense against our bodies.

We must be aware, however, that in doing this the craving for pleasures can prevent a sensible accounting, and paint a false picture of the correlation between pleasures and suffering. The only sure solution is to tell the body that we have decided to work on spirituality without any gain to ourselves.

In this case, we cut off all the connections between the action and the body, and the body can no longer interfere with its calculations or whether it is worthwhile or not to work. This answer is called "the work of the heart," since the heart longs for pleasures.

16

Inner Qualities and Outer Aspects

The answer to the intellect must be in this manner: "I believe that the Creator listens to all of my requests and prayers for help." If we are able to stand firm on our answers to both intellect and heart, then the Creator will reveal Himself to us, so that we will see and sense only the Creator.

Within each of us are seventy fundamental desires. These are called "the seventy nations of the world." Therefore, our souls correspond to the *partzuf* of *Zeir Anpin* in the world of *Atzilut*, which includes 70 Sefirot. After we begin to seek more closeness with the Creator, and receive the Light of the Kabbalah, we are given feelings and desires that we never imagined existed.

The seventy desires derive from two sources, since we move forward in combinations of the two lines—the right and the left. Our actions in accordance with the right line are countered by our evil (egoistic) inclinations (the husk, *klipa*) against the work of the heart, which is called *Klipat Yishmael*.

The work in the left line is countered by an evil force against the work of the intellect, called the *Klipat Eisav*. However, when we progress further in our work, we see that in order to enter into the spiritual realm we must rid ourselves of both *klipot*, because they do not want to receive the laws of the spiritual realm—just as it is mentioned in the Bible that the Creator offered the *Torah*, the laws of the spiritual realm, to Eisav and Yishmael before he gave it to

Israel, but they did not want to receive it. Only after we see that we are not able to receive the altruistic-spiritual laws with either the right or left force, do we carefully progress to the middle line, which is called "We will do, and then we will hear," which is called "for the sake of bestowal," and is then called *Israel*.

Since all of us, along with our thoughts, intentions and desires, are entirely immersed in our egoism, we are unable to think independently, objectively and non-egoistically. Thus, we are unable to criticize ourselves.

In general, we have no need to criticize ourselves, since we already know that everything we do is based on our egoistic desires. However, in working on ourselves,, doing work which goes against our desires, when we invest efforts to develop spiritual yearnings, we need to examine our situation. We ourselves must examine the situation, not the Creator, Who already knows what our situation is.

The surest way to test our true spiritual state is to see whether we feel joy when we work for the sake of the Creator. If so, we see that the test is not to determine if we exert great physical or emotional strength, but rather to examine our inner state. Do we retain the same joy regardless of whether we receive from the Creator what we imagine is necessary for us, or not?

Kabbalah speaks of an individual as being like a whole world, since inside each of us is to be found everything around us: the universe, the nations, gentiles, the righteous people of the nations of the world, Israel, the temple and even the Creator Himself—the point that is in our hearts.

In the first place, Kabbalah teaches of our inner qualities, and then proceeds to the outer aspects that are considered consequences of the inner qualities, and thus are designated with respective names. In addition, the spiritual state of the inner qualities directly affects the spiritual state of the outer aspects and the influence of the latter upon us.

As human beings, our initial spiritual state is egoism. One who begins to strive for closeness with the Creator is known as "a righteous person of the peoples of the world." How can one verify if one is, in fact, already at this level? Since Man possesses only egoistic desires, everything that is missing from the gratification of the ego is perceived to have been taken away, as if what was desired had been possessed, and then stolen from the individual.

We have this feeling because of our spiritual "past": on previous spiritual levels, our souls were completely filled with good, but with our spiritual descent into this world, all of it was lost. Therefore, the moment we feel a desire for something, it is equivalent to being filled with complaints towards the Creator about what was taken away, or was never given—that for which one longs.

Thus, if we are able to say from our hearts that everything the Creator did is for the good of all of us, and feel joy and love towards our Creator, as if we had, indeed, received from Him everything we could possibly imagine for ourselves, and justify everything the Creator supervises, then we have successfully completed the test of our intentions (kavana). One who has succeeded in this way is known as a "righteous person of the peoples of the world."

If, with the help of the Creator, we work further on correcting our desire to receive, then the object of verification is no longer our thoughts, but our actions. The Creator gives us everything that we ever desired, but we must be prepared to return everything, while at the same time receiving only the part that we are capable of receiving for the sake of the Creator.

In many situations, we experience the tests as a choice between two possibilities: we feel as if half of our desires draw us to one side, and the other half draws us to the second side. In general, we do not feel within us any struggle between the opposing forces of good and evil, as only the forces of evil rule within, and the problem that continues to arise is which force will deliver the maximum benefit to us.

When the opposing forces are equal, we cannot choose or prefer one over the other, as we feel we are between two forces that are influencing us. At this point, our only solution is to turn to the Creator, so that He should draw us to the good side.

Thus we are obligated to consider everything that happens to us as if it were a trial from Above.

When we do so, we will speedily rise to the goal of creation. To understand the Creation in general, and the particulars of what has happened to us, we must understand the creation's final goal. Then we will understand the actions of the Creator, since all of them depend on and emerge from the final goal.

This is similar to our world, where, if we do not recognize the future result, we are incapable of understanding anyone else's actions. It is said: "Don't show something completely in the middle of its work."

The Creator represents the entire creation, the Light. His goal is to please us with this Light. Thus, the only thing that He must create is the desire to be pleased . All that exists represents the Light and the desire to be pleased. All else created besides us has only one purpose—to aid us in reaching the final goal of creation.

We exist within the Creator, in the ocean of Light that fills everything with Itself. But we can perceive the Creator only to the degree to which we are comparable to Him in qualities. The Light can enter only those desires we hold that are similar to those of the Creator.

To the degree that we differ in qualities and desires from the Creator, we do not perceive Him, because His Light does not penetrate us. If all our qualities are opposite to His qualities, then we do not perceive Him at all, and imagine ourselves to be the only ones in this world.

The Creator strives to give us pleasure through His quality of "the desire to give." For this reason, He created all the worlds and their inhabitants with the opposite quality, "the desire to receive."

The Creator generated all of our egoistic qualities; thus, our lowly state is not our own fault. But the Creator wishes for us to correct ourselves and thus become like Him.

The Light gives life to all substances: inanimate, plant, animal, and human. In our world, the Light is obscured and thus we cannot feel it. As we swim in the ocean of the Creator's Light, if a part of that Light enters us, it is called "the soul."

Since the Light of the Creator brings life, emits vital energy and pleasure, then those who do not receive the Light, but only obtain an insignificant glow to sustain their physical existence, are considered spiritually dead and lacking a soul.

Only a few in this world, known as *Kabbalists* (*Kabbalah* deriving from the word *lekabbel*: "to receive the teaching about the way to acquire the Light") gain the ability to acquire the Light. Each of us starts from our original state, during which we are completely unaware of the ocean of Light in which we "swim."

We must, therefore, attain a complete replenishment of Light. Such a state is known as "the goal of creation" or "the final correction." In addition, this state must be reached during one of our earthly lifetimes.

Spiritual Gradations

When we are gradually filled with the Light of the Creator, the stages of this process are called "spiritual gradations" or "worlds." Life's trials and tribulations force us to move towards the goal of creation. However, if instead of pleasure the ego experiences great suffering, it is willing to forfeit the desire to "receive" in order to end the suffering, since receiving nothing is preferable to receiving torment.

Various afflictions pursue us until we forgo the urge "to receive" and want only "to give." The only difference between people is the kind of pleasure that each hopes to receive: animalistic (bodily pleasures, also found in animals), human (fame, honor, power), and cognitive (discoveries, achievements).

In everyone, the drive towards each of these pleasures is composed of proportions unique to the specific person. The human intellect presents itself merely as a tool to help us achieve our desires. While these desires may change, the intellect helps to find ways to attain a variety of goals.

When the ego begins to suffer, it abandons the desire for enjoyment and becomes inclined to "give." The period necessary to completely eradicate the ego is said to be 6,000 years. However, this number has no relationship to our concept of time.

Egoism is known as the "body." When we are under its influence, we sense that it is spiritually dead. Thus, we "kill" the body by departing from it in five stages, from the simplest stage to the most egoistic stages.

For those egoistic desires we manage to resist, we receive the Light of the Creator. In this manner we sequentially receive five types of Light: *nefesh, ruach, neshama, haya* and *yehida.*

The stages of our spiritual elevation include:

1. The pursuit of the egoistic pleasures of this world. We may finish our lives without leaving this stage, unless we begin to study Kabbalah. Then we will proceed to Stage 2.

2. The recognition of egoism as harmful to us, and evil, followed by our renunciation of its use. Precisely at the center of our egoistic desires is the source, or seed, of our spirituality.

   At a certain moment in our lives, we begin to feel a desire and longing for an understanding and sensing of spirituality. If we behave in accordance with these desires and develop and cultivate them, rather than suppress them, these desires will begin to grow.

   Later, by adding the proper intention acquired from our teacher's guidance, we begin to sense for the first time, the spiritual Light in our new spiritual desires. Its presence helps us attain the confidence and strength we need to further correct our egoism.

3. The attainment of the state in which we desire only to please the Creator with our every action.

4. The correction of the newly acquired desire to "give" into desires "to receive for the sake of the Creator." To do this, we must use our desires for pleasure, but with an intention "for the sake of the Creator."

   The commencement of this task is called the "revival of the dead." In this state, we transform the rejected egoistic desires into the opposite, thus winning doubly. We are able to both enjoy the Creator and our likeness to Him. The conclusion of the process of changing egoism into altruism is known as "the end of correction."

Every time we correct a part of our desires, we receive a part of our souls, and this Light allows us to continue until we completely alter ourselves and regain our souls. The amount of Light, that part of the Creator, corresponds exactly to our prototypical egoism, as was created by the Creator.

By completely transforming our egoism into altruism, we can wholly eliminate any remaining barriers to receiving the Light of the Creator. We may now fill ourselves with the Creator, fully merging with the Creator by perceiving the entire ocean of Light around us and by enjoying it.

We have repeatedly been made aware of our limited potential to understand the world.

The less we understand ourselves, the less we can understand the Creator.

All our perceptions are the result of subjective sensations, the reactions of our bodies to external stimuli.

In other words, we receive and perceive only the amount of information that is selectively sent to us, in accordance with the quality and quantity, or depth, of our potential to perceive it.

Four Fundamental Outlooks

Because we lack concrete information about the structure and function of higher, elusive notions we cannot feel, we permit ourselves to philosophize and argue about how they might be constructed and how they might function. This is similar to children's arguments over who is right about some completely unknown subject.

When religious, secular, scientific and pseudoscientific philosophies try to define "soul" and "body," they all focus on four fundamental outlooks:

Religious

All that "exists" in any object is its "soul." Each soul differs from another by its qualities, known as the "spiritual qualities" of a person. Souls exist independently of the body before the body's birth, before being garbed in the body, and after the body's death. The latter is a completely biological process of albumen breaking down into its parts. (The notion of a "believer" is not the same as the notion of one who is religious").

Thus, the death of the physical body does not affect the soul itself, but only serves to separate the soul from the body.

The soul represents something eternal, since it is not composed of materials from this world. By its nature, the soul is undivided. It does not consist of several parts, and therefore cannot be divided, cannot disintegrate and, ultimately, cannot die.

The physical, biological body is the outer "clothing" of the soul. It is the garment in which the soul dresses and, acting through the body, displays its intellectual and spiritual qualities, as well as its character. This can be compared to when we drive a car, displaying our own wishes, character and intellect in the way we operate the car.

In addition, the soul gives the body life and motion, and protects the body to such an extent that, without the soul, the body lacks life and movement. The body itself is dead material, just as it appears to us after the soul leaves it at the moment of death.

We call the moment of death "the departure of the soul from the body." As a result, all signs of life depend on and are determined by the presence of the soul.

Dualistic

As a result of scientific developments, a new outlook on the physical body has emerged: the belief that our bodies can also exist without any kind of spiritual component to invigorate them.

In fact, the body can exist absolutely independently of the soul. This has been proven with the use of biological and medical experiments that are now able to revive the body or its parts.

But the body in a state like this is no more than an independently existing biological object, composed of albumen substances. The factor that determines various personal qualities is the soul, which descends into the body from Above, as in the first approach. The difference between the Dualistic approach and the Religious point of view centers on the fact that the Religious approach proposes that, just as the soul endows the body with life, it also bestows upon it intellectual and spiritual qualities.

The Dualistic point of view argues that the soul bestows only spiritual qualities on the body, since it is evident from experiments that the body can exist by itself, without the help of any additional upper powers. Thus, the soul's only function is to be the source of all of the good qualities that are "spiritual," but not material.

Moreover, this approach maintains that, despite the body's ability to exist independently, it is nevertheless the product of the soul. The soul is seen as primary, since it is responsible for the birth and maintenance of the body.

Non-Believer

A non-believer is one who denies the existence of any spiritual structures, as well as the presence of the soul in the body. The non-believer only recognizes the existence of material substances and their properties.

Thus, it is reasoned, since there is no soul, the human intellect, as well as all other properties of the human being, is the result of the body that generated it. The view is that the body is a system that controls its characteristics by sending commands through electrical signals via nerve conductors. (A non-believer is not the same thing as non-religious).

Non-believers say that all the sensations of the body occur by the interaction of nerve endings equipped with outer stimulators. The sensations pass via the nerve conductors to the brain, where they are then analyzed and classified as either "pain" or "pleasure."

The mind reacts to a particular organ in response to whether it perceives it as painful or pleasurable. In addition, it is believed that everything is constructed as in a mechanism with sensors, whereby signals are transmitted to, processed and emitted by the brain device.

They are also controlled by means of reverse feedback. The brain operates according to the principle of distancing itself from pain, and coming closer to pleasure. The pain vs. pleasure signals will determine the person's attitude towards life, and one's consequent actions.

We perceive reason as a reflection of our physical processes, similar to a photograph. The main difference between a human being and an animal is the fact that the human brain is so well developed. In fact, all the processes taking place in human beings are condensed into such an exhaustive picture that we perceive these processes as reason and logic. But our entire intellect is the result of our physical perceptions and awareness.

Undoubtedly, of all the approaches to understanding the problem, this approach is the most logical, scientific and understandable, since it relies solely on experience, and hence concerns itself only with our bodies, rather than some ephemeral notion known as "the soul." Thus, this approach is most reliable in that it deals with our bodies.

However, the flaw of this approach is that it is unsatisfactory and repellent—even to non-believers. This concept presents human beings as robots in the hands of blind nature (predetermined qualities of character, laws of social evolution, demands of our bodies to sustain life and search for pleasure, etc). All these deprive us of the status of reasoning beings.

Thus, if a human being is merely a mechanism, forced to act in accordance with data initially prepared in it, and with the accepted norms of society, then this theory negates the whole idea of free will and the right to choose our actions (objective thinking).

Though human beings are created by nature, we consider ourselves to be wiser.

As a result, this view cannot be accepted even by those who do not believe in the Upper Intellect, since people appear to be completely governed by blind nature that lacks any design or goal, simply toying with people (with reasonable beings) without any purpose, giving no reason for their life or for their death.

In order to somehow soften such a scientifically logical, yet spiritually unacceptable, approach to the question of our existence, in our time humanity has gradually adopted a "modern" outlook on itself.

Modern

This has become fashionable, especially today (despite our tendency to accept the previous, materialistic approach to creation as the most scientifically reliable and understandable). It is also fashionable to concede that something eternal, undying and spiritual in us exists that drapes itself in the material bodily casing. Specifically, this is our spiritual essence, known as the soul, whereas the body is only the garb.

Still, the adherents to this view cannot explain how the soul becomes clothed by the body, the relationship between soul and body, the source of the soul, and the essence of the soul. Thus, closing their eyes to all these questions, human beings resort to an old, tested method of complacency: they forget about all their concerns in the torrent of daily petty burdens and delights, living today just as they did yesterday.

Who can understand such questions as: What is the body and what is the soul? What is the relation between them? Why do we perceive ourselves as being comprised of two parts, the material and the spiritual? In which of these two can we find ourselves, our eternal "I?" What happens to our "I" before our birth and after our death? Does it remain the same "I" as we perceive now? Is it the same as the one felt within our body and outside of it, before birth and after death?

Most important, we use our physical intellect to analyze all these questions and possible alternatives. This is how we assess how our souls are transformed and circulated, and how our bodies became material.

Are these images true, or are they merely the products of our imagination, produced by our material minds. The mind creates pictures of the spiritual world, of the path from that world to ours and the return from ours to the spiritual, in accordance with its earthly understanding and lack of any other information.

The mind can operate only on the basis of how it perceives the world imprinted in it, and thus produces our fantasies and assumptions.

Similarly, we cannot conceive of an extraterrestrial being that is completely unlike us in all aspects and has no elements of our physical make-up.

We are then faced with the question, "What if all that we are able to imagine, which is the basis of our theories of life, is nothing more than our minds' attempt to grasp something beyond our capacity to grasp?

If we accept as truth the notions that our minds produce, based on our experiences in this world (lacking any better alternative), then we must ask if, within our abilities to perceive in this world, there exists an answer to the question, "What are the soul and the body"?

I have already mentioned in other parts of the book the issue of our limited ability to understand. To the degree that we cannot truly see, perceive or examine any object in this world, we also cannot truly judge our souls or, for that matter, our bodies.

Given the four categories of how we understand an object—its material composition; its outer form; its abstract form, and its essence—we can only perceive the outer form of the object as it appears to us and, after examining it, the material of which it consists. But we have no understanding of the removed form of the object, that is, its non-material qualities (its essence).

17

Merging with the Creator

Kabbalah is called "the science of the hidden" because it reveals to the one who learns it that which was previously hidden. The true picture of existence is revealed only to the one who apprehends it, as is written in the poem by Rabbi Ashlag:

The miracle truth will radiate,
And the mouth will only utter that truth,
And all that will be revealed in confidence
You will see, but no other!

Kabbalah is the teaching of that which is secret, since it is hidden from the average reader and becomes revealed only under very special conditions. Those who study it will find these secrets gradually become clearer from the teachings themselves, along with special guidance to direct the reader's desires and thoughts.

Only the one for whom Kabbalah ceases to be a hidden teaching and becomes revealed can see and understand the construction of the world, and the so-called "soul" and "body" can only be seen and understood by those for whom Kabbalah ceases to be a hidden teaching, and becomes revealed. Yet, even they are unable to transmit their perceived views of creation to anyone else, having no right to pass on this information, with one exception: During one's gradual spiritual ascent, one learns the truth of creation: There is nothing except the Creator!

The sensory organs we were created with are able to perceive only a small part of the entire creation, known as "our world." All the mechanisms we have invented widen the range of our sensory organs. We are unable to imagine which sensory organs we lack because we do not feel any deprivation from their absence.

This can be compared with not feeling the need for a sixth finger on one's hand. Since we don't have the senses required to perceive other worlds, we cannot sense them. Therefore, despite our being surrounded by such a rich environment, we are able to see only a small fragment of it. In addition, even the fragment we perceive is quite distorted, since we can only grasp a small portion of it.

However, using what we perceive as a foundation, we create our views of the whole of existence. Like those who see only in x-ray mode, where all is perceived as a skeletal picture obstructing the x-rays, we, too, have a distorted view of the universe. Just as we cannot receive a true picture of this universe according to x-ray vision, neither can we fathom the true picture of creation through our limited senses.

No amount of imagination can compensate for our lack of ability to perceive, since even our fantasies are built on past experiences. Despite all this, let us try to create a simple concept of the so-called "other world," which exists on the other side of our conception, the one beyond the range of our sensory organs.

First, imagine that you are in a vacuum. Before you stretches a road. Along the road at certain intervals are markings from zero, where you stand now, to the end. These markings divide the road into three parts.

We do not move along the road by the alternate advancement of our feet, but by alternate changes in desires.

In the spiritual world, place, space or motion do not exist as we understand them. The spiritual world is the world of emotions that exist outside the realm of physical bodies.

Objects are emotions. Motion is the change of qualities. Place is a certain quality. Place in the spiritual world is defined by its characteristics. Therefore, "motion" is defined as "the change of one's emotions, similar to the concept of spiritual motion in our world, the movement of emotions, but not physical movement.

Thus, the path we are trying to understand is the gradual alteration of our inner qualities, our desires.

The distance between spiritual objects is defined and measured by the difference in their qualities. The more similar the qualities are, the closer the objects are considered to be. The closeness or distance of objects is defined by the relative change in their properties. If two objects are identical, then they will merge into one. However, if a new quality appears in one of the spiritual objects, that particular quality separates from the first one, and in this manner a new spiritual object is born.

At the end of the path before us is the Creator Himself. His attribute—the complete Will to bestow—determines His distance from us. Since we are born into this world with only egoistic characteristics, we are as distanced from the Creator as east is from west. And the goal the Creator places before us is to attain His qualities while living in this world, that is, to spiritually merge with Him.

Our path is to lead us to a gradual alteration of our qualities until they are exactly like those of the Creator. The only quality of the Creator that defines His Essence is the complete absence of any trace of egoism.

This is followed by the lack of any thought about oneself, or one's condition and power—a lack of all that comprises the essence of our thoughts and our aspirations. But since we exist in this world in a specific outer covering, we must care for the bare essentials to maintain this casing. This is not considered to be a sign of egoism.

In general, we can determine whether a thought or a desire of the body is egoistic by a simple test: If we want to be free from a thought, but our survival depends on it, then such a thought or action is considered to be involuntary, not egoistic, and thus does not separate us from the Creator. The Creator advances us towards our goal in the following manner: He endows us with a "bad" desire or with suffering, which can be compared to moving forward with the left foot.

If we find within us the strength to ask the Creator for help, then the Creator will give us a "good" desire or pleasure, which can be compared to the forward movement with the right foot. Once again, we receive from Above an even stronger bad desire or doubts about the Creator, and once again, with an even greater effort of the will, we must ask Him to help us.

The Creator will help by giving us an even greater good desire, and so on.

In such a manner, we move forward. There is no backward motion. The purer the desires, the farther a person is from the initial point of absolute egoism. The motion forward can be described in many ways, but it is always an alternating advancement through all the feelings.

After a feeling of something spiritual, a subconscious sensing of the existence of the Creator, it is followed by a feeling of trust, which then brings about a feeling of joy. Afterwards, this feeling begins to fade away, indicating that we rose to another step of spiritual ascension, which we cannot perceive because of our lack of sensory organs with which we could fully experience it. Since we have not yet achieved the next level through suffering, toil and work (have not built the appropriate vessels), the perception of the next level has not yet been born.

The new sensory organs for the next stage (the desire for pleasure, and the feeling of suffering due to the lack of this pleasure) can be developed in two ways:

1. *The Way of Kabbalah*: Here, we begin to perceive the Creator, then lose our connection. In its place appears suffering because we cannot feel pleasure.

   The suffering is necessary in order for us to eventually feel pleasure.

   In such a manner, then, are born new sensory organs to allow us to perceive the Creator at each consecutive stage. As in our world, without a desire for a goal or object, we are not able to experience pleasure from it .
   The differences between people, and between man and animal, are determined by what they choose to bring them pleasure. Therefore, spiritual advancement is not possible without first feeling a lack. We must suffer from the lack of what we desire.

2. *The Way of Suffering*: If one were unable through effort, studies, appeals to the Creator, and entreaties of friends to elevate oneself to new desires to love and fear the Creator; if one displayed shallowness of thought, disrespect for the spiritual, and a pull towards base pleasures, then that person would descend to the level of evil powers.
   In this case, the person would step along the left lane in the corresponding levels of the evil (egoistic) worlds *ABYA* (*Azilut, Beria, Yetzira, Assiya*). However, the suffering would become a vessel into which a new perception of the Creator can be received.

Progress made through the way of Kabbalah differs from the way of suffering, in that we are given the Light of the

Creator. This is a feeling of the Creator's Presence, which is then taken from us.

When we lack this pleasure, we begin to long for the Light. This longing is the vessel, or new set of sensory organs, through which we can try to receive a perception of the Creator. These goals pull us forward until we receive the desired perceptions.

When we advance by means of suffering, we are pushed from behind by the suffering, unlike the path of Kabbalah, where we advance by way of the desire for pleasure. The Creator directs us in accordance with His Plan—to bring us, to transfer each and every one of us and all of mankind, in this life or in coming lives, to the final point of this path at which He is found.

This path represents steps we will take to draw closer to Him as we take on more of His characteristics. Only by merging our qualities with those of the Creator will we gain a true perception of the creation of the world and see that nothing else exists but the Creator.

All the worlds and their inhabitants, all that we feel around us, as well as we ourselves, comprise only a part of Him. More precisely, we *are* Him. All of our thoughts and actions are determined by our desires. The intellect only serves to help us achieve that which we desire.

When we receive our desires, they are bestowed upon us from Above, and only the Creator Himself can change them.

The Creator did this intentionally in order for us to understand that everything that happened to us in the past, present, and future in every area of life is absolutely dependent upon Him. Our situations can only improve if He so wishes, since only He is the cause of what happened, happens and will happen.

This is necessary in order for us to recognize and feel the need for a connection with Him. We can trace this process from the original lack of desire to recognize Him at the beginning of the path, until the end of the path, when we have become fully attached to Him.

If someone suddenly experiences a desire to come closer to the Creator, a desire and pull towards the spiritual, then this is the result of the Creator drawing that person closer to Him by instilling these feelings in the individual. In a reversed situation, we see that by "falling" in one's aspirations, or even in one's material, social or other status, through failures and deprivations, we gradually begin to understand that this is done intentionally by the Creator.

In this way, the individual can feel dependent on the Source of all that occurs, creating an understanding that "only the Creator can help, otherwise one will perish." The Creator does this purposely to arouse in us a firm need for Him, so we will encourage Him to change our spiritual state. In this way, we crave more closeness with Him, and He can, in accordance with our wishes, bring us closer to Him.

From this, we see that the Creator helps save us from (a spiritual) sleep or a situation where we are content with our present state. In order for us to progress to the goal specified by the Creator, He sends us suffering and failure, both physical and spiritual, through our surroundings, family, friends, colleagues and acquaintances.

We have been created so that we perceive that anything pleasant is a result of our drawing close to Him. We also feel the opposite: that everything unpleasant is caused by our being distanced from Him. For this reason, our world is constructed in such a way that we depend on health, family, and the love and respect of those surrounding us.

For the Creator, all these serve as messengers, so that He can exert negative influences that would force us to search for solutions to these pressures, finally recognizing that all the world depends only on the Creator. Then, with sufficient strength and patience, we can become worthy to associate all that happens in life with the desire of the Creator, rather than with some other cause, or even with our own actions and thoughts in the past. In time, it will be clear that only the Creator is the cause of all that happens.

The path presented above is the way for each of us, as well as for humanity in general. Starting from the initial point at which we find ourselves in accordance with our present desires ("our world") until the final destination at which we must arrive even against our will ("the world to come"), our path is divided into four stages or states:

1. Absolute lack of perception (the absolute concealment) of the Creator.

The consequences of this state are: absence of belief in the Creator and in Divine Supervision from Above; belief in one's own power, in the power of nature, of circumstances; and of chance.

All of humanity is at this stage (at this spiritual level). When we are at this stage, our lives become a process of accumulating experiences in our souls through various sufferings sent to us.

The soul accumulates experiences through repeated returns of the same soul into this world in different bodies.

Once the soul acquires a sufficient amount of experience, the person is able to perceive the first spiritual level.

2. Unclear perception of the Creator.

The consequences of this state are a belief in punishment and reward, and a belief that suffering is a result of distance from the Creator. Pleasure is seen as the result of closeness to the Creator.

Under the influence of these great hardships, we might return to a previous stage. However, as we accumulate experience, unaware of this process, we continue to learn until we realize that only our complete awareness of the Creator's Management will give us strength to progress.

In these two situations, we have the ability to believe in the Upper Supervision. If we attempt, despite all the disturbances sent from Above, to strengthen our faith and work to perceive the Creator's Management in His world, then after a specific number and intensity of efforts, the Creator will help us by revealing both Himself and the picture of existence.

3. Partial Revelation of His Management in the world.

Here, we are able to see the reward for good actions and the punishment for bad deeds. Therefore, we are incapable of doing other than good and refraining from bad, just as each one of us is unable to refrain from doing good or harming ourselves.

However, this stage of spiritual development is not the final one, since at this stage all our actions are involuntary, as a result of our awareness of reward and punishment. Thus, there is one more stage of spiritual development—gaining the perception that all that is done by the Creator is done with absolute and eternal love for His created beings.

4. The Revelation of the complete picture of the Creator's Management of the world.

This offers a clear perception that the management of the world by the Creator is based not on reward and punishment for a person's deeds, but is instead based on His unbounded love for His creations. We attain this stage of spiritual development when we see clearly that in all circumstances, with all the creations in general and with each in particular, without judging whether their actions are good or bad, the Creator always manages and supervises them only with absolute and unbounded love.

When we sense this Upper Spiritual Level, we already perceive everyone's future state. We can perceive the situation of those who have not yet reached this state, along with those in the past and in the present who have already reached it; we also apprehend the knowledge to experience the same stage, both as individuals and as a whole.

This apprehension is a result of the Creator revealing the entire design of creation and His relation to every soul in every generation, for the entire duration of the existence of all the worlds. These worlds were created for a single purpose— to give pleasure to His created beings. It is the sole purpose that determines all the actions of the Creator towards His created beings.

This continues from the beginning to the end of creation, so that all of them together, and each one separately, may experience an unbounded pleasure from their attachment to Him. As a result, when we can clearly see that the Creator's actions are only to do good and benefit His created beings, there becomes formed within us the deeds of the Creator towards His creations.

We are consequently imbued with a feeling of boundless love for the Creator, and as a result of similarity of feelings, the Creator and the person merge into one entity. Since that stage represents the end goal of creation, the first three stages comprise preliminary steps necessary to attain the fourth one.

All the desires of an individual are as if lodged in the heart, because they are felt there in a physiological form. Therefore, our hearts are considered representative of all of the desires of the body, and of our essence. The changes in one's heart's desires reveal the changes in one's personality.

From our birth, that is, from the time we appeared in this world, our hearts are occupied only with worries of the body; and only the desires of the body concern it. The heart is filled only with the desires of the body, and from them it lives.

But deep inside the heart, in the depth of all the desires, is a point that is hidden behind all the petty and temporary desires and is not perceived by us. It is the need for spiritual sensation. This point is a part of the Creator Himself.

If we consciously, through the power of our efforts to overcome and leap over the indifference and laziness of the body, seek in Kabbalah the ways to draw closer to the Creator, this point gradually becomes filled with pure and good desires. Thus, we gain the perception of the Creator on the first spiritual level, the level of the world *Assiya*.

Then, passing in his perceptions all the stages of the world *Assiya*, we can begin to perceive the Creator on the level of the world *Yetzira*, and so on, until we reach the Highest Level— the perception of the Creator on the level of the world *Atzilut*.

Every time, we experience all our perceptions in the same inner point of our hearts. In the past, when our hearts were under the influence of the desires of the body, so the inner point in the heart received absolutely no perception of the

Creator. We could only think about the desires that the body forced us to think about, and desire only that which the body forced us to desire.

Now, if we fill our hearts with pure and altruistic desires through prayers and requests and demands to the Creator for our spiritual redemption, we will begin to perceive the Creator. Then, we will be capable of thinking only about Him, since there have been born in us thoughts and desires related to that spiritual level.

Consequently, we always desire only that which we are forced to desire by the spiritual influence that we receive, in accordance with the stage at which we find ourselves.

Given the above, it becomes clear that we should not strive to alter our own thoughts, but must ask the Creator to alter them, since all our desires and thoughts are merely consequences of what we receive, or more exactly, of the degree to which we perceive the Creator.

In regard to the entire creation, it is evident that all derives from the Creator, but the Creator created us with a certain degree of freedom of will. The ability to direct our desires appears only in those who reach the stages of *ABYA*. The higher we ascend spiritually, the higher our degree of freedom.

For the sake of clarification, we can compare the process of our spiritual development with the development of the material nature of our world. All of nature and the universe represent but a single desire for self-gratification. This exists in each individual to a varying degree, and as this desire increases, more advanced beings come into our world, because the desire induces the mind to work and develop the intellect for the satisfaction of one's needs.

Our thoughts are always a result of our desires. They follow after them and are directed only towards the attainment of these desires, and nothing else. Along with this, thoughts possess a special role—with their help, we can increase our desires.

If we constantly deepen and expand our thoughts about something, and strive to constantly return to this thought, gradually this desire will begin to increase with respect to the other desires. In this way, we can alter the correlation of our desires. With constant thoughts about a small desire, we can increase it into such a large desire, it will overshadow all the other desires and determine our essence.

Phases of Revelation

The lowest level on the scale of the spiritual resembles the inanimate part of nature, similar to bodies in space, or minerals, and so on. This inanimate level is also called "not alive."

The inanimate level in the spiritual (or someone who is found there) is not capable of acting in an independent fashion. Nor can it reveal characteristics of its own, since the desire to have pleasure within it is so small that it is defined as merely guarding its characteristics and not furthering their development.

Lack of individuality at that level of creation is pronounced in the fact that it possesses nothing independent. It focuses on its function blindly, automatically carrying out the desires of its Creator, since it cannot conceive of anything else because it has no individual desires.

Since the Creator wanted inanimate objects to behave in precisely this manner, He gave them the lowest level of desires, which did not require these objects to develop. Thus, having no other desires but those originally implanted in them by the Creator, these objects blindly perform their tasks, caring only for their needs of a spiritually inanimate nature, not sensing their surroundings. Similarly, in people as yet spiritually inanimate, there is also a lack of any individual desires. Only the desires of the Creator guide them, and because of their nature they must follow this guidance meticulously and subconsciously, in accordance with the program implanted in them by the Creator.

Therefore, in spite of the fact that the Creator devised human nature in this manner for His own purpose, in this spiritual state people cannot perceive anything but themselves. Consequently, they cannot do anything for others, but can only work for their own benefit. Thus, this level of spiritual development is called "inanimate."

A higher degree of development can be found in the nature of plants. Since the Creator conferred on this group of objects a greater desire for pleasure than given to inanimate objects, plants require certain movement and growth in order to satisfy their needs.

But this movement and growth is an attribute of a group, not an individual aspiration. In people who belong to the vegetative level of desire, there appears a certain level of spiritual independence from the Creator Who sets the program. Since the Creator constructed all of nature on the basis of absolute egoism (the desire for self-gratification), on the vegetative level these individuals begin to develop inclinations to distance themselves from the desires already implanted in them.

Consequently, they begin to act out of consideration for others, that is, as if against their nature. However, regardless of the fact that the plants in this world grow in all directions and possess a certain freedom of movement, their movement is still considered to be a collective movement. After all, no one plant is capable, due to a complete lack of appropriate desire, even to fathom the possibility of individual movement.

Similarly, a person belonging to the vegetative level of desires is not capable of aspiring to individual endeavors that diverge from the norms of the collective, society and one's upbringing. On the contrary, this person aims to preserve and to obey all the norms and the laws of its "vegetative" environment. This is comprised of a similar group of people belonging to the "vegetative" level of development.

Therefore, just like the plant, the person at this level has no individual, separate life, but lives as part of a community, residing among numerous others who are similar in nature.

Among all the plants and among all the people at this level there can be found only one common life, rather than an individual life for every being. All the plants in general can be compared to a single vegetative organism, in which each plant can be likened to a separate branch of this body.

The people belonging to the "vegetative" spiritual level can also be compared to this example. Though they do sometimes deviate from their egoistic natures, nevertheless, because their spiritual development is minor, they remain confined by the laws of society and by their surroundings. They have no individual desires or strength to oppose society or their upbringing, even though in some matters they already go against their own basic nature and act for the benefit of others.

On the spiritual gradation of development, the vegetative level is followed by the animal level. This is considered higher because desires, allotted by the Creator to this level, develop those at this level to such a degree that they find satisfaction in the ability to move independently of others, and think independently for the purpose of satisfying their desires, much more so than at the vegetative level.

Each animal has an individual character and feelings irrespective of the surrounding environment. Consequently, a person at this stage of development possesses a greater ability to function contrary to egoistic inclinations and for the good of others.

But even though a degree of independence has been gained, from the collective, leading to a personal individual life not shaped by the opinions of the community, feelings for the self are still paramount.

Those who exist on the human ("speaking") level of development are already capable of acting against their nature and contrary to the collective (unlike the plant).

These people are completely independent from society in the choice of their desires.

They can feel for any other being and can thus care for others. They can help them in their quest to better themselves by identifying with their suffering. Those on this level, unlike the animals, can sense the past and the future, and can, thus, act, being guided by the recognition of a central purpose.

All the worlds and the stages ascribed to these worlds can be seen as a sequence of screens that conceal from us (the Light of) the Creator. As we acquire the spiritual strength to overcome our own natures, each of its forces, each consecutive screen, disappears as if dissolved.

The following tale illustrates the progression of our spiritual quest to dissolve the screens and live as one with the Creator.

18

The Omnipotent Magician

Who Could Not Be Alone

A Tale for Grown-Ups

Do you know why only old folk tell stories and legends? Because legends are the cleverest thing in the world! Everything in the world changes, and only real legends remain. Legends are wisdom and in order to tell them, one needs to have great knowledge, and to see things others do not.

For that, one needs to have lived a lot. That is why only old people know how to tell legends. As is written in the greatest, oldest magical book, "An old person is someone who has acquired wisdom."

Children love to hear legends because they have the imagination and brains to envision everything, not just what others see. If a child grows up and still sees what others do not, he becomes wise and clever, and "acquires wisdom."

Because children see what others do not, they know that imagination is real. They remain as a "wise child," as is written in the greatest, oldest magical book, "The Zohar."

There once was a magician, great and noble and good-hearted, with all the attributes usually given in children's books. But because he was so goodhearted, he did not know who to share his goodness with. He did not have anyone to pour his affections on, to play with, to spend time with, to think about.

The magician also needed to feel wanted, for it is very sad to be alone.

What should he do? He thought he would make a stone, just a small one, but beautiful, and perhaps that would be the answer.

"I will stroke the stone and feel there is something constantly by my side, and we will both feel good because it is very sad to be alone." He waved his wand and in an instant there was a stone exactly as he wanted.

He began to stroke the stone, to hug it and talk to it, but the stone did not respond. It remained cold and did nothing in return. Whatever he did to the stone, it remained the same unfeeling object.

This did not suit the magician at all. How can the stone not respond? He tried creating some more stones, then rocks, hills, mountains, land, the Earth, the Moon and the Galaxy. But they were all the same... nothing.

He still felt sad and all alone. In his sadness, he thought that instead of stones, he would make a plant that would blossom beautifully. He would water it, give it some air, some sun, play it some music, and the plant would be happy. Then they would both be content, because it was sad to be alone.

He waved his wand and in an instant there was a plant, exactly as he wanted. He was so happy be began to dance around it, but the plant did not move. It did not dance with him or follow his movements. It only responded to what the magician gave it in the simplest terms.

If he gave it water, it grew; if he did not, it died. It was not enough for such a good-hearted magician who wanted to give with all his heart.

He had to do something more, because it is very sad to be alone. He then created all sorts of plants in all sorts of sizes, fields, forests, orchards, plantations and groves. But they all behaved the same way as the first plant, and again he was alone in his sadness.

The magician thought and thought. What should he do? Create an animal! What sort of animal? A dog? Yes, a cute little dog that would be with him constantly. He would take him for walks and the dog would jump and prance and run along.

When he came home to his palace (or rather, being a magician, his castle), the dog would be so pleased to see him he would run to greet him. They would both be happy, because it is very sad to be alone. He waved his wand and there was a dog, just as he wanted. He began to take care of the dog, fed it, gave it to drink, and stroked it. He even ran with it and washed it and took it for walks.

But a dog's love is summed up in being next to its owner, wherever he is. The magician was sad to see that a dog cannot reciprocate, even if he plays with him so well and goes everywhere with him. A dog cannot be his true friend, cannot appreciate what he does for it, does not comprehend his thoughts and desires, and how much effort he makes for it.

But that was what the magician wanted. So he made other creatures: fish, fowl, mammals, all to no avail—none of them understood him. It was very sad to be so alone.

The magician sat and thought. He then realized that in order to have a true friend, he must be someone who would look for the magician, would want him very much, would be like the magician, able to love like him, understand him, resemble him, be his partner. Partner? True friend?

It would have to be something that was close to him, that understood what he gave him and could reciprocate by giving him everything in return. Magicians also want to love and be loved. Then they would both be content, because it is very sad to be alone.

The magician then thought about creating a man. He could be his true friend! He could be like the magician. He would merely need help to be like his creator. Then the two of them would feel good, because it is very sad to be alone.

But in order for them to feel good, man must first feel lonely, and be sad without the magician. The magician waved his wand again and made a man in the distance. The man did not feel there was a magician who had made all the stones, plants, hills, fields and moon, rain, winds, etc. He did not know that he had made an entire world filled with beautiful things, such as computers and football that made him feel good and lacking nothing.

The magician, on the other hand, continued to feel sad that he was alone. The man did not know there was a magician who had made him, loved him, was waiting for him and said that together they would feel good because it is very sad to be alone.

Yet how would a man who feels content, who has everything, even a computer and football, who does not know the magician, want to find him, get acquainted with him, become close to him, love him, be his friend and say, "Come, we will both feel good, because it is very sad to be alone, without you."

One knows only one's surroundings, and does what everyone else nearby does, speaks as they speak, wants what they want, tries not to offend, asks nicely for presents, a computer, or a football. How can the person possibly know there is a magician who is sad to be alone?

But the magician is goodhearted and constantly looks out for man, and when the time is ripe, he waves his wand and calls to the man's heart very quietly. Man thinks he is looking for something and does not realize it is the magician who is calling him, saying, "Come, we will both feel good, because it is very sad to be alone without you."

Then, the magician waves his wand again and the man feels his presence. He begins to think of the magician, to think that it will be good together, because it is very sad to be alone, without the magician.

Another wave of the wand and the man feels there is a magic tower full of goodness and might in which the magician waits for him and that only there will they feel good, because it is very sad to be alone.

"But where is this tower? How can I reach it? Which is the way?" he asks himself, puzzled and confused. How can he meet the magician? He keeps feeling the wave of the wand in his heart and he cannot sleep. He constantly sees magicians and mighty towers and cannot even eat.

That is what happens when a person wants something very much and cannot find it, and is sad to be alone. But in order to be like the magician—wise, great, noble, good-hearted, loving and a friend—a wave of the wand is not enough. One must learn to make wonders oneself.

So the magician secretly and subtly, gently and innocuously, leads the man to the greatest, oldest magical book, the Book of Zohar, and shows him the way to the mighty tower. The man grasps it so he can swiftly meet the magician, meet his friend, and tell him, "Come, we will feel good together, because it is very sad to be alone."

Yet there is a high wall surrounding the tower, and many guards repel the man, not letting him and the magician be together and feel good. The man despairs, the magician hides away in the tower behind locked gates, the wall is high, the guards vigilantly repel, nothing can pass.

What will happen...? How can they be together, feel good together because it is sad to be alone?

Every time the man weakens and despairs, he suddenly feels a wave of the wand and he rushes to the walls again to try to circumvent the guards, no matter what! He wants to break into the gates, reach the tower, climb the rungs of the ladder and reach the magician.

And every time he surges forward and moves nearer the tower and the magician, the guards become more vigilant, stronger and arduous, mercilessly flaying him. But with each round the man becomes braver, stronger and wiser. He learns to accomplish all sorts of tricks himself, to invent things only a magician can.

Every time he is pushed back, he wants the magician more, feels his love for him more, and wants more than anything else in the world to be with the magician and see his face, because it will be good to be together. Even if he is given everything in the world, without the magician, he will feel alone.

Then, when he can no longer bear to be without him, the gates of the tower open, and the magician, his magician, rushes towards him and says, "Come, we will be good together, because it is very sad to be alone."

And ever since, they are faithful friends, closely acquainted, and there is no finer pleasure than that which is between them, forever into infinity. They feel so good together that they never remember, even occasionally, how sad it was to be alone.

The End.

The sequence of the screens conceals the Creator from us. These screens exist in ourselves and in our souls. However, the Creator is everything outside of ourselves and our souls with their interfering screens. We can only perceive that minute part of the outer surroundings that can permeate our screen.

Everything that is outside of us is completely lost to our perception. In the same manner, in this world we see only those objects that are reflected on the inner surface of the eye, once they fall within the range of our vision.

Our knowledge of the spiritual worlds comes from the perceptions and sensations gained by the souls of the Kabbalists, which are passed on to us.

However, their achievements are restricted by the range of their spiritual vision. Hence, all the spiritual worlds known to us exist only in relation to these souls.

Given the aforesaid, the entire creation can be divided into three parts:

1. The Creator

We cannot discuss Him due to the fact that we can only judge those phenomena that fall within the range of our spiritual perception after passing through the interfering screens.

2. The Purpose of Creation

This is our starting point, from which we can begin to explore the Creator's intention. While some argue that its essence centers on pleasing His creations, we cannot say anything else about the Creator's relation to us for lack of information.

The Creator wished that we should feel His influence upon us as Pleasure, and so He created our sensory receptors in such a way as to permit us to sense His influence upon us as Pleasure. But since all perception is accomplished by the soul, it is senseless to talk about the other worlds without connecting this subject to those who perceive these worlds. Without the soul's ability to perceive, the other worlds do not exist.

The interfering screens that stand between us and the Creator actually present these worlds. *Olam* derives from the word *alama*, which means "concealment." The worlds exist only for the purpose of transmitting even a small part of the Pleasure (Light) emanating from the Creator to the soul.

3. Souls

These are entities generated by the Creator that perceive themselves as existing independently. This feeling is highly subjective and essentially translates into the soul, that is our individual self, having been specifically made in this manner by the Creator. However, in reality we are actually an integral part of Him.

A person's entire path of development, from the initial stage to the final stage at which one completely merges with the Creator in all his qualities, can be divided into five stages. Each of these can in turn be divided into five sub-stages that are, in turn, further comprised of five sub-stages.

In total, there are 125 stages. Every person at a particular stage experiences the same feelings and influences as every other person at the same stage. And every person possesses the same spiritual sensory organs, and hence can feel the same as everyone else at the same stage.

Similarly, every person in our world possesses the same perceptual organs that yield identical perceptions, but do not allow the perception of other worlds.

Therefore, the books on Kabbalah can be understood only by those who reach the stage of the author, since then the author and the reader will have common experiences. This also applies to the readers and authors who describe the events of this world.

From the spiritual worlds, the soul receives the awareness of the Creator's closeness, as well as spiritual gratification and the enlightenment that accompanies unification with Him. The soul also receives, from the understanding gained of His wishes and the laws of His Dominion, the so-called "Light of the Creator," or the ability to perceive Him.

As we advance on our spiritual path, we gradually perceive that we are being drawn closer to the Creator. That is the reason for gaining a new perspective on the Revelation of the Creator at every phase of our journey.

For those who can grasp only our world, the Bible appears as a collection of laws and historical events that describe the behavior of human beings in this world. However, those who are more advanced along their spiritual path begin to perceive the spiritual actions of the Creator behind the names of objects and actions of our world.

From all the above, it becomes clear that in creation there are two participants: the Creator and the human being, who was created by the Almighty. All the other visions that arise before us, whether our perception of our world or even our perception of Higher Worlds, are only the different phases of revelation and disclosure of the Creator on His way to coming closer to us.

19

Spiritual Levels

The entire creation can be described as a function of four parameters: time, soul, world, and Source of existence. These are regulated from the inside by the Will and the Wishes of the Creator.

Time: a cause-and-effect progression of events that takes place with every single soul and with all humanity in its entirety, similar to the historical development of humanity.

Soul: everything organic (live), including human beings.

World: the entire inorganic (lifeless) universe. In the spiritual worlds, this corresponds to the inorganic level of desires .

Source of Existence: the plan for the development of events. This occurs with each of us and with humanity in general, and is the plan for governing the entire creation and bringing it to the initially predetermined condition.

When He decided to create all the worlds and the human beings in them to bring them closer to Him, the Creator gradually decreased his presence by diminishing His Light in order to create our world. The four phases of gradual (from above downwards) concealment of the Creator's Presence are known as "the worlds." These are:

Atzilut: a world in which those present are completely unified with the Creator.

Beria: a world in which those present have a connection with the Creator.

Yetzira: a world in which those present perceive the Creator.

Assiya: a world in which those present almost completely or completely do not perceive the Creator. This level includes our world as the last, the lowest and the most removed from the Creator.

All the above worlds have emerged one from the other and, in a way, are replicas of one another. Each lower world, the one further removed from the Creator, is a cruder version, yet an exact replica, of the previous one.

Interestingly, each world is a replica in all four parameters: world, soul, time, and Source of existence. Thus, everything in our world is the direct result of processes that have already taken place in the past in a higher world, and all that has taken place there is the result of what took place even earlier, and so on, up to the point where all four parameters—world, time, soul, and the Source of existence—merge in a single Source of existence, in the Creator!

This "place" is known as *Atzilut*. The clothing of the Creator in the garments of the worlds *Atzilut, Beria, Yetzira* (His appearance to us by means of illuminations of Light through screens which weaken these worlds) is known as Kabbalah. The clothing of the Creator in the garment of our world, the world of *Assiya,* is known as the written *Torah.*

In truth, however, there is no difference between Kabbalah and the Torah of this world. The Source of everything is the Creator.

In other words, to study and to live according to the Torah, or to study and to live according to Kabbalah, is determined by the spiritual level of the student. If one is on the level of this world, then one sees and perceives this world and the *Torah* as everything.

However, should the student move to a higher level, a different picture will emerge. The sheath of this world will vanish and what will be left are the sheaths of the worlds,

Yetzira and *Beria.* Then the *Torah* and all reality will appear different, as it does to those who reach the level of the world, *Yetzira.*

At that point, the Bible, with all its stories about animals, wars and the objects of this world, will be transformed into Kabbalah—the description of the world, *Yetzira.*

If the person elevates himself even further into the world of *Beria* or *Atzilut*, then an entirely new picture of the world and of the mechanism that governs it will appear, in accordance with one's spiritual state.

There is no difference between the events of the Bible and Kabbalah, the Bible of the spiritual world. The difference is in the spiritual level of those who are involved. In fact, if two people were reading the same book, one would see in it historical events, and the other, the depiction of the dominion over the worlds, which is clearly perceived from the Creator.

Those from whom the Creator is in complete concealment exist in the world of *Assiya.* That is why, in the end, all appears to them as not good: the world appears as full of suffering, since they cannot perceive it otherwise due to the concealment of the Creator.

If they do, in fact, experience pleasure, it appears merely as pleasure that follows suffering. It is only when one attains the level of *Yetzira* that the Creator partially reveals Himself and allows a person to see His governing by reward and punishment; thus is born love (dependent on the reward) and fear (dependent on punishment) in that person.

The third step—unconditional love—appears when one realizes that the Creator has never caused one harm, but only good. This corresponds to the level of *Beria.* When the Creator reveals the entire picture of creation and His Dominion over all the creations, then there arises in one an absolute love for the Creator, since His absolute love towards all His creations is now visible.

This understanding elevates one to the level of the world, *Atzilut*. Therefore, our ability to understand His actions depends only on the degree to which the Creator will reveal Himself to us, since we are created in such a way that the conduct of the Creator affects us (our thoughts, our qualities, our acts) automatically. Thus, we can only ask that He alter us.

Regardless of the fact that all acts of the Creator are inherently good, there are forces, also originating from the Creator, that appear to operate contrary to His desires. These forces often invoke criticism of His acts and thus are known as "impure."

At every step, from the first to the final points on our path, there exist two opposing forces. Both were created by the Creator. These are pure and *impure*. The impure force deliberately invokes in us mistrust and pushes us away from the Creator. But if, ignoring this impure force, we nevertheless strain ourselves in our plea to the Creator to help us, then we strengthen our bond with Him and instead receive a pure force. This elevates us to a higher spiritual level, and at that moment the impure force stops affecting us, since it has already performed its role.

The impure force of the world *Assiya* (step 1)

This force aspires to instill events through the denial of the existence of the Creator.

The impure force of the world *Yetzira* (step 2)

This force aspires to convince us that the world is governed not through reward and punishment, but by means of arbitrariness.

The impure force of the world *Beria* (step 3)

This force aspires to neutralize our perception of the Creator's love for us, which in turn invokes our love for the Creator.

The impure force of the world *Atzilut* (step 4)

This force aspires to prove to us that the Creator does not always act in accordance with absolute love towards all His creations, thus attempting to prevent our feelings of absolute love towards the Creator.

Thus, it becomes clear that our elevation to each consecutive spiritual level, the Revelation of the Creator and the attainment of pleasure from getting closer to Him, requires our overcoming the corresponding opposite forces. These arise in the forms of thought and desire. Only when they are overcome can we ascend to the next level and take another step forward on our path.

From the above, we can conclude that the range of spiritual forces and senses of the four worlds, *Assiya-Yetzira- Beria-Atzilut*, has a corresponding range of opposite and parallel forces and senses from the four impure worlds of *Assiya-Yetzira-Beria-Atzilut*. Movement forward is an alternating process.

Only after overcoming all the impure forces and obstacles sent to us by the Creator, and then asking the Creator to reveal Himself, thus endowing us with the strength needed to withstand the power of impure forces, thoughts and desires, can we reach the pure stage.

From birth, each of us is found in a state where the Creator is absolutely concealed from us. In order to begin the advance on the described spiritual path it is necessary to:

1. Perceive our present state as unbearable.
2. Feel, at least to some extent, that the Creator exists.

3. Feel that we depend only on the Creator.

4. Recognize that only the Creator can help us.

By revealing Himself, the Creator can immediately alter our desires and form within us an intelligence with a new essence. The appearance of these strong desires immediately awakens within us the powers to fulfill them.

The only thing that defines our essence is the combination and collection of our desires.

Our reason exists solely to aid us in attaining these desires. In truth, reason serves as nothing more than an assisting tool.

We advance along our path in stages, moving forward step by step, alternately being influenced by the impure (left) egoistic force and by the pure (right) altruistic one. By overcoming the forces of the left with the help of the Creator, we will acquire the characteristics of the right.

The path, then, is like two rails: the left and the right, like two forces repelling from and attracting to the Creator, similar to two desires: egoism and altruism. The farther we move away from our starting point, the stronger the opposing forces become.

By becoming more like the Creator in both desires and love, we will move forward, since the love of the Creator is the only divine feeling towards us, from which emerge all other feelings. The Creator desires to do only good for us, to bring us to the ideal state, which can only be a state resembling that of the Creator.

This is the state of immortality, filled with limitless pleasure from feeling infinite love of the Creator, Who emits a similar feeling. Since attaining this state is the purpose of creation, all other desires are considered to be impure.

The Creator's goal is to bring us to the state of likeness to his own state. This goal is imperative for each of us and for humanity in general, whether we want it or not. We cannot possibly desire this goal simply because we can only perceive all pleasures, and find redemption from all suffering, by unifying with the Creator.

The suffering is sent by the Creator Himself to push us forward, to force us to change our environments, habits, actions and outlook, since we are instinctively ready to free ourselves from suffering. Furthermore, we cannot experience pleasure without first experiencing suffering, just as there can be no answer if there were no question; no satiation if there were no hunger.

Thus, in order to experience any sensation we must first experience its opposite. Therefore, to experience the drawing power and love for the Creator, we must experience the exact opposite feelings, such as hatred and alienation from ideas, habits and desires.

No feeling can be born out of a vacuum; there must be a definite desire to attain that feeling. For instance, a person should be taught to understand, and thus to love, music. An uneducated person cannot grasp the happiness of the educated one, who after strenuous efforts discovers something new that was being sought for a long time.

The desire for something is known in the terminology of Kabbalah as a "vessel" (kli), since specifically the feeling of lack is a necessary condition for pleasure to fill it. The magnitude of the pleasure one will receive in the future depends, of course, on the magnitude of the vessel.

Even in our world, we can see that it is not the size of the stomach, but the desire, the sensation of hunger, that determines how much pleasure will be derived from food. The level of suffering from the absence of what is desired determines the size of the vessel, and this in turn determines the amount of pleasure to be received.

The pleasure that fulfills the desire to be gratified is known as Light, because it endows the vessel with a feeling of fulfillment and satisfaction.

Therefore, a desire must exist that is so strong that one suffers by its lack. Only then can it be said that the vessel is prepared to receive the abundance that the person so waited for.

The purpose of the creation of impure forces (desires), known as *klipot*, is to create in a person a desire of infinite magnitude. If not for the desires of *klipot*, we would never experience the urge for more than the basic needs of the body.

Thus, we would remain on the child's level of development. It is the *klipot* that compel us to search for new pleasures, since they constantly create new desires that require fulfillment and that force us to develop.

The attainment of the qualities characteristic of the world, *Atzilut*, is known as "the resurrection of the dead," since in this manner we transform all the impure (dead) desires into pure form. Prior to the world of *Atzilut*, a person, as if moving on two rail tracks, can only alter the desires to opposite ones, but cannot transform all the desires into pure ones.

Upon entering the world of *Atzilut*, we can correct past desires, thereby reaching higher stages of spiritual elevation. This process is known as *"the resurrection of the dead"* (desires).

Of course, resurrection in this case does not refer to our physical bodies. They, like those of all other creations that populate this world, will disintegrate once the soul departs from them, and have no value without the presence of the soul.

If, as a result of working on self, we are no longer controlled by impure desires, yet are still distracted by them, and unable to connect with the Creator, this situation is called *Shabbat* (the Sabbath). But if our thoughts and longings for the

Creator were diverted either by us, or through the influence of others' thoughts, and we allowed these foreign thoughts or desires to enter ("desecration of the Sabbath") then we do not consider these thoughts as foreign, but consider them as our own. We are certain that they are the correct thoughts, rather than those that previously brought us directly, without doubts on our path, towards the Creator.

If a great man who is an expert in a certain field joins a group of others from the same field who are second rate, and they convince him that it is better to work halfheartedly than with all of one's soul, then this great expert will gradually lose his talent.

If, however, such an expert is found amidst mediocre workers, but comes from a different field of expertise, then that person will not be damaged, since there is no association between that person and the other workers. Therefore, one who truly desires to succeed in a particular field of expertise should strive to become part of an environment of experts who treat their jobs as an art.

Apart from this, the most remarkable difference between an expert and a common worker is that an expert derives pleasure from the work itself and its results, rather than from the wages for that work. Consequently, those who truly desire to elevate themselves spiritually should carefully check the environment and those who surround them.

If it is an environment of people who lack faith in the Creator, then those who seek spiritual elevation are like experts amongst specialists in a different field. The goal of the expert is to grow spiritually, whereas the goal of the specialists is to acquire the greatest pleasure from this world.

Therefore, the specialists' opinions pose no great danger. Even if for an instant one were to adopt the other point of view, in the next moment it would become apparent that this point of view originated from non-believers. At that point, it would be discarded and the original goals would be restored.

However, one should beware of others who believe but do not pay proper attention to the correct reasons for fulfilling the commandments.

These people anticipate the reward that awaits them in the world to come, and observe the commandments for that purpose only. They should be studiously avoided.

One should be especially cautious of those who call themselves "Kabbalists" or mystics, and move as far away as possible from them. These people can cause damage to one's newly acquired abilities in this area.

Kabbalah presents the creation as consisting of two components: the Creator and His desire to be gratified with closeness to Him. This desire for such gratification, as the Source of infinite, absolute pleasure, is known as *"the soul."* It is similar to all our desires but exists without physical form.

The cause and goal of creation is the Creator's desire to gratify our souls. The desire of the soul is to be gratified by the Creator. The desire of the Creator and the desire of the soul are resolved as each approaches the other and they unify. When qualities and desires concur, the result is unification and closeness.

Similarly, in our world we consider another person to be close to us because of the *feeling* of closeness we experience, rather than the person's proximity to us. As in our world, the greater the initial distance of separation, the greater the obstacles standing in the way of the desired, and the greater pleasure we receive from attaining that for which we strive.

For this reason, the Creator places the soul in a condition that is most distanced and opposite from Him: He absolutely conceals Himself as the Source of all pleasures and plants the soul in a body with the desire to derive pleasure from everything that surrounds it.

Despite the concealment of the Creator and the obstacles set up by our body's desires, we may develop a desire within to draw close and cling to the Creator. Then, precisely because of these obstacles caused by the opposition of the body, we will feel a much greater desire to receive pleasure from the Creator than was possible prior to the encasing of our souls into our bodies.

The method or instruction for how we can cling to the Creator is known as Kabbalah, derived from the verb "lekabel"—to receive pleasure from the Creator. With the help of words and descriptions of our world, Kabbalah relates to us the experiences of the spiritual world.

According to Kabbalah, all that is said in the Bible (which includes the Five Books of Moses, the Writings and the Prophets) is said to teach us how to achieve the goal of creation.

Kabbalah sees this meaning in the following words: "In the beginning" (in the beginning of working on oneself, in the beginning of drawing closer to the Creator) "our forefathers" (the initial state of a person's desires) "were idol worshippers" (all personal desires were directed towards deriving plea-sure) "And afterwards, the Creator chose one of them" (from all of one's desires, we choose one desire, which is to unite with the Creator) "and commanded him to separate from his land and people and to settle in a different place" (in order to perceive the Creator, we must raise one desire above all others—the desire to perceive the Creator—and to distance ourselves from other desires).

If we can choose just one of the desires, cultivate it and live by it alone, that is the desire to unite with the Creator. Then, it is as if we pass on to a different life, a life of spirituality. If we want to move forward, or are already on the path directly towards the Creator, then we are called "Israel," derived from the words *yashar* (directly), *le'El* (to the Creator).

The creation of the world, including its conception and management, enables the world to exist and advance according to the predetermined plan towards the end for which it was created.

20

The Return to the Creator

In order to implement the Divine Supervision, and thus allow free choice in man's actions, two systems of governing were created. Opposite each positive, pure force there is always an opposing, negative, impure force. Four worlds of *ABYA de kedusha* (positive) were created, opposed by four negative, impure worlds of *ABYA de tum'a* (impurity).

In our world, the difference between the pure and the impure powers is not apparent, just as there appears to be no difference between one who is spiritually ascending towards the Creator and one who does not develop spiritually. We ourselves are not capable of knowing the truth as to whether we are progressing or remain static, and cannot determine whether a positive or a negative force is acting upon us. Therefore, an awareness and confidence that our paths are true and correct is extremely deceptive, and often we may not have chosen correctly.

But if we are at the very beginning of our spiritual journey, how can we advance correctly in order to achieve the goal of creation and the goal of our existence? Without a definite understanding of what constitutes good and evil for our final destination and for our true and eternal well being—rather than for the illusory and ephemeral gratification—how can we find the right path in this world?

All of humanity is wandering lost, as in a forest, creating mistaken theories of life's essential goal, and how to achieve it.

Even those of us at the beginning point of the proper path have no milestones and are incapable of determining whether our thoughts and desires are correct or not.

Is it possible that the Creator would have created us without preparing us with any help for our hopeless and unsolvable state? Common sense says that it is not reasonable to create something with a clear goal and afterwards to abandon the process to the hands of such weak and blind creatures as we.

Certainly, the Creator would not have acted like this. Thus, presumably in all situations, He gave us a way to find the proper path. In fact, the only way is to go above reason. In all our paths, we experience failures and learn how not to go. We do not succeed in an action unless we first stumble. When we feel we have reached a state of despair, we need the Creator.

In fact, there exists one very important confirmation of the correctness of the chosen path, and that is the help of the Creator! Those who choose the way of the impure and egoistic *ABYA* do not reach their spiritual destination, lose all their strength in the process, and finally reach the barrier of ultimate despair, since they do not earn the Creator's disclosure of the entire picture of creation.

On the other hand, those who follow the ways of the pure worlds *ABYA* are rewarded by the awareness and understanding of the entire Creation is given as a blessing from the Creator. These people are able to reach the highest spiritual state.

Therefore, this is the only test in our world (in our state) as to which path we should take, how we should act, and which thoughts we should choose that will help us achieve our goals, regardless of the thoughts and desires we receive from both the pure world of *Assiya* and the impure world of *Assiya*.

The difference between those who follow the right path and those who err is that the Creator will reveal Himself to the former and draw them closer, unlike the latter.

Thus, if we see that the secrets of Kabbalah do not become apparent to us, then we must conclude that this path is incorrect, though enthusiasm, strong conviction and imagination may point to another direction and indicate that we have already reached certain spiritual heights. Such an end is common among those involved in amateur studies of Kabbalah and "mystical" philosophies.

Our entire path of spiritual ascension along the stages of the worlds *ABYA* can be described as an alternating exertion of force, emanating from each consecutive stage at which we find ourselves at any given moment. Each of these forces is denoted by a particular letter of the Hebrew alphabet. That is, each letter symbolizes a spiritual force that governs a certain stage in the worlds *ABYA*. But only one force is able to save us and free us from the domain of egoistic desires. That force is the blessing of the Creator, denoted by the letter *bet*.

There is no opposite corresponding force in the impure worlds of *ABYA*, since the blessing originates from the one and only Creator, and there can be nothing equal to Him in any impure world of *ABYA*. Therefore, the world exists only through the blessing of the Creator, and only this blessing can illuminate the distinction between good and evil, or more precisely, between that which brings good to a person and that which works to the person's detriment.

Only with the Creator's blessing can one distinguish pure forces from impure forces, and overcome the impure along one's entire life path towards the end of creation. This clearly demonstrates whether one is deceiving oneself, or is truly moving into the spiritual worlds.

Every force in the realm of impure forces of evil exists only because it receives sustenance from a force corresponding to, but opposite the one existing in the realm of pure forces. The only exception is the Force derived from the blessing of the Creator.

Thus, this world could not have been created with any Force except the One springing from the blessing of the Creator. Without being diminished in the process, this Force emanates from the Creator and permeates the entire spectrum of the worlds, reaching all the way down to the lowest stage of the worlds—ours.

This Force is able to rectify the creations, giving them the strength to improve themselves and begin to ascend spiritually. It is with the aid of this Force that the universe was created; therefore impure egoistic forces can neither diminish its power nor use it to their own advantage, since the impure forces have an effect only where the pure forces are weak.

Hence, the ultimately pure Force helps us distinguish between pure and impure thoughts, since as soon as our thoughts are directed away from the Creator, the power of the Force of the blessing disappears.

The sounds of the letters (*nekudot*) symbolize the outpouring of Light, the perception of the Creator. Any perception of the Creator, any spiritual sentiment comprises ten *Sefirot*. Starting from the highest of these (*Keter*), the sounds correspond to the following gradation: 1 - *kamatz*; 2 - *patah*; 3 - *segol*; 4 - *tseireh*; 5 - *shva*; 6 - *holam*; 7 - *hirek*; 8 - *kubutz*; 9 - *shuruk*; 10 - without sound, that is, corresponding to *Malchut*—the last stage of perception, which never becomes filled. Sometimes, in the process of advancing towards the goal to draw closer to the Creator, we suddenly feel weak, since we lack knowledge of Kabbalah and are unable to perform any unselfish acts. Instead, our thoughts are only concerned with our success in this world.

We then fall into despair and tell ourselves that the ability to draw close to the Creator was given to special people with special powers from birth, as well as qualities, thoughts and desires appropriate to this goal, and whose hearts yearn for Kabbalah and for self-improvement.

But afterwards another feeling arises—the awareness that everyone has a place prepared for them beside the Creator, and that everyone, sooner or later will merit spiritual pleasures by clinging to the Creator. We will then rise out of our despair, and become aware that the Creator is "All Able" and plans the path of every one, knows what each one of us feels, leads us, and awaits our turning towards Him with a request to draw closer to Him.

Afterwards, we will recall that more than once we had said this to ourselves, but nothing had changed. In the end, we remain immersed in thoughts of our despicable weakness and insignificance. Later, we come to realize that this feeling was sent to us by the Creator in order that we can overcome it.

We then begin working on improving ourselves, using all the will we possess. Suddenly, we receive from the future condition to which we aspire. This means that the Light of the future state is shining from afar, since it cannot shine from within as long as our desires remain egoistic in nature. The Light (spiritual pleasure) cannot enter and shine (please us) in such desires.

As creations, we are a concentrated essence of egoistic desires, and are known as "human beings."

The Creator, on the other hand, is totally removed from anything egoistic. Therefore, returning to the Creator, clinging to Him, and becoming aware of Him, all come as a result of becoming equivalent in form to Him. Such a return to the Creator is called a "higher return."

This is the reason that a return to the Creator, a merging with the Creator, an awareness of the Creator can be considered as nothing other than concurring with Him in certain qualities. It is this return to the Creator that is known as *tshuva*.

One can determine that such a return has been achieved only if the Creator Himself "testifies" to it. What is this testimony? It is that one now has the ability to constantly feel His Presence, which makes it possible to be with the Creator in all thoughts.

In this manner, one can tear oneself away from the desires of the body.

Only we as individuals can feel whether indeed we have returned to the Creator.

The strength gained when we perceive the Creator enables us to gradually return to the Creator completely, and to alter all the egoistic desires to altruistic ones.

The more "bad" desires we possess at the beginning of our path, the more self-improvement we can undertake, and consequently, the closer we can come to the Creator. This is why we should never lament our bad qualities, but rather ask for their correction. We should turn to this way of thinking every time thoughts of worthlessness come to mind.

All of these thoughts are awakened in us as a result of feeling distant from the Creator, and the Creator sends these feelings to us, and not to others, but only if we are ready to receive them. Others don't consider themselves wicked, and don't perceive their egoism. On the contrary, they are convinced that they are righteous.

These thoughts are not sent by the Creator to make us suffer or fall into despair, but rather to encourage us to call out to the Creator, demanding to be liberated from ourselves and our weaknesses.

Every time we again feel worthless and weak—having already experienced the same feelings in the past—we will remember that we need not return to those feelings of failure and defeat. We must be reminded that each time we go through this process, we undergo new corrections, which accumulate until the Creator Himself gathers them together.

All of these negative feelings of ours concerning our distance from the Creator, our dissatisfaction with our spiritual path, our complaints about the many deadlocked states—we experience all of these to the degree required for us to merit the awareness of the Creator and the pleasures emanating from Him. It is then that the "gates of tears" are flung open, and it is only through them that we can enter the halls of the Creator.

Even if we become overwhelmed by the powerful reactions and stubbornness of our egos, we should not decide that the Creator did not give us sufficient strength to cope with them, or that we were born lacking talent, patience, equanimity and sharpness of mind. Nor should we lament that the Creator did not give us the appropriate conditions for correcting ourselves, thus being unable to accomplish that which someone else could have done.

It is also forbidden for us to decide that these sufferings are a result of our former sins, or that this is "our lot," or that actions in a previous incarnation have led to this state. We are also forbidden to give up hope and do nothing, since if we properly use the minimal strength and talents that we have, we will be very successful.

We will need every trait that the Creator gave us, even the most lowly, both today and in the future, to accomplish our goal: the correction of the soul. This process is similar to planting a seed. If it is planted in fertile soil and is properly cared for, then the seed will sprout, grow, and bring forth its fruit. Therefore, we need both a good mentor and good soil (environment) in order that all of our traits should develop and balance, with each and every trait combining to create a proper relationship to help us achieve our main goal.

Every question that is awakened in us is sent by the Creator, Who awaits the correct answer from us. The answer to the questions of the body and the mind, the egotistic questions such as "What for?" and "What do I gain from it?" have only one answer—an answer that the body does not understand: "It is the Will of the Creator that I should reach Him in this way."

All the words of Kabbalah and all the advice it provides are concerned with only one issue: how we can reach the Creator and unite with Him. All our deficiencies stem from our inability to sense the greatness of the Creator. Having just begun to aspire to come closer to Him, we already want to experience Him in our senses.

But this is impossible until we have a screen (masach) that refuses the Light of the Creator. This exists as long as we do not have vessels of bestowal. And as long as we do not have these qualities of bestowal, we are only able to have a feeling of the Creator from afar, which is called "Surrounding Light," which can shine from afar on who is still distant in qualities from those of the Creator.

The Surrounding Light is always greater than the Inner Light, which is gained through the help of a screen, given that one possesses certain altruistic qualities. The Surrounding Light is the Creator Himself, while the Inner Light (the soul) is only that "part" of the Creator that an individual can acquire after improving one's own qualities to a certain degree.

So how can we receive the Light of the Creator when we have not yet repaired our dispositions? The answer is simple: *only by intensifying the illumination of the Surrounding Light.* In other words, we will achieve this only by increasing the exaltedness and importance of the Creator in our eyes by constantly yearning to sense the Creator as the Source of all existence and everything that is done.

We must understand that everything that happens to us is an act of God, and that there is nothing in the world other than Him. All of our efforts should be concentrated on this: to not think that what happens to us is through chance, or fate, or a consequence of our prior actions, or the will of others. We must exert ourselves not to forget the Creator.

Under no circumstance should we interpret the text of any section of the Bible (The Five Books of Moses) according to our own perceptions, likening the description of events to the events in our own world.

For example, as I have written in my previous books, "the evil Lavan" mentioned in the Bible is the highest level of the soul being filled with the Light of the Creator. "Pharaoh" is a symbol of the totality of our egoism.

Another example can be found in the Bible where it tells how a certain person by the name of Ptachia came into a city and gathered around him empty people, and all of them went with him to the desert. The name Ptachia derives from the verb *"liftoach"* (to open)—a person who opens people's eyes.

He gathered all the "empty" people—people who feel emptiness in their lives. "He took them from the city to the desert"—he opened up the desert in their lives in order, as it is written in the Bible: *"Lech acharai ba midbar."*

"Lech" (Go) says the Creator to the person, *"acharai ba midbar"* (after me in the desert)—with the feeling that your life without perception of the spiritual is like a desert without a drop of water, that the small spark of redemption from the feeling of emptiness will seem to you like "a cool spring on your exhausted soul."

A further example can be found in the Passover Haggada (story) on the exodus from Egypt, from the spiritual captivity of Pharaoh—our egoism. "Pharaoh died"—finally the person sees that his egoism is not for his good, that it kills him, and obligates him to serve it all of his life. This principle now, in his eyes, "dies." And as long as he does not recognize that his egoism is his sole enemy, he thinks that his life and servitude in Egypt (captivity to the desires of the body) was a good and favorable condition. And even afterwards, occasionally (during spiritual downfalls) he cries for the "plates of meat and bread" that he had in Egypt, namely, that served his egoism in abundance.

As long as Pharaoh (the egoism in the heart of a person), the king (who ruled over all the thoughts and desires of a person) of Egypt was alive, he dictated against the person's will what all of the person's desires and actions would be. This person is said to be found "in the exile (imprisonment) of Egypt," captive to various egoistic desires (*mitsraim* deriving from the words *mitz-ra*—"a concentration of evil").

We, ourselves, are not able to understand that the nature that rules over us is bad. And this is only as long as the Creator has not yet created good for the person of "And behold, Pharaoh died."

He gives us those life experiences that allow us to recognize that egoism is our enemy. Only then will this symbol of evil die, and we will feel that we are incapable of existing as we once did, working for nothing.

And "the sons of Israel groaned because of the servitude and they cried out"—they did this only after realizing they were not even able to move without some egoistic benefit for themselves, and had not yet gained a spiritual, altruistic nature.

"And their cry for help from their servitude rose up to God, and God heard our voice"—this occurs only if one truly cries out from the very depths of the soul, and this is possible only if the person reached the outermost limits of patience and suffering.

Only then does the Creator send help, and this help always arrives unexpectedly. An individual can never know in advance which tear will be the last one; all tears should be shed as if they were the last. As for the help of the Creator— "yeshuat haShem keheref ay'in"—it appears suddenly and always unexpectedly!

The Zohar is considered by many to be a moral teaching based on Kabbalah, since it is written in the language of the commandments, prescribing what an individual should do. It is clear that by defining the book of Zohar in such way, people attempt to deny its mystical, concealed essence.

The authors of the Zohar have written this book, which deals only with the composition and the operation of the spiritual worlds, in a deliberately scholastic and legalistic language. This was intended to leave no doubt in the readers' minds that the main purpose of Kabbalah is not the wisdom itself, but the "dispenser of the wisdom." In fact, the main purpose of Kabbalah and of the spiritual laws is to develop our need for the Creator, and for us to wish to come closer to Him in the qualities of the soul.

All the obstacles that we encounter in our path towards the Creator, in order to enter the spiritual realm, are actually signs of our drawing closer to the Creator, to the gates of the spiritual. This is because there is no situation that is further removed from the Creator than when we do not think at all about the existence of the spiritual realm, or are incapable of wanting to experience it.

When we feel distant from the spiritual realm, this is because the Creator has let us become aware of our true state, and in this way awakens in us a desire for closeness to Him. And if these feelings of distance from the Creator were not awakened within us, we would have no chance whatsoever to begin to draw close to Him.

Therefore, these feelings of distance are a sign of beginning to draw closer. And so it goes throughout the entire path of one's advance towards the Creator: we constantly experience all types of obstacles. In reality, these obstacles are nothing other than the Creator helping us by awakening in us feelings of anger and dissatisfaction with our present state, to cause us to request Him to change it.

All of the obstacles that we must overcome in drawing closer to the Creator are necessary for getting used to following the path of being distanced—recognizing our egoism and separation from the Creator. Still, this feeling should not really alter our actions.

Instead, we should recognize in advance that this feeling reveals our true state, and that the previous state was no better than the present one, although there was no awareness of this fact at the time. And so it goes, until we stop focusing on our concerns about our condition, and replace them with thoughts and desires concentrating on a single desire: to care only about how the Creator looks upon us.

This desire should determine all our actions and thoughts. And what the Creator wishes to see in each of us becomes clear as one studies Kabbalah and follows all the directions of the spiritual laws in order to reach this ultimate goal. Then all the spiritual laws become a tool for unification with the Creator.

Until we begin to measure all of our actions and thoughts against the desires of the Creator, we are actually measuring all the actions against the desires of others who impose their will upon us, thus defining our thoughts and actions. Never are we free to act on our own.

Either we are influenced by others who determine our behavior and actions, or our thoughts and actions are dictated by the Will of the Creator. Never can we act in absolute freedom. The concealment of the Creator from us is done for our own benefit.

Just as in our own world every object not fully explored attracts us more than an object thoroughly examined, so the veiling of the spiritual world is indispensable to induce us to heighten our desire to nurture a sense of importance of attaining the understanding of the spiritual world.

We are never truly able to comprehend the greatness of the Creator and the spiritual worlds that constitute a partial Revelation of the Creator. But precisely due to His conceal-ment, or the extent to which the Creator grants us a sense of concealment and distance, our desire to perceive the Creator becomes aroused, as well as how important it is to strive to understand that which is concealed.

On the other hand, the degree of concealment is determined by a particular person's need to attain that which is hidden. Thus, one gradually becomes aware of how important it is to reach that which is concealed, until one begins to feel removed from the object of one's passionate desire .

The path to attaining what is hidden through Kabbalah is unlike any other experience in this world. For example, when one is honored, this fills the ego and consequently causes great damage to the soul. The damage is considered to be so great that prominent righteous people who gained immense popularity and acquired followers considered that such fame had actually been a punishment from the Creator.

On the other hand, there are those great ones whom the Creator wishes to protect so that they do not forfeit even the slightest amount of their spiritual level. To these, the Creator sends not only followers but also those who hate them, envy them, oppose their views, and are ever ready to slander them. Thus the Creator balances the praise and honor received by these great ones with the suffering they experience at the hands of their contemporaries.

It is difficult for one who has not yet entered the spiritual realm and has not yet perceived spiritual strength and desires, to sustain actions and thoughts in the right direction. In contrast, it is easy and natural for a person to act in accordance with the nature of the spiritual worlds if that person has received spiritual strength and entered the spiritual realm, thus acquiring a higher disposition.

At the time of a spiritual decline, all former spiritual achievements disappear.

The wish to serve the Creator and to reunite with Him, the wish to battle with oneself and to remain only in the state of spiritual ascent—all these disappear. Even the memory of these spiritual achievements disappears, as well as the awareness that a desire for spiritual ascent can exist.

One feels that, if these things truly exist, it is only by lofty and exalted thoughts that they can be maintained, while shielding oneself from the multitude of petty and minor pleasures of this world. But most ordinary people, to whose ranks one feels that one belongs at such a time, have other worries and aims in this world besides spiritual yearnings.

And how can a simple person such as myself, one asks, even dream of having a bond with the Creator, not to mention a close attachment with Him? The possibility itself seems absurd and remote.

It is of moments like these that it has been said: "Where you find the greatness of the Creator, you will also find His modesty," since the Creator gives to each of His creations the possibility to unite with Him. And after the passage of some time, when those who were dejected soar spiritually once again, they must never forget this state of moral decline, so that they can truly appreciate the highly spiritual state of aspiring to unite with the Creator—the personal, individual gift from the Creator.

In such a case, there will be no need to experience this state of spiritual decline ever again, because through constant work on oneself, through an elevation of faith over reason, through learning and the observance of an established order of actions and thoughts, a person will thus create a spiritual vessel for a gradual spiritual ascent.

The Path of Kabbalah

The desirable path of spiritual ascent is the path of Kabbalah. The path of suffering awaits us only if there is no other way to prompt us to reach perfection. As was stated earlier, the path of Kabbalah is an opportunity given from Above to each of us to create in ourselves the desires necessary for spiritual growth, demonstrating through spiritual ascents and declines that the spiritual Light is pleasure and its absence is suffering.

In this way, we begin to desire the Light and spiritual ascent and the perception of the Creator. Without first receiving the Upper Spiritual Light and then having it taken away, we cannot feel a desire for the Light.

The greater the Light initially sent us by the Creator, and then "taken away," the greater will be our desire to receive that Light once again. This path is known as "the path of Kabbalah," or the path of the Light. But there is also "the path of suffering," when one searches for a way to escape from unbearable suffering constantly in one's life, and not from a desire to have lost pleasures restored.

With the path of Kabbalah, there awakens a desire to become filled by the spiritual Light as the vitalizing Source of redemption. Both paths lead to one goal, but one draws by the pleasure and the perfection that lie ahead, and the other pushes from behind, prompting an escape from pain.

In order for a human being to be able to analyze external factors and internal sensations, two means of perception are given: the bitter and sweet—perceived by the heart, and the false and true—perceived by the intellect.

Spiritual attainment cannot be appreciated by the heart, since it is absolutely contrary to the heart's true nature . This is why this attainment is always perceived as bitter, while any personal pleasure is perceived as sweet. For this reason, work on oneself in redirecting one's desires is considered to be the work of the heart.

The work of the mind is of a completely different nature, because we cannot rely on our own minds and logic to analyze the surrounding events. In such a case, we are forced, in spite of ourselves, to rely on the egoistic, natural mind.

We are unable to break away from it because each of us was created in this manner by the Almighty. That is why there is only one path: to completely turn away from the typical inclination to analyze one's surroundings and instead to accept the advice of the sages, expounded in the books of

Kabbalah and explained by teachers who have reached the spiritual level of awareness.

If we are capable, with the Creator's help, of making even the slightest attempt to analyze through faith, rather than by reason, and to discern with our hearts the bitterness of egoism, we will immediately be sent a spiritual understanding of the attained level, which comprises both spiritual Light and strength (*screen*).

The Creator then reveals the next lower stage of egoism, which was previously hidden because if we immediately grasped the entire extent of our own egoism, we would not have had the strength to overcome it. Instead, we would surely have become despondent from the overwhelming task lying ahead.

However, we should realize that this mountainous ego was always there within us from the beginning, but was hidden and is revealed gradually, as the Creator gives us the ability to correct it and the strength to do so. That is why those who ascend the spiritual levels, gradually overcoming "our own" reason, feel increasingly more perplexed and dense in relation to the guidance of the sages in the Kabbalistic books and of the Kabbalist instructors.

But to the degree that we diminish the significance of our "own" understanding, we are granted a higher understanding. In the end, rather than becoming more baffled by turning away from this world's egoistic logic, we become incomparably wiser.

If we have not yet reached a higher understanding, or altered our way of analysis, begun to feel the sweetness, rather than the bitterness, of non-egoistic thoughts, or have not begun to see the truth of faith compared to the falseness of the intellect which is bound by the nature of our world, we can still progress through an already amended method of analysis derived from our teachers, by listening and following the example of the teacher in all things. Therein lies the counsel of the sages: If only a single Kabbalist, possessing the true spiritual understanding of the mind and heart, leads humanity, everyone can reach the goal of creation not by the path of suffering but by the easy and painless path of Kabbalah!

On the other hand, misfortune and constant failures will be our lot if those who were chosen to travel this path first, with whom the Creator first settles all accounts, and from whom the most is demanded, have chosen as their leaders those who do not understand His higher purpose or the design of His Dominion.

Only during wars, catastrophes, or other great misfortunes, when it seems that our problems cannot be resolved, do we all clearly see the hand of the Creator and His help. But this transpires only during critical moments in which we find ourselves, since we refuse to acquire and use Kabbalistic knowledge to recognize the Divine Providence in the world.

Why are people born with different capacities to perceive the subtler forces around us, as well as with different capacities to prudently and logically grasp the nature of things? And whose fault is it that a person was not created in the same manner as were geniuses, those of deep thought and deep emotions? Why is it that when we are born, we receive from the Creator unequal mental and spiritual desires and capacities?

Individuals born with grand aspirations, with big hearts, and with sharp minds, are referred in the Bible as "the intelligent" because they are capable of receiving the highest understanding. On the other hand, those born with limited mental and spiritual capacities in the Bible are referred to as "foolish people." But since every soul has its own special purpose for which it has "descended" into this world, no one should be ashamed of the particular inclinations with which one was born.

Nor should we be ashamed of our bad thoughts, since they, too, were sent to us by the Creator.

However, we should pay special attention to and be conscious of how we react to bad thoughts, whether we fight them or follow them blindly, whether we correct ourselves— each to the extent of the capacities that we were born with, and what we do towards correcting ourselves.

It is this that each of us should be ashamed and it is for this that each will have to answer to the Creator. But still, how can a foolish person reach spiritual heights? The Creator has said: "I have created the wise, and I have created the foolish. And I have placed the wise in every generation, to help the foolish, so that having fastened their hearts to the ones ascending, they could also reach a complete union with Me."

Why are foolish people needed in this world? After all, compared to the few wise men of the world, there is an overwhelming multitude of fools!

The reason lies in the fact that every spiritual quality requires its own separate carrier. Those people with limited spiritual capacities are the carriers of egoism. The wise, on the other hand, desiring to ascend infinitely in their service to the Creator, and having corrected their own egoism, need to help the foolish work on their egoism.

To continue ascending, the wise must continuously absorb "extraneous" egoism and correct it. Thus, both the foolish and the wise need each other.

But because the masses can give the wise only their own insignificant egoism consisting of a desire for the petty, transitory pleasures of our world, for every wise person in this world there are billions of fools.

Nevertheless, if the foolish ones act in accordance with the directives of the wise, consciously following the wise in all they do, everyone can still reach the goal of their existence: absolute unity with the Creator.

Even though the spiritual work of raising altruism above egoism is carried out within the heart, while that of raising faith over the assertions of the intellect is carried out within the mind, both are contingent upon our rejection of the intellect that was given to each of us at birth, as well as upon the rejection of self-gratification and self-affirmation.

This is because, even while working towards altruistic aims, one still prefers to see and know to whom one gives and who receives the fruits of one's labor—and in such a case one has nothing but the faith in the existence of the Creator and the faith that He is accepting the fruits of one's work.

Here we find the notion of the oneness of the Creator, in accordance with the principle that "there exists nothing but the Creator." We must recognize the Creator as the One sending everything that we sense and perceive in our minds, bringing us to a particular line of thought, which in turn leads us to certain decisions and resolutions.

Only after we acknowledge all of the above can we gain a proper perspective on everything that transpires. Then, we can correct our desires and thoughts in accordance with the design of the Creator.

Kabbalah in its entirety concentrates on the Creator and on His actions. For this reason, Kabbalah is called by the names of the Creator. Similar to an individual's name indicating who is being referred to, so every word of Kabbalah is a name of the Creator, since it expresses His action and indicates what He is sending us at any given moment.

Kabbalah speaks about us as being a part of the Creator that He distanced from Himself, having bestowed egoism upon us. For this reason, our souls are comprised of two opposing parts. The first of these is the divine part, which exhibits its own desire to perceive the Creator (in some of us), thus causing people to begin searching for something spiritual in order to be fulfilled internally. At the same time, the pleasures pursued by others around us no longer satisfy to those seeking spiritual fulfillment.

The second part of the soul is that specially created egoistic nature that people experience in full measure: the desire to possess everything, to know everything, to do everything, to see the result of all their actions, that is, to see a part of the "self" in all one's surroundings. The egoistic part of the soul is the only part that was created, since the altruistic part of the soul is a part of the Creator Himself. Having taken His desire from within Himself and having endowed it with egoism, He thereby distanced this part from Himself and it became the soul, a creation separate from Him.

The soul is considered a creation precisely because it contains a part of something new—its egoism—a quality that had not existed before, as nothing of the kind exists within the Creator. It is the notion of the soul, which consists of a part of the Creator and a part of the newly created egoistic feeling "to receive everything into oneself, that Kabbalah deals with. It is the soul, rather than the body, that is discussed in the Bible, because the body, consisting of flesh and bone, is like the flesh and bone of the animals, and its end is decay and a return to the elements of this world.

We sense ourselves as bodies because we do not perceive our souls.

But as we begin to perceive the soul, the sense of the physical body, of its desires and of its pains, diminishes, when the soul asserts itself more and more. When we are further advanced on the spiritual path, we do not sense the desires of the body altogether, because we pay attention only to the soul—the part of the Creator within us.

Thus, the "body" begins to represent the spiritual desires, rather than the desires of the flesh and bone, which one almost doesn't sense any longer.

The Bible tells not of our physical bodies, the mass of flesh and bone, but of the two aspirations of the soul—of the desire of the divine part to perceive the Creator and to unite with Him, and of the desire of the egotistical part towards self-gratification, self-satiation, and a perception of oneself instead of the Creator.

Both of these aspirations are known in Kabbalah as "the "body." This refers to both the egoistic body and the physical body, i.e., the body of our world, since only our world is characterized by ego, and the spiritual body, since altruistic desires are the desires of the Creator, characteristic of the spiritual world.

In all instances, the Bible describes how our souls are affected in various settings and circumstances. It also deals with our desires, focusing on how the Creator alters them, and on how each of us can alter them, or rather, how we can ask Him to alter them, since we ourselves are incapable of changing them.

But the beginner's main challenge is to hold on by willpower and to concentrate upon the fact that in spite of one's multitude of thoughts and desires, all of these emanate from the Creator; all these thoughts and desires, so vastly different, and at times so low, are sent by the Creator.

The Creator does this so that, in spite of all obstructions, the individual persistently continues to uphold the bond with the Creator by preserving one's faith that all these thoughts and desires are sent by the Creator. Thus, struggling with them should strengthen our faith that all emanates from the Creator.

As we strengthen this conviction within ourselves, we can reach such a level that this sense will always be present, despite the ever-increasing obstacles that will be sent by the Creator. These are intended to further strengthen this very sense.

Then, our constant faith in the Omnipresence of the Creator will combine with the feeling of His Presence within us, and the Creator will be "robed" in us, thus determining all of our thoughts and desires. At this point, we will become part of the Creator.

We must come to the realization that the very feeling of being distanced from the Creator is specifically the means by which we will be able to perceive the Creator. These two senses are known in Kabbalah as *kli* (vessel) and *or* (light). The first of these is a desire to experience the Creator, which is gradually born in us while experiencing obstacles (thoughts and desires).

These deliberately distract us from thoughts of the Creator and His Oneness, and make us increase our power of faith by exerting our willpower and thus retaining our thoughts of the Creator.

Light is itself an answer to our desire to receive the perception of the Creator. When the Creator garbs Himself in this desire of a person, the Light enters the vessel, and the order of spiritual growth is such that a person awakens to the desire for the spiritual, to the perception of the Creator, to the need to discover oneself, only under the effect of the Light, to the immense feeling of life, to inspiration derived from becoming closer to spiritual sensations, to the feeling of wholeness.

But then the individual is invariably visited by extraneous thoughts. Through their influence a descent begins from the level one had achieved back to the level of ordinary desires and thoughts. And then, after a while, one begins to regret these transitory and petty cares and thoughts.

This in turn brings about bitterness and anger on oneself, and sometimes even on the Creator, Who sends that person such thoughts and desires that cause a turning away from the spiritual. It is as a response to this bitter feeling of regret about one's own spiritual state that one receives the Light from Above, the feeling of coming closer to the One above.

And then arises the willingness to give up everything for that sense of the Creator, for the feelings of security, self-confidence, eternity that one feels when drawing nearer to the eternity and perfection conveyed from the Creator. At that moment, all shame in one's former thoughts is gone, along with fears of anything in this world.

When one perceives the soul as a part of the Creator and therefore immortal, and agrees with the Creator in everything and justifies everything that the Creator does with His creations, and is ready to deny his own intellect and to follow his Creator, the individual is filled with the Light of the Creator, and becomes a willing servant of the spiritual perceptions.

But once again, after a passage of time, one is visited by an extraneous thought. And so, gradually, after many cycles of disturbing thoughts and spiritual ascents, such a steadfast feeling of spiritual need arises that one finally receives the ever-present Light of the Creator.

Rabbi Baruch once asked his grandfather, the Baal Shem Tov: "It is known that in ancient times, those desiring to experience the Creator were constantly subjecting themselves to restrictions of all sorts, but you have annulled this according to the saying that if anyone voluntarily submits to privations, one transgresses the spiritual laws and must be held responsible. So what then is the most important thing in the work that an individual must do on oneself?"

The Baal Shem Tov answered, "I have come into this world to show the other path; a person must strive to master three things: love of the Creator, love of the people, and love of the spiritual. Then there is no need for voluntary privations."

The capacity to thank the Creator is already a goodness bestowed by the Creator.

The benevolence of the Creator is in the fact that we can love Him. His strength is in the fact that we can fear Him.

Why, then, does an individual who strives to approach the Creator and senses that he is coming closer to Him suddenly feel distant?

The Baal Shem Tov answers this as follows: "This is like teaching a toddler to walk; while the toddler is being supported he makes several steps towards the father, but the father, wishing to teach the child to walk independently, moves away until the child learns to walk on its own."

The Baal Shem Tov said: "An individual's work on oneself consists of a constant struggle with egoism, a struggle to the very last breath that should result time after time in the replacement of egoism with the Creator.

"The Creator, like a great ruler, sits at the center of His palace. He has erected many walls and obstacles around

Himself. He has scattered within the walls of His palace a great wealth and He gives out honors and titles to those who overcome the obstacles. Upon receiving the latter from the Creator, a person becomes content. But only the one who rejects everything, desiring to be with the Creator Himself, earns the right to enter into His Presence."

In nature, there is a transitory state between the seed and the sprout, when the complete decay of the seed, its absolute disappearance, is necessary. Similarly, until we reach the state of complete denial of the "self," we cannot receive the new spiritual nature.

The Creator has generated the human "self" from "nothing," and because of this, we must return from the state of the "self" into the state of "nothing" in order to unite with the Creator. This is why it is said that the savior (Messiah) was born the day of the destruction of the Temple.

Therefore, every time we reach the state of complete despair, we realize that all is "dust and vanity of vanities." Precisely from this state arises a new step in our spiritual ascent, because at this point we can forsake everything.

The Maggid of Mezrich, a great Kabbalist of the previous century, proclaimed: "There are ten rules of spiritual work. Three of these rules can be learned from an infant and seven of them can be learned from a thief."

The infant:

1. is happy for no reason,

2. does not rest even for a minute,

3. demands what he wants with all his might.

The thief:

1. works at night,

2. attempts to gain this night what has not been gained the previous night,

3. is loyal to his comrades,

4. risks his life to gain even the most insignificant things,

5. does not value that which was stolen, and sells it for pennies,

6. is beaten, but does not turn from his path,

7. sees the advantages of his occupation and does not wish to change it.

He also added: "There is a key to every lock, but if the lock does not give, a courageous thief will break it. The Creator loves a person who breaks his own heart to enter the house of the Creator."

When we learn the spiritual levels, only then do we become insignificant in our own eyes, and can then bow before the Creator, sensing that we have no need of anything: not our own spiritual redemption, nor any spiritual ascent, nor eternity, but only the Creator.

During the time of a spiritual decline, it may appear that the Creator is concealing Himself, and it is difficult for us to sustain faith in His existence and His Providence. But if we indeed feel that the Creator conceals Himself, then we are not truly experiencing the concealment of the Creator, but rather a condition in which the Creator expects us to make an effort to advance toward Him.

The Creator is considered to be The Place (*HaMakom*), precisely because one should enter Him with one's whole being, so that the Creator should surround one and be one's dwelling place. (As was already noted, we dwell in an ocean of the Light of the Creator, and we should become aware of this fact.)

During the time of prayer, we should constantly control where we are directing our attention and efforts: to the reading of the text and to the following of a strict order of the text fragments in a particular prayer book; to the in-depth examination of the meaning of names and of letter combinations; to the distinct pronunciation the words; to the strict following of the mental intentions (*kavanot*) in a particular prayer book; or to the most important—directing one's heart towards an attachment with the Creator.

Most important is our intention: a prayer to perceive the Creator! Those who pray acknowledge the existence of the Creator, but those who pray for the ability to perceive the Creator, experience Him!

21

Correcting Egoism

The entire spiritual body of law is intended to help us overcome our egoism. Therefore, the spiritual law, "love thy neighbor as thyself" is a natural result of attachment with the Creator. Since there is nothing else besides Him, when a person understands this, all the creations, including our world, merge in our perception of the One Creator.

Thus it becomes clear how our forefathers were able to obey all the spiritual laws long before they were actually passed down. A consequence of spiritual elevation is found when we begin to love our worst enemies and the foes of all the nations. Thus, the greatest work can entail praying for our enemies.

When Rabbi Levi Yitzhak of Berdichev was attacked for his extensive work in teaching the correct manner of serving the Creator, the rumors of this reached Rabbi Elimelech of Lizhensk. He exclaimed, "What is there to be surprised about! This happens constantly! If this did not occur, not a single nation could ever enslave us."

There are two stages of battle against egoistic desires: First, we pursue them. Then, we attempt to escape them, only to realize that these desires continue to pursue us.

Those of us who deny the Oneness of the Creator do not yet sense that He and all that happens in the world, including all that happens to each individual, are one and the same. Rabbi Yichiel Michal (Maggid mi Zlotchiv), a Kabbalist of the last century, lived in great poverty.

His students asked him, "How can you recite the blessing to the Creator for having given you all the necessary things when you have so little?" He answered, "I can bless the Creator who gave me everything, because apparently it is poverty that I need to come closer to Him, which is why He gives it to me."

There is nothing that denies the Rule of the Creator more than depression. Notably, every person arrives at this feeling for different reasons: suffering, a feeling of personal help-lessness, absence of what is desired, etc. It is impossible to feel joy over the blows one receives unless one realizes their necessity and immense value; then, every blow can be taken as medicine.

A person's only worry should be why one is worrying. "One should not consider suffering to be bad," explained Rabbi Moshe of Kovrin, "since there is nothing bad in the world, but rather that it is bitter, because medicine is always bitter."

The most earnest effort should be made to "cure" the feelings of depression, because the consequence of faith is joy, and only by increasing one's faith can one save oneself from dejection. For this reason, when it is said in Mishna that, "A person must be grateful for the bad," the Talmud immediately adds: "And must receive it with joy," because there is no evil in the world!

Because we perceive only what actually enters our senses and not what remains outside us, we can grasp the Creator only to the degree that He acts upon us. Hence, we need our senses to deny the oneness of their source; they are specifically in order for the person to ultimately sense and reveal the Oneness of the Creator.

It is said that after the crossing of the Red Sea, people believed in the Creator and began to sing. Only faith allows one to sing out. If an individual feels that through self-improvement he will be able to correct himself, he should examine his attitude towards the belief in the omnipotence and the Oneness of the Creator, because only through the Creator, through prayer for change, is it possible to alter something in oneself.

It is said that the world was created for the delight of the created beings. *Olam* (the world) derives from the word *he'elem* or *ha'alama*—meaning "concealment." It is by experiencing the opposing tendencies of concealment and revelation that a person experiences pleasure. And this is the meaning of the expression, "I created a help against you" (*ezer ke-negdo*).

Egoism was created as an aid to humankind.

Gradually, while struggling against it, each person acquires all the senses necessary to experience the spiritual. For this reason, each person should look upon all obstacles and suffering with a full consciousness of their purpose, that is, to induce one to ask for the Creator's help in receiving redemption from that suffering. Then, egoism and other unpleasant aspects transform into "help against you"—which is actually against egoism itself.

It is also possible to offer an alternative rendition. Imagine egoism standing "opposite us," instead of the Creator, screening and covering the Creator from us, as if saying: "I stand between the Creator and you."

Thus does the "I" or "self" of a person stand between that person and the Creator. For this purpose, there is a commandment first to "remember what was done" to us by *Amalek*, and then to "erase all memory" of Him.

We should not search within ourselves for thoughts that serve as obstacles, but rather should take the first thing that arises in our hearts and minds from the moment of awakening, and tie it to the Creator. This is how "obstacles" help us return our thoughts to the Creator. From this, we see that the worst thing is when we forget about the Creator.

To the extent that egoism pushes us to sin, it also pushes us to be exceptionally righteous. In both cases, it tears us away from the truth. To the same extent that we can pretend to be righteous before others, so sometimes, without realizing we are deceiving ourselves, we begin to believe that we are truly righteous.

Rabbi Jacob Yitzhak of Lyublin (Hoseh mi Lyublin) said, "I have more love for sinners who know that they are sinners, than for the righteous who know that they are righteous. But sinners who think that they are righteous will never find the right path, because even on the threshold of hell they think that they have been brought there to save others."

A true Kabbalist wants students to fear and respect the Creator more than they fear and respect their teacher. So, too, are they encouraged to depend on and trust the Creator more than they depend on and trust their teacher.

When Rabbi Nahum of Ruzhin, a Kabbalist of the last century, found his students playing checkers, he told them of the similarity between the rules of the game at hand and the rules of spirituality: first of all, you cannot make two moves simultaneously; secondly, you can move forward but not backward; thirdly, one who reaches the end can move as one likes, according to one's desires.

If we believe that someone is talking about us, we become interested in what they are saying. That which is desired but is concealed is known as a "secret." If we read the Bible and feel that it is talking about us, then we are considered to have begun studying the hidden wisdom of Kabbalah, where we will read about ourselves, although we are not yet aware of this.

As we progress on the spiritual path, we will realize that the Bible speaks about us, and then the Bible will transform from being concealed to being revealed. Those who read the Bible without posing questions about themselves cannot discern in the Bible either the hidden or the revealed parts; to those individuals, the Bible appears simply as a historical account or a collection of legal statutes.

For those who study Kabbalah, it is said the Bible speaks only of the present. From the point of view of egoism, there is nothing more strange and unnatural, unreal and absurd, then "selling" oneself into slavery to the Creator, to erase in oneself all thoughts and desires, and to enslave oneself to His Will, whatever it may be, without knowing in advance what it is.

All spiritual demands seem equally pointless to one who is distant from the Creator.

And conversely, as soon as one experiences spiritual ascent, one agrees to that state of being without resistance or critique of reason. Then, one is no longer ashamed of one's thoughts and aspirations directed towards committing oneself to the Creator.

These contradictory predicaments are given to us specifically to help us realize that our redemption from egoism is above nature, and is awarded only by the Will of the Creator. Until then, we exist in a state of dissatisfaction, because we either compare our present state to that of the past, or we compare our present with our hopes for the future, and thus suffer from the absence of the desired experience.

If we had only known great pleasures we could receive from Above, and were not actually receiving them, we would suffer immeasurably more. However, it can be said that in regard to spiritual pleasures, they are kept from our awareness, and we remain in a state of unconsciousness and do not perceive their absence.

Thus, it is vital for us to feel the Presence of the Creator. If we were to subsequently lose that perception, it is already clear that we would once again yearn for it. As it is said in Psalms, number 42, "As a deer pants for streams of water, so my soul cries out for You, God."

The desire to perceive the Creator is called "the aspiration to 'lift' the Creator's Presence from the dust," that is, from the lowest state in our understanding, when everything in our world appears to us more precious than being able to sense the Creator.

Those who keep the commandments due to their upbringing (which in itself is a manifestation of the Creator's desire) do so in the same manner as those who aspire to grasp the Creator. The difference lies in the perception of the individual in question. This is of primary importance, since the desire of the Creator is to benefit His creations by giving them the feeling of His closeness.

Thus, in order to forsake the habitual observance of commandments and become freely acting, we must clearly understand what we received as a result of our upbringing and from society, and what we now aspire to as independent individuals.

For instance, consider someone who received an upbringing in accordance with the system of "Mussar," which teaches that our world is nothing. In such a case, the spiritual world is perceived as only slightly greater than nothing. On the other hand, Kabbalah teaches that this world, just as it is perceived, is full of pleasures. However, the spiritual world, the world of sensing the Creator, is incomparably more beautiful.

Hence, the spiritual emerges not as simply more than nothing, but as greater than all the pleasures of our world. It is impossible to force oneself to benefit the Creator in the same way as the Creator benefits us, because such inclinations are not found in human beings.

Nevertheless, we should be clear about "to whom" we must aspire. When we seek the truth behind our desire to approach the Creator, we should keep in mind that, when we sincerely desire the Creator, all other thoughts and desires disappear, just as the light of a candle is overwhelmed by the light of a torch.

Until we have perceived the Creator, each of us feels as if we were alone in the world. But since only the Creator is One and Unique, and since only He is able to give, and gives to all of the world, and as we are absolutely opposite to this characteristic of giving, immediately upon receiving the perception of the Creator we acquire, if only temporarily, these same characteristics, as explained above in the analogy of a candle in front of a torch.

By living in accordance with the laws of the spiritual world, we are able to accomplish everything that we need to while still in this world.

When we believe that everything, even the bad that we experience, was sent by the Creator, we remain continuously attached to Him.

There is the Creator and the creation—the human being that is not able to perceive the Creator but can only "believe" in His existence and oneness, and in the fact that only the Creator exists and holds domain over everything (the word "believe" is placed in quotation marks because, in the Kabbalistic sense, faith refers to one's perception of the Creator).

The only thing that one desires is to receive pleasure. Such was the design of the Creator. Such was also the aim of the creation, the Will of the Creator. However, one should experience pleasure in the same manner as the Creator. Everything that has ever happened, is happening, or will happen to each of us, everything both good and bad, is predestined and sent to us by the Creator.

At the end of the correction, it will become perfectly clear that all that happened was necessary for our benefit. But while each of us is on the path of rectification, to each of us this path appears to span many thousands of years, to be extremely long, bitter, bloody, and extraordinarily painful. No matter how prepared we may be for the next blow, as soon as we perceive a trial approaching, we forget that it comes from that Singular Power in the world from which everything derives.

We forget that we are merely instruments in the hands of the Creator, and begin to imagine ourselves to be independently acting units. Consequently, we believe that unpleasant circumstances are caused by other humans, rather than recognizing them as instruments of the Creator's Will.

Thus, the most important concept we need to understand should go beyond mere acceptance that everything comes from the Creator. It should also focus on the idea that we must not succumb to harmful feelings and thoughts during our most difficult moments.

Nor should we suddenly begin to think "independently" and fall into believing that the events in our lives at that moment are in any way caused by other human beings, rather than by the Creator; nor should we even consider that the outcome of any phenomenon is determined by other people or circumstances, rather than by the Creator.

It is possible to learn this through our own experiences alone, but while we are learning we tend to forget why events in our lives occur. Everything that happens in our lives is in order to develop and prompt our spiritual growth. If we forget this, we may fall into a false belief that there is a lack of Divine Supervision and a complete concealment of the Creator.

This process occurs in the following manner: the Creator gives us the knowledge that only He, the Creator, rules the world, and then He places us amidst frightening and unfortunate events that bring about various disagreeable consequences. The disagreeable feelings grip us so strongly, we forget from Whom they were sent, and for what purpose these harsh blows are delivered.

From time to time during the course of this "experiment," we are given the understanding of why this is happening to us, but when these dreadful occurrences increase, our understanding disappears. Even when we suddenly "remember" Who sends us such sufferings and why they are sent, we are incapable of convincing ourselves to attribute them to the Creator, and appeal to Him for help.

Rather, at the same time we realize that everything originates from the Creator, we still attempt to help ourselves. We can visualize this process in the following manner:

1. On our path to the Creator stands an impure, distracting force or thought, which compels us to break through it in order to cling to the Creator;

2. When we are close to the Creator, we are like a child held by our mother, but the extraneous thoughts/forces try to tear us away from the Creator to keep us from sensing Him and feeling His Rule;

3. It is as if the Creator bestows on us something important to guard us from our enemy. Then, the enemy attacks and we valiantly struggle against that enemy.

4. When the struggle is over, it becomes very clear that we were merely struggling against obstacles sent by the Creator in order to attain understanding and elevation.

In the end, we acquire knowledge about ourselves and about the Creator's Divine Management, as well as cultivate love for the Creator, finally understanding why He sent us all the obstacles.

Our upbringing should not be one that forced or suppressed us, but rather should help us develop the skills necessary to form a critical perspective on our own internal states and desires. Proper upbringing should include instructions on how to develop the skills to think and analyze, while traditional upbringing, on the contrary, usually attempts to instill in us automatic actions and reactions that we can draw upon in the future.

In fact, the entire goal of upbringing should center on establishing a habitual practice to constantly and independently analyze and appraise our independent actions. These are actions freely chosen, and not those into which we have been coerced by an outside force, nor influenced by our upbringing.

How can we reach the truth when the ego perceives trust as bitterness or pain? Who is prepared to undergo such an ordeal willingly?

We receive vitality and energy from passion, honor, and envy.

For example, if we are dressed in shabby clothing, we are ashamed because others are better dressed. But if others are also dressed poorly, then we are left with only half of the unpleasant feeling. For this reason, it is said that "a shared misfortune is half the consolation."

If we receive pleasure only from one of these three sources, we could never advance in our spiritual development. For example, if we possessed only the drive for pleasure but not for honor, we would walk naked in hot weather because we would feel no shame. The yearning for honor and for high standing in society can decrease if people moderate their needs, as they do during significant ordeals or wars.

But in the desire to receive pleasure or to decrease our suffering, we have little dependence on the opinions of others, just as our toothache does not lessen because someone else also experiences a similar pain. Thus, the work "for the sake of the Creator" should be based on pleasure, not honor; otherwise, one can become content and stop in the middle of the way.

It is said that "the envy of the scholars increases wisdom." Even if one has no desire for honor, one will still wonder why someone else is honored, rather than oneself. For this reason, people devote great efforts to science to ensure that others will not receive greater honors than they do.

Such efforts do expand knowledge, and a similar pattern can be observed among new students. One sees that others rise before sunrise to study, so one forces oneself to also rise early, even if deep down there is a strong desire not to do so.

But if we realize that every thought is truly not our own but actually comes from the outside, then it becomes easier to withstand these thoughts. Society affects people in such a way that they accept all thoughts and desires impressed upon them by others as their own. Thus, it is crucial that we choose an appropriate environment for ourselves that will be characterized by proper goals and aspirations.

If, however, we wish to be influenced by and to receive thoughts from a particular circle of people, the surest method to achieve this goal is to place ourselves among them; moreover, to serve and assist them, since the process of receiving takes place from the higher one to the lower one.

Thus, in a study group, it is crucial to perceive everyone else as more knowledgeable than oneself.

This is known as "acquiring from the authors," because this is gained through communication with others. Moreover, when we are among others at work and at home, it is desirable that we mentally remain on the level of our peers. This will ensure that no extraneous thoughts should enter us unwittingly, thus causing us to reason in the manner of our neighbors, spouse, or colleagues.

Yearning for Spiritual Qualities

It is utterly impossible for a beginner to distinguish a true Kabbalist from a false one, because each one champions the same truths about the necessity of improving oneself and renouncing egoism.

But these words, like the Light of the Creator that shines over everything, can be compared to a Light without a vessel, that is to say, one might utter the most profound words, but unless one possesses *kelim*—the vessels for containing the sense of that Light—the speaker may not comprehend the internal meaning. It is much more difficult to receive ideas and notions from the books of a Kabbalist writer, the process known as *"mi sfarim,"* [lit. from books] than to acquire knowledge directly from a teacher. This is due to the fact that if one wishes to absorb the thoughts of the author, one must believe that the author is a great Kabbalist.

The greater respect one has for the author, the more one will be able to absorb from the author's books. From the thousands who have perceived the Creator, only Rabbi Shimon Bar Yochai (Rashbi), Rabbi Ashkenazi Yitzhak (Ari) and Rabbi Yehuda Ashlag (Baal HaSulam) were granted permission to write about Kabbalah in a language understandable to those who had not yet acquired the perceptions of the spiritual levels.

Other Kabbalistic works use imagery that is understandable only to those who have already entered the spiritual realms, and therefore cannot be used by beginners.

By relying on one's choice of companions and one's choice of books as the source of knowledge—an individual may gradually gain the ability to think independently. Prior to this stage the individual remains in the state common to all human beings in this world, that is, in the state of desiring to be independent, but unable to do so.

It is said that envy, pleasure, and a yearning for honor take a person out from this world. This simply means that these three human desires induce a person to act. Though not considered good desires, they nevertheless motivate a person to change, grow, and wish to attain more and more, until one acquires an understanding that the real gain is the gain of the spiritual kind, and decides to leave this world for the spiritual one.

Thus, it is said of these three desires that they "take" a person from this world and into the spiritual world to come. As a result of the accumulation of knowledge and intelligence, an individual begins to discern what is most valuable in this world, and to understand that one should attempt to reach that most valuable goal. In this manner, one moves away from the desires "for oneself" and reaches the desires "for the sake of the Creator."

The entire creation can be viewed as *the yearning to receive pleasure, or the suffering caused by the absence of the pleasure that emanates from the Creator*. There are two conditions that are necessary to feel pleasure:

1. The pleasure should appear and disappear, leaving an impression, a memory (*reshimo* from *ro'shem*—an imprint).

2. One must attain the necessary knowledge and strength to break through the outer shell and thus become worthy to partake of the fruit.

There are several types of impure, distracting forces that are known as *klipot*, meaning "shells" or "peels." Their name reflects their purpose. These forces (1) protect the spiritually pure forces (the fruit in the shell) from piercing elements that damage the spiritual realm—the unenlightened who could harm both themselves and others after gaining the spiritual and (2) create obstacles for those who truly desire to possess the fruit.

Consequently, by struggling with them, one gains the necessary knowledge and strength to break through the outer shell and thus becomes worthy of partaking of the fruit. Under no circumstances should one feel that any thoughts against the Creator, against the path, and against faith, emanate from a source other than the Creator.

Only the Creator, the singular Force encompassing a human being, acts in the entire creation, whereas a human being is accorded the role of an active observer.

In other words, human beings are left to experience the full range of forces acting upon them, and to struggle against believing that that these forces came from a source other than the Creator. In fact, unless the Creator confers such obstructive thoughts to block one's study of Kabbalah and self-improvement, one cannot move forward.

The main *klipot* are the *klipat mitzraim* (Egypt), which turns one away from the desire to continue on the spiritual path, and *klipat noga*, which gives one the false sense that everything is fine the way it is, and that there is no need to move forward. In this case, one feels as if in a slumber, although the heart does not agree with this condition (*"ani yeshena ve libi er"*—I sleep, but my heart is awake).

True Kabbalistic texts, especially the texts of Rabbi Yehuda Ashlag, are written in such a way that the one who delves into them can no longer derive pleasure from the false glow of the *klipat noga,* once an understanding of the goal of creation has become clear.

Those few who are chosen by the Creator to be brought closer to Himself are sent the suffering of love (*isurei ahava*). This is suffering intended to induce these people to overcome the difficulties of their condition and move closer towards the Creator.

This internal striving of the individual, which one feels to be one's own, is called "the pressure from within" (*dahaf pnimi*). When we act, this is considered to be "revealed," since it is available for all to see and cannot be subjected to various interpretations.

On the other hand, our thoughts and intentions are considered to be "concealed." They can differ greatly from the way others perceive them, and can even differ from our owns perception of our intentions. Sometimes, we are not aware of exactly what prompts us towards this or that action.

Our true inner intentions that motivate us are often concealed from us, as well as from outside observers. For this reason Kabbalah is known as the hidden part of the Bible, the hidden wisdom, since it instructs us about intentions and how to direct them towards the Creator.

Thus, this knowledge should be concealed from everyone, sometimes even from the individual in question. It is imperative to believe that everything in this world happens according to the Will of the Creator, is governed by Him, sent by Him, and controlled by Him.

There are those who maintain that our sufferings are not sufferings, but rewards.

This is true only with respect to those righteous people who can relate all circumstances and all ensuing consequences to the Rule of the Creator. Only in such cases when people can live by their faith in the ultimate justice of the Creator's Rule, despite great trials and suffering, will curses be transformed into blessings.

However, those trials that we cannot overcome by going beyond our reason's limitations bring us a spiritual decline, since only in maintaining faith above reason can we find support. Once we have fallen out of faith and back to our dependence on reason, we must then wait to be saved.

On the other hand, those who can withstand these trials will ascend, since the suffering and trials increase the strength of one's faith. It is in these cases that the trials and the suffering will transform into blessings.

A real plea to the Creator must come from the depths of one's heart, which means that the entire heart must be in agreement about that which it wants to say to the Creator. The plea must be said not with words, but with feelings, since only that which takes place in the person's heart is heard by the Creator. The Creator hears even more than one might prefer, because He understands all the causes and all the feelings that He, Himself, sends.

Not a single creation can avoid the predestined goal—to begin yearning for spiritual qualities. But what should be done by a person who feels a lack of sufficient desire to part with the pleasures of this world? How can one deal with the idea of parting with relatives, family, and the entire world so full of life and of small delights, with all that the egoistic desires so vividly paint in that person's mind? What should one do if, even while asking for the Creator's help, one does not truly wish the Creator to hear and grant this plea?

To help and support those in this position requires special preparation and the realization how vital it is to acquire altruistic qualities. Such a realization develops gradually as one realizes how remote one is from the spiritual joys and inner peace that attract that person from afar.

This can be likened to a host who must appease the appetite of his guests with appetizers so they will enjoy the meal that lies in store for them. Without first being prepared for the meal, the guests will never experience true delight from it, no matter how delicious or plentiful it may be. This approach is also effective in arousing an appetite for such unnatural and unfamiliar delights, such as receiving pleasure from altruism.

Our need for closeness with the Creator is gradually born in us when under the influence of our efforts inspired during times of extreme remoteness from spiritual redemption. These include times of severe deprivation and darkness, when we need the Creator for personal salvation, so that the Creator delivers us from the hopeless situations in which He placed us.

If we are truly in need of the Creator's help, then this can be considered as the sign that we are ready to receive this help, since we have developed an "appetite" for accepting the pleasures prepared for us by the Creator.

The degree to which we have experienced suffering will parallel the degree to which we will be able to receive pleasure. However, if we must go through suffering, and receive joy from Above to the same degree that we have suffered, then this is the path of suffering, not the path of Kabbalah.

In addition, a question arises: is there really a need to ask the Creator for anything at all? Maybe one should experience suffering to the point that the body desires complete redemption and cries out to the Creator with such strength that He will save it.

The answer is simple: a prayer, even if does not spring from the depths of one's heart, still prepares the individual for salvation.

In a prayer, we promise the Creator that after we receive spiritual strength, we will concentrate all our efforts on returning the spiritual aspirations that are presently lacking. In this lies the great power of the prayer.

The Creator accepts a plea of this kind, and as a result, we will advance by the path of Kabbalah, rather than by the path of suffering. For this reason, we should never agree to the path of suffering, even if we are certain that the suffering is being sent by the Creator; and even if we firmly believe that everything that is sent by the Creator is sent for our benefit.

The Creator does not want us to passively accept suffering. On the contrary, He expects us to prevent suffering, to avoid the condition in which He must push us from behind by suffering. He wants us to strive by ourselves through the means of faith, and ask for this opportunity to move forward.

Even if we do not yet possess a true desire to attain the right state, we should still ask the Creator to grant the true desire and faith through the power of prayer. That is, we should ask the Creator to give us a desire to ask, which is now lacking.

Our souls, the "self" of each of us, exist in a perfect condition from the moment the Creator decided how they should exist. This condition may be described as "the condition of absolute peace" (since every action is initiated by the desire to gain a more perfect state), and the condition of absolute happiness (since all the desires created in us by the Creator are absolutely fulfilled).

In order to reach this state, we must acquire the desire to reach it. That is, we should resolve to transform our present aspirations to perfect, altruistic ones. There is no other alternative: "Thus says the Creator: 'If you will not make the right choice of your own accord, then I will place cruel rulers over you, who will force you to return to Me.'"

Every individual simultaneously possesses two perfect states: the present and the future. At any given time, we experience only the present, but a transformation to the "future" state can be achieved in an instant by altering our natures from being egotistical and materialistic, to being altruistic and spiritual.

The Creator is able to perform such a miracle within each one of us at any given moment, since both states exist simultaneously. The difference is in the fact that we can perceive one state immediately, but not the other perfect state, which exists parallel to the first one, despite our existence in both states simultaneously.

The reason for this occurrence can be explained by the fact that our qualities-desires do not coincide with the qualities of the perfect unperceived state. As the Creator declares, "It is impossible for Me and for you to exist in the same place," as we are opposite in our desires.

For this reason, each of us possesses two conditions, or, as is referred to in Kabbalah, two bodies. Notably, there is the physical body, which we occupy at the present moment and which in Kabbalah is known as "the material sheath."

On the other hand, it is our desires and our qualities that are considered to be the body in the Kabbalistic sense, since in them is found our souls, which is a part of the Creator. If in our present state, our bodies consist of entirely egotistical desires and thoughts, then only a microscopic particle of our souls, the so-called *ner dakik*, can penetrate into us as a spark of the Greater Light, which gives us life.

The second body, which exists parallel to the first one, is the spiritual body, which we do not yet sense. It consists of our future altruistic desires and qualities that constitute our absolute soul, that is, that part of the Creator which will be unveiled in the future, once the correction process is complete.

The qualities of both the egoistic and the altruistic bodies, and their life-giving forces, are divided into feelings and intellect, which we perceive with our hearts and our minds. The egoistic body desires to receive with the heart and to grasp with the mind, whereas the altruistic body desires to give with the heart and to believe with the mind.

We are not able to alter either of these two bodies. The spiritual one cannot be changed because it is completely perfect, and the present one is completely immutable and cannot be corrected at all because it was designed as such by the Creator.

But there exists a third body, which serves as a connecting link between the other two. The middle body, directed from Above, consists of constantly changing desires and thoughts, which we should strive to correct ourselves and to ask the Creator for their correction. It is in this way that we connect the middle body, known as *klipat noga*, with the spiritual body.

When we become able to link all the constantly emerging desires and thoughts with the spiritual body, our egoistic body will then depart and we will acquire a spiritual body. At that point, the Creator will alter all the qualities of the egoistic body to become opposite ones, and the entire innate egoism will transform into absolute altruism.

In all the situations that face us in life, we should strive to see everything as coming directly from the Creator, and to see His point of view as if it were ours. We should assert that "it is He who stands between everything else and me; it is through Him that I look upon everyone in this world, including myself. All that is perceived by me emanates from Him, and all that emanates from me goes only to Him. For this reason all that surrounds us is He." As it is said, "You are both before me and behind me, and You have placed Your hand on me." "All that is in me," one should say, "all that I think and feel, comes from You, and is a dialogue with You."

The most horrifying feeling is our perception of the endless abyss.

This strikes us when a sudden void seems to open up right beneath our feet; a void characterized by hopelessness, fear, lack of any support, and a complete departure of the Surrounding Light that has given us a sense of the future, of tomorrow, of the next moment.

All variations of this dreadful negative feeling stem from the greater original sensation and, actually, can be considered aspects of it. All of them are sent to us from the same source, *Malchut*, the empty soul put forth by the Creator so that each of us will fill each part of that soul with Light.

All the sensations of darkness we experience emanate from this empty soul and can be overcome only by faith in the Creator, by perceiving Him. It is for this reason that all suffering is sent by the Creator.

King David, the embodiment of our souls, describes the condition of the soul in every line of his psalms, depicting all its impressions as it ascends the various levels. It is astonishing how much we must bear before we have the understanding, the awareness, and the way to the right path. No one can tell us what the next step should be.

Only by necessity, having stumbled on the previous step, will we choose the right action. The more we are spurred on by hardships, the faster we can grow spiritually. Thus, it is said, "Happy is the one who is afflicted by the Creator."

We should not know our next step, or our future; the prohibition against fortune-telling in the Bible should not be taken lightly.

Spiritual growth occurs only through the growth of faith. This is supported by the fact that everything we live through at a given moment, and everything that we will live through in the next moment, emanates from the Creator and can be overcome only by attaining closeness with Him. This occurs by necessity, since our nature refuses to admit that He has domain over us.

The knowledge of our future state, or merely our confidence in our knowledge of it, takes away our opportunity to close our eyes, keep quiet, and accept any sudden manifestation of the Higher Rule as true and just. This is possible only when we come closer to the Creator.

The Bible describes all of our progressive states of spiritual ascent in the everyday language of our world. As we already know, there are only two qualities in all creation: altruism and egoism, the quality of the Creator and the quality of His creations. Kabbalah, on the other hand, describes the stages of spiritual ascent in the language of direct feelings, as is done in this part of the book, or in the language of *Sefirot*, the physics-mathematical description of spiritual objects.

This language is universal, compact, and precise. Its external form is discernable by beginners. It also helps us to understand others and be understood by them, since it focuses on abstract spiritual objects and on events that, to a certain degree, are removed from us.

When we have moved to the spiritual stages, we can use this "scientific" language to describe our own actions and feelings, because the Light that we perceive already carries the information about the action itself, the name of the action, and the spiritual level.

However, a Kabbalist can convey feelings and sensations about a particular spiritual level only to one who has already experienced that level, since another person will not understand these concepts. Similarly, in our world, an individual who has not undergone a particular sensation and who does not know it through an analogous sensation will not be capable of understanding it.

There are two consecutive stages of correcting egoism. The first stage is not to use it at all, but to think and act only with the desire to "give," without any thought to possible gain from the results of one's actions. When we are capable of acting in such a way, we then proceed to the second stage: we begin to gradually employ our egoism by gradually incorporating it into our altruistic actions and thoughts, thereby correcting it.

For example, a person gives away everything to others, without getting anything back in return; this is the first step of development. If one is truly able to act in this way in all cases, then, in order to be able to give even more, the rich will provide this individual with even more.

Riches will thus pass through that individual in order to be given away to others. The amount of wealth that will be received from others will depend on whether one can give away everything that was received without being tempted by such bounty. In such a case, egoism will be employed for a noble cause: the more one receives, the more will be given away. But can one give away everything?

The amount of wealth passing through one's hands determines the level of one's correction.

The first stage is known as "the correction of creation" (of egoism), and the second stage is known as "the goal of creation," or one's ability to use egoism in altruistic actions, for altruistic goals.

Kabbalah centers on these two stages of spiritual development. However, the desires and pleasures mentioned in Kabbalah are billions of times greater than all the pleasures of our world combined.

These two steps are also in constant conflict with one another, because the first completely rejects the use of egoism and its correction, while the second uses it in small quantities, determined by the strength of one's ability to counteract it for one's correction. Thus, the actions in these two conditions are opposite to one another, even though both are altruistic in purpose.

Even in our world, an individual who gives away everything is opposite in action to the one who receives, even in order to give away. In this light, many of the contradictions and conflicts depicted in the Bible become more understandable.

For example, the conflict between Saul and David, the arguments and the contradictions between the schools of Shamai and Hilel, the conflict between Mashiach Ben-Joseph (the Kabbalist Ari) and Mashiach Ben-David, and other, almost all of the contentious issues and wars, which are interpreted by those who are not in the spiritual realm as the conflicts between nations, tribes, families, and egoistic individuals.

After a period of undertaking intense work on ourselves, learning and striving for spiritual perception, we will feel a desire to see some results. It will seem that, after all the work we have done (especially compared with the work done by others around us) we have earned the right to experience the Revelation of the Creator, to see a clear manifestation of the spiritual laws we studied so ardently, and to perceive the pleasures of the spiritual worlds.

In reality, however, all things appear to be exactly opposite to our expectations: we might feel that we are regressing, rather than progressing, in comparison to others who do not study Kabbalah. We might feel that instead of perceiving the Creator, and instead of the Creator hearkening to us, that we are moving farther and farther away from the Creator.

Moreover, the increasing hiatus from spiritual achievements and our lowering of spiritual aspirations would appear to be the direct result of our studies. Thus, a legitimate question arises: looking at those studying the Bible in a simple, ordinary manner, we can see that they come to feel their superiority over others, while we who study Kabbalah grow more discontented, seeing how much worse we have become in our desires and thoughts, and how much further away we have moved from the good spiritual desires which led us to Kabbalah in the first place!

Perhaps it would be better not to start engaging in the study of Kabbalah at all! Maybe all the time devoted to these studies will be spent in vain! On the other hand, we may already feel that only here can we find the truth and the answers to the questions within us.

This feeling only adds to the building pressure: we cannot abandon Kabbalah because it is the truth, but we seem to have nothing in common with it and, thus, we are moving further away from it, with the perception that our desires are much lower than those of our contemporaries.

It seems to us that if another were in our place, the Creator would have answered that person long ago and would have brought that person closer to Himself. Another would not have complained and become embittered because the Creator was inconsiderate towards them, or possibly, not reacting to their actions at all.

However, in essence, these emotions are experienced only by those who are in the process of true spiritual work on themselves, rather than by those who merely pore over the study of Bible, only to learn its simple meanings and to keep the commandments.

This is because those who aspire to ascend will strive to attain a spiritual state in which all personal aspirations, thoughts, and desires are devoid of personal interests. For this purpose, the quintessence of one's true thoughts and motivations is revealed from Above.

We can prove that we can endure our testing after having gone through suffering, having found within ourselves the enormity of our egoism, and having seen the great distance between the self and even the most insignificant spiritual quality. We will prove ourselves worthy of glimpsing the spiritual worlds, however, if we can still, in spite of everything we have endured, silence the heart, and express love for the Creator without demanding a reward for one's efforts and suffering.

And if, despite all that has been endured, these conditions are dearer than animal pleasures and tranquility.

In general, whenever we begin to do real work on ourselves, we immediately begin to see the obstacles on our path to the perception of the spiritual.

These obstacles appear as various extraneous thoughts and desires, as the loss of confidence in the correctness of the chosen path, as discouragement in the face of our real desires.

All these obstacles are sent to us to test us from Above. They will determine whether we really possess a thirst for the truth, no matter how contradictory it is to our own egoistic nature, or how distressing it is to give up our own comforts for the sake of the Creator.

On the other hand, ordinary people are not being tested, and feel very comfortable with the accustomed way of life, even thinking that a place in the next world is guaranteed because these people keep the commandments of the Bible.

Thus, such individuals feel that both this world and the world to come are assured, and so rejoice at the thought of the future reward, feeling that it is well deserved because they are carrying out the Will of the Creator, and thus have earned compensation both in this world and in the world to come.

That is, the egoism of the observant person increases many times in comparison to the egoism of the nonobservant person, who expects no reward from the Creator in the spiritual realm.

But the Creator tests us not to find out where we stand spiritually. The Creator knows this without testing, because it is He who gives a particular position to every person. He tests us to make *us* aware of our own spiritual state. By creating in us the desire for earthly pleasures, the Creator pushes away those who are unworthy, and gives those whom He wants to approach Him the opportunity to come closer to the gates of the spiritual world by overcoming all obstacles.

In order for the chosen individual to feel hatred towards egoism, the Creator gradually reveals one's *real enemy* and shows the real culprit standing in the way of one's entering the spiritual realms, until the feeling of hatred develops to such a degree that one manages to tear away from it completely.

Everything that exists outside one's "self" is the Creator Himself, since the foundation of the creation is the perception of the "self" by each of us. This illusion of the personal "self" constitutes the creation and is felt only by us alone. But outside of this sense of the personal "self," only the Creator exists.

Thus, our attitude towards the world and everyone around us reflects our attitude to the Creator. If we grow accustomed to such an attitude towards everything, we thereby reinstate a direct bond with the Creator. But if there is no one except the Creator, then what is this "self"? The "self" is the sense of "I," the sense of our own being, which does not actually exist.

However, in accordance with the wishes of the Creator, the soul (which is a part of Himself), feels this way because it is removed from the Creator. The Creator conceals Himself from the soul, but as that part of the Creator senses the Creator more and more, the "self" begins to feel increasingly that it is a part of the Creator, rather than an independent creation.

The stages of our gradual perception of the Creator are known as "the *worlds*," or *Sefirot*.

Usually, we are born without any sense of the Creator, and perceive everything around us to be "reality." This condition forms "our world."

If the Creator wishes to bring us closer to Him, we will at times begin to sense a vague existence of an Upper Force. We do not yet see this Force with our inner sight, but we sense that from afar, from the outside, something illuminates, bringing us feelings of confidence, of spiritual elation, and of inspiration.

But the Creator can once again become distant and imperceptible. In such a case, we feel this to be a return to our original state, and somehow manage to forget that at one time we were certain of the Creator's existence, and even perceived Him.

The Creator may also distance Himself in such a way that we feel the departure of a spiritual Presence, and as a result become despondent. This feeling is sent by the Creator to those whom He wishes to bring even closer to Himself, because a sense of yearning for the wonderful feeling that disappeared makes us attempt to bring that feeling back.

If we make an effort and begin to study Kabbalah, and find ourselves a true teacher, then the Creator alternatively either reveals Himself to a greater extent through our spiritual ascension, or conceals Himself, prompting us to find a way out of our state of downfall.

If, by exerting our willpower, we are capable of overcoming this unpleasant state of the concealment of the Creator, then we will receive help from Above in the form of spiritual uplift and inspiration. On the other hand, if we do not try to move out of that state through our own strengths, the Creator might approach us Himself, or He might leave us entirely (after prompting us several times to make an independent effort to advance towards Him), although we are still unable to perceive Him.

22

Spiritual Development

All that we desire to know about our world can be defined as the result of creation and His Providence, or as scientists refer to it, as "the laws of nature." Humankind in its inventions attempts to replicate some details of the creation and utilize its knowledge of the laws of nature. That is, it tries to replicate the actions of the Creator on a lower level and with baser materials.

The depth of humankind's understanding of nature is limited, though the boundary is gradually expanding. Still, to this day, one's body is equated with one's material body. But such a perspective does not differentiate between people, since the individuality of each person is determined by one's spiritual strengths and qualities, rather than by the forms of one's body.

Thus, it can be said that all bodies, irrespective of their multitude, form only one body from the perspective of the creation, since there is no individual difference between them to differentiate one from the other. From this perspective, in order to understand others and the entire world around us, and to understand how to relate to what is outside our own bodies, it is enough for us to look within and to understand the self.

In fact, this is how we behave, since we were created to grasp that which enters us from the outside, that is, to react to outside forces. Thus, if we do not differ from others spiritually, and all our actions are standard and within the framework of the various animal qualities of our material bodies, then it is as if we do not exist at all.

Without a distinct spiritual individuality, it is as if we were part of one common body that represents all our bodies. In other words, the only way that we can differ from another is by our souls. Therefore, if we do not possess a soul, we cannot be said to exist individually.

The more spiritual differences we possess, the more important we are, but if these differences do not exist, then we do not exist either.

But as soon as the first small spiritual distinction is formed within us, that moment, that spiritual state is called our birth, because for the first time something individual appeared in us, something that differentiates us from everyone else.

Thus, the birth of individuality occurs through our individual spiritual separation from the general mass. Like a grain that has been planted, two conflicting processes occur in sequence: the process of decay and the process of growth. There is a complete liberation from the previous form. However, until it is repudiated completely, until one's physical form is shed, one cannot change from a physical body to a spiritual force.

Until all these states are passed (called "the procreation of the fruit from above to below") the first spiritual force from below to above cannot be born within us, proceed to grow, and reach the level and form of the One who begat us.

Similar processes occur in inorganic, vegetative, animal and human natures, though they assume different forms. Kabbalah defines "spiritual birth" as the first manifestation within the individual of the lowest quality of the lowest spiritual world—the passage of the individual outside the boundaries of "our" world onto the first and the lowest spiritual levels.

But unlike a newborn in this world, a spiritual newborn does not die but continuously develops. A person can begin to comprehend himself only from the moment of self-awareness, but never earlier.

For example, we do not remember ourselves in our former states, such as the moment of conception, the moment of birth, or even earlier states. We can only grasp our development, but we cannot grasp our previous forms.

However, Kabbalah describes all the preceding states of creation, beginning from the state of the existence of only the Creator, to His creation of a general soul—a spiritual being. It then follows the gradual descent of the spiritual worlds from the highest to the lowest level, to the last state of the lowest spiritual realm.

Kabbalah does not describe all the following stages (how an individual of our world apprehends the lowest level of the spiritual realm, and then one's further ascent from the bottom to the top, to one's ultimate goal—the return to the original point of creation). This is because the ascent follows the same laws and levels as the descent of the soul, and everyone who seeks to understand must independently experience every stage of spiritual birth, up to the final spiritual level of completion.

But all souls, having reached, at the end of their growth, the absolutely corrected state of their original qualities, will return to the Creator and merge with Him into an absolutely indivisible state because of their complete similarity.

In other words, from the moment of one's spiritual birth to one's complete attachment with the Creator, the soul must ascend from the bottom to the top through the same 125 levels that it descended from the top to the bottom, from the Creator to us.

In Kabbalah, the first level from the bottom is known as "the birth," the last, at the very top, is known as "the final correction," and all the levels in between are designated either by the names of places or people in the Bible, by Kabbalistic symbols, the names of the *Sefirot* or the worlds.

From all of the above, it becomes clear that we are incapable of completely comprehending the creation and ourselves without fully realizing the goal of creation, the act of creation, and all the stages of development up to the end of correction. Since we examine the world only from within, we can only explore that part of existence that we perceive. Thus, we cannot attain complete knowledge of ourselves.

Moreover, our understanding is limited because, in order to understand an object, we must explore its negative qualities, and we are incapable of seeing our own short-comings. Despite any desires to the contrary, our nature automatically excludes them from our consciousness, because if we are aware of these shortcomings we will feel tremendous pain, and our nature automatically avoids such feelings.

Only the Kabbalists, working on the correction of their natures in order to attain the qualities of the Creator, gradually uncover the shortcomings of their own nature to the degree to which they can correct themselves. Since these characteristics are already undergoing correction, the un-corrected attributes are as if no longer belonging to the individual. Only then will the intellect and the nature of the Kabbalist permit recognition of these shortcomings.

Our tendency to see primarily negative qualities in others does not help us analyze ourselves. Because human nature automatically avoids negative sensations, we are incapable of transferring onto ourselves negative qualities we recognize in others. Our nature will never allow us to perceive in ourselves the same negative aspects.

In fact, we are able to detect negative qualities in others because it gives us pleasure!

Thus, it can be confidently asserted that not a single person in this world knows himself.

A Kabbalist, on the other hand, grasps the full scope of a person's nature, of its root, comprehending a person in the primary form, which is the soul.

In accordance with this, in order to gain a real under-standing of creation, one must analyze it from above to below, from the Creator to our world, and then from below to above. The path from above to below is called "the gradual descent of the soul into our world." This is the conception and development of the soul according to an analogy with our own world—the point at which the fetus is conceived in the body of the mother with the seed of the father.

Until the last lowest level manifests in a person, a level at which one is completely removed from the Creator, as the fruit of the parents, as a seed, which has completely lost its primary form, one cannot become a physically independent organism. But as in our world, so in the spiritual realm one continues to be completely dependent on its Source until, with the help of the Source, one finally becomes an independent spiritual being.

Having just been born spiritually, a person arrives at a spiritual level which is furthermost removed from the Creator, and gradually begins to master the levels of ascent to the Creator. The path from below to above, is known as "personal comprehension and ascent" in stages of spiritual growth in accordance with the laws of the spiritual realms.

This parallels our world, where a newborn develops in accordance with the laws of this world.

The stages of one's growth from below to above precisely correspond to the stages of the soul's descent from the Creator into our world, from above to below.

For this reason, Kabbalah focuses on the descent of the soul, whereas the stages of ascent must be learned independently by each person making this ascent, in order to be able to grow spiritually.

Hence, under no circumstances should one interfere with one's pupil, nor force upon that pupil any spiritual actions. The latter must be dictated by the pupil's own awareness of the surrounding events in order to explore and correct all qualities in need of correction. This is also the reason why Kabbalists are prohibited from sharing with each other information about their own personal ascensions and descents.

Because the two paths—from above to below and from below to above—are absolutely identical, by comprehending the path from below to above, one can comprehend the path from above to below. In this way, in the course of one's own development, a person arrives at the understanding of one's prenatal state.

The program of creation descends into our world from above downward; the highest level begets the lower one, all the way to our world, where it is born in an individual of our world at a particular moment during one of the individual's lives. From that moment the process reverses and forces one to grow spiritually, until one reaches the highest level.

But those who are growing spiritually must include their own efforts while they grow and add their own personal actions into creation for its development and conclusion. These actions consist only of a complete reconstruction of the process of the creation, because a person cannot invent something that is absent from nature, whether it is physical or spiritual. In the same way, everything that we do is nothing more than ideas and patterns taken from nature. Therefore, the entire path of spiritual development consists only of the aspiration to repeat and reconstruct the spiritual realm that has already been implanted into the spiritual nature by the Creator.

As already indicated in the first part of this book, all the creations of this world and all that surrounds them were created in perfect correspondence to the conditions necessary for each and every kind. As in our world, nature has prepared a secure and appropriate place for the development of offspring, and the coming of the newborn stimulates in the parents the need to take care of it.

Similarly, in the spiritual world, until the spiritual birth of an individual, everything happens without the individual's knowledge and interference.

But as soon as the individual grows up, difficulties and discomfort arise, requiring efforts to continue one's existence.

As one matures, a greater number of negative qualities appear.

Likewise, in the spiritual world, with gradual spiritual growth a person's negative qualities become more and more apparent. This structure is specifically created and prepared by the Creator through nature, both in our world and in the spiritual worlds. It brings us to the necessary level of development, so that we will realize through ceaseless privations that only through loving our neighbor as ourselves can we attain happiness. Only then will we discover anew the correspondence between the self and the acts of "nature" from above to below.

Therefore, any time we find "miscalculations" of nature or "incompletions" of the Creator, we can take that opportunity to complete our own natures and correct our attitude to the world around us.

We must love everyone and everything outside us as ourselves, in accordance with their descent from the spiritual levels from above to below.

Then, we will completely concur with the Creator, and thus, will attain the goal of creation—absolute pleasure and good. All this is within our reach, and in no case will the Creator deviate from His own plan, because He designed the plan for us with the Will to impart to us absolute pleasure and good.

Our task is merely to study the levels of spiritual descent from above to below, and to gain the understanding of how to conduct ourselves in our own ascent from below to above. The seemingly unnatural feeling of love towards others like us that the Creator demands of us (not those "close" to us, but those *like* us, because those close to us are already dearly loved), makes us feel an internal contraction of the "self," just like any other altruistic feeling or any other denial of egoism will do.

But if we can relinquish, or contract, our own personal interests, then the spiritual space vacated by egoism can be used to receive the Upper Light, which will act upon the vacuum by filling and expanding it. These two actions together are called "the *pulsation of life*" or "the *soul*," and are already able to bring about further actions of contracting and expanding.

Only in this manner can the spiritual vessel of a human being receive the Light of the Creator, and having expanded the soul, ascend. The contraction can be caused by an external force, or by the actions of the internal qualities of the vessel. In the case of contraction from the effects of the painful pressure of an external force, the nature of the vessel prompts it to raise the forces to withstand this contraction. It expands and thereby returns to its original condition, removing itself from this external pressure.

Should this contraction be caused by the vessel itself, then the vessel is incapable of expanding to its original state on its own. But if the Light of the Creator enters this vessel and fills it, the vessel is then enabled to expand to its previous state. And this Light is called "*Life*."

Life itself is the attaining of the essence of life, which can be achieved only through the previous contractions, since one is unable to surpass the spiritual boundaries in which one was created. A person can contract for the first time only under the influence of an external force, or by having prayed to the Creator for the help of the higher spiritual forces, because until one receives the first help—life—into the soul, one is powerless to generate such an unnatural action of the soul.

While one depends on the external force and is unable to "contract" independently, one is not considered to be alive, because "live nature" is defined as having the ability to act independently.

The teachings in Kabbalah clearly describe the entire creation. Kabbalah divides everything in Creation into two concepts: the Light (*Ohr*) and the vessel *(kli)*.

Light is pleasure, vessel is the desire to receive pleasure. When pleasure enters the desire to receive pleasure, it imparts upon this desire the specific urge to take pleasure in it. In the absence of Light, the vessel does not know what it wants to take pleasure in. Thus, the vessel itself is never independent, and only the Light dictates the type of pleasure it will receive—the thoughts, the aspirations, and all its qualities. For this reason, the spiritual worth of a vessel and its importance is completely determined by the amount of Light filling it.

Moreover, the greater the desire of the vessel to receive pleasure, the "coarser" it is, because it depends on the Light to a greater extent and is less independent.

On the other hand, the "coarser" it is, the greater the amount of pleasure it can receive. Growth and development depend precisely on great desires. This paradox occurs as a result of the opposing qualities of the light and the vessel.

The reward for our spiritual efforts is recognition of the Creator, but it is our "self" that screens the Creator from us.

Since it is the desire that determines an individual and not one's physiological body, then with the appearance of each new will it is as if a new individual is *born*. This is how we can understand the concept of the circulation of souls, that is, with each new thought and desire a person is born anew, because the desire is new.

Thus, if the desire of the individual is animalistic, then it is said that one's soul has become enclothed in an animal. But if the desire is elevated, then it is said that the person became a sage. Only in this manner should one understand the circulation of souls. The individual is capable of clearly perceiving within himself how contradictory his opinions and desires may be at various times, as if the individual were not one, but several different people.

But every time a person experiences certain desires, if these desires are truly strong, that person cannot imagine that there might be another condition, completely opposite to the one in which the person finds himself at the moment. This is due to the fact that the soul of a person is eternal because it is part of the Creator. For this reason, a person expects to remain in any given state forever.

But the Creator alters one's soul from Above, which constitutes the circulation of souls. Thus, the previous state dies and "a new individual is born." Similarly, in our spiritual ascents, inspirations, and declines, in our joys and depressions, it appears inconceivable to us that we could shift from one state into the next, when in a state of spiritual elation, we cannot imagine how there can be any other interest but that of spiritual growth.

As the dead cannot imagine that there is such a state as life, so the living do not think about death. All this takes place because of the existence of the Divine, and hence, of the eternal nature of our soul.

Our entire reality has been especially created in order to distract us from perceiving the spiritual worlds. A thousand thoughts constantly distract us from our aim, and the more we try to concentrate, the greater the obstacles we experience.

The only remedy against all these obstacles is the Creator. This is His purpose in creating them—so we will turn to the Creator in search of the path for personal salvation.

Just as we attempt to distract young children with fairy tales while feeding them, so the Creator, in order to lead us to the good, is forced to embed the altruistic truth into egoistic causes, so that we will want to experience the spiritual. Then, once having experienced it, we ourselves will want to partake of this spiritual food.

The entire path of our rectification is constructed on the principle of uniting with the Creator, of connection with spiritual objects, so as to acquire from them their spiritual qualities. Only while in contact with the spiritual are we able to partake from it.

For this reason, it is very important to have a teacher and fellow classmates in pursuit of the same goal: even in daily contact, unnoticeable for oneself, and therefore without being impeded by the body, one can acquire spiritual desires. Notably, the more one strives to be with those who have elevated spiritual goals, the greater the chance that one will be influenced by their thoughts and desires.

Since a real effort is considered to be the one that is done against the desires of the body, it is easier to make the effort if there is a set example, and many are doing it, even if it seems unnatural. (The majority determines consciousness; where everyone is naked, as in a sauna or in a "primitive" society, it takes no effort to shed one's clothing.)

But a group of friends and a teacher are only helpful tools. In the process of spiritual ascent, the Creator will still make certain that a person will be forced to turn for help only to Him.

Why is there both a written *Torah*, the written form of spiritual laws—like the Bible—and an oral one? The answer is simple: the written form gives us the descriptions of spiritual processes that are carried out from above to below. It relays only this process, though it employs the language of the narrative, of historical chronicles and of legal documents, the language of prophecy and of Kabbalistic learning.

But the main purpose for the giving of the spiritual laws is *for the spiritual ascent of a person from below to above, to the Creator Himself,* and this is an individual path for each person, a path determined by the qualities and particularities of the individual soul.

Thus, each person comprehends the ascent along the levels of the spiritual realms in one's own way. The revelation of the spiritual laws from below to above to the individual is called the *"oral Torah,"* because there is neither need nor possibility to give a single version of it to every person. Each one should grasp it individually by praying to the Creator (orally).

All the efforts expended by us in studying and working on self-improvement are needed only so that we will realize our helplessness, and turn to the Creator for help. But we cannot evaluate our own actions, and call out to the Creator for help, until we feel a need for that help.

The more we study and work on ourselves, the greater our grievances against the Creator.

Even though, ultimately, help emanates from the Creator, we will not receive it without praying for it. Thus, the one who wishes to progress forward should exert one's efforts in all possible actions, while the one who sits and waits is described as a "fool, who sits with arms folded and gnaws at himself."

An "effort" is defined as anything that the individual does against the desires of the body, irrespective of what action it is. For example, if an individual sleeps in spite of the desires of the body, this is an effort. But the main problem lies in the fact that an individual always anticipates a reward for efforts made. To overcome egoism, one must strive to make an effort without being compensated for it.

One should, therefore, ask the Creator for strength to do so, because the body cannot work without a reward. But just as a master who loves his craft thinks only of his craft while working, and not the reward, so one who loves the Creator desires strength to suppress egoism. In this way, one would be closer to the Creator because the Creator wishes it, and not because, as a result of the closeness, the person will receive unbounded pleasure.

Should an individual not strive for reward, that person is constantly happy, because the greater the efforts one can exert with the help of the Creator, the more happiness there is both for himself and for the Creator. In a way then, it is as if such an individual is constantly rewarded.

For this reason, if an individual feels that self-improvement is still very difficult and that no pleasure is derived from it, this is a sign that egoism is still present. The individual has not yet made the transition from the masses of society to those few in this world who work for the Creator and not for themselves.

But the one who feels how difficult it is to make the smallest effort not for one's own sake, but for the sake of the Creator, is already midway between the masses and the Kabbalists.

The masses, however, cannot be educated properly, because they are incapable of accepting the concept of working without reward. The education of the masses is built on the foundation of *rewarding egoism*. For this reason it is not difficult for these people to observe the commandments in the strictest sense, and even to seek additional difficulties.

However, a preliminary stage, to be simply a believer, is necessary for everyone. Accordingly, the great Kabbalist Rambam (12th century) wrote that at first everyone is taught as little children are taught. They are shown that observance should be kept for egoistic benefits, for the reward in the world to come. Later, when a few of them grow up, become wiser, and learn the truth from a teacher, they can gradually be taught how to depart from egoism.

Generally, that which one wishes to see as a result of one's actions is called a reward, even as the actions themselves may be in many different areas. One cannot work without a reward, but one can alter the reward itself by replacing egoistic pleasure for altruistic pleasures.

For example, there is no difference in the pleasure extracted by a child from a toy, and the pleasure the adult receives from the spiritual. The difference is only in the outer form of pleasure, in its garb. But in order to change the form, just as in our world, one has to grow up.

Then, instead of the desire for a toy, one will have a desire for the spiritual, thus, the egoistic form of desire will be replaced by an altruistic one. It is, therefore, completely incorrect to maintain that Kabbalah teaches one to abstain from pleasure. It is just the opposite: according to the laws of Kabbalah, a person who denies himself several kinds of pleasure must bring a sacrifice as a kind of a fine to atone the sin of not using everything that the Creator awarded to human beings.

The goal of creation is precisely to delight the souls with absolute pleasure, and such pleasure may be found only in an altruistic form. Kabbalah is given to us so that with its help we can be convinced that it is necessary to change the external form of our pleasure, so that the truth will seem sweet to us, rather than bitter, as it appears at the moment.

In the course of our lives, we are forced to alter the external clothing of pleasure because of our increasing age or because of our community. There is no word in our vocabulary to define pleasure. Instead, there are words describing the form, the garb, and the objects from which we receive pleasure: from food, from nature, from a toy. We describe our striving for pleasure according to its type, as in "I like fish."

The preferred pleasure of those who study Kabbalah can be determined by the question: is it Kabbalah that is important to the person, or is it the One who Gives the Kabbalah? Is Kabbalah important because it emanates from the Creator? Is it the Creator who is important, or is the observance of the spiritual laws and the reward ensuing from that observance, the most important thing?

The complexity of the entire problem is in the fact that there is a short and easy path to the attainment of the spiritual condition, but our egoism does not allow us to take that path. As a rule, we tend to choose the difficult and tortuous path dictated to us by our egoism; we return to the initial point after much suffering, and only then do we follow the correct path.

The short and easy path is the path of faith, while the long and difficult one is the *path of suffering*. But just as it is difficult to choose the path of faith, so is it easy to follow it once it has been chosen.

An obstacle in the guise of a demand from our own lower intellect first to comprehend and only then to proceed, is called a "stumbling block" or a "stone" (*even*). Everyone stumbles on that stone.

Kabbalah talks only of one soul, the soul of any one of us, and about that soul's ascent to the final stage. It is said in the Bible that when the arms (faith) of Moses (*Moshe*, deriving from the verb *limshoch*—to pull, to take oneself out of egoism) became weak, he began to lose the battle with the enemies (those he thought were his enemies were his own egotistical thoughts and desires).

Then the elders (his wise thoughts) sat him down (lowered his own intellect) on a stone (above egoism) and raised his arms (faith) and put a stone beneath them (lifted faith above the demands of the egoistic common sense), so that Israel would triumph (the aspiration to the spiritual ascent).

It is also said that the forefathers were idol-worshippers (the initial aspirations of a person are egoistic and are aimed to the benefit one's own body) and that they were escapees

(Zion derives from the word *yetzia*, which tells us that through *yetziot*—escape from egoism—the Light is received).

In the world of a beginning Kabbalist, there are only two states: that of suffering or that of perceiving the Creator.

However, until an individual corrects one's egoism, and can turn all personal thoughts and desires toward the benefit of the Creator, the world around him will be perceived only as a source of suffering.

But then, having sensed the Creator, one sees that the Creator fills the world with Himself, as the entire world consists of corrected spiritual objects. This picture of the world appears only if one gains spiritual sight. At that point, all former suffering begins to appear as necessary and pleasant because one has received a correction in the past.

Most important, an individual must know who is the Master in the world, and must realize that everything in the world transpires only in accordance with His wishes, despite the fact that the body, with the Will of the Creator, continuously professes that everything in this world happens by chance.

Yet, in spite of the body, an individual must firmly believe that all actions in this world are followed by either a punishment or a reward. For example, if one suddenly feels a desire to elevate spiritually, it may seem to be by chance. After asking the Creator for help to act properly, no immediate answer is received and because of this, not enough importance is allotted to past prayer, which was forgotten. But the desire is the reward for former good deeds—the act of asking the Creator for help to act properly.

Or, if one declares that at the present stage, when one feels spiritually elevated, there are no other cares in life except the lofty ones, one must understand that (1) this state is sent by the Creator as an answer to earlier prayers, and (2) that by such an assertion, one proclaims the self capable of working independently.

This means the individual's spiritual ascent depends on personal actions, rather than on those of the Creator. Moreover, if during one's studies, one suddenly begins to perceive the object of learning, once again it must be reinforced that this is not accidental, but that the Creator sends one such a state.

Thus, while studying, we should place ourselves in a position of dependence on the Will of the Creator, so that we can strengthen our faith in the Upper Providence. Becoming dependent on the Creator, we thus form a bond with Him, which eventually lead to complete attachment to the Creator.

There are two opposite forces acting upon us: the *altruistic* force, which professes that living the Will of the Creator should be the ultimate purpose in this world, and that all should be for His sake; and the *egoistic* force, which maintains that everything in this world is created for human beings and because of them.

Although, in all cases, the higher altruistic force prevails, there exists the long path of suffering. However, there is also a short path, known as the path of Kabbalah.

Every person should voluntarily strive to radically shorten the path and the time for self-correction, otherwise involuntarily one will be forced to accept the path of suffering in order to arrive at the same destination. The Creator will inevitably force one to accept the ways of Kabbalah.

The most natural feeling of a person is love of oneself, which is ultimately epitomized in newborns and in children. But no less natural is the feeling of love for another being born out of love for oneself, which provides countless themes for art and poetry. There is no scientific explanation for love and the processes that bring it about.

In our lives, we have all encountered the natural phenomenon, inherent to our lives, of mutual love, of the surge of this feeling, and then, oddly, of its decline. Precisely in the case of mutual love, the stronger the feeling, the quicker it passes.

Conversely, a faint feeling of one person often spurs a very intense feeling of the other, but a sudden return of emotion may very well lessen the original feeling of love. This paradox can be observed in the examples of various types of love: love between the sexes, between parents and children, and so on.

Moreover, it can be said that if one exhibits a great love for another, one does not give the other the opportunity to long for and to love the other more intensely. That is, the display of great love does not allow the loved one to respond to the full extent of one's feelings, but, on the contrary, gradually transforms the feelings of love into hatred. This is due to the fact that the one who is loved stops fearing to lose the one who loves, experiencing the eternal unconditional love of the latter.

But if in our world, one rarely gets a chance to love another, even egoistically, it is not surprising that the feeling of *altruistic love* is completely foreign and unattainable for us. Since it is precisely this love that is bestowed upon us by the Creator, He conceals His feeling until we develop the qualities needed to answer Him with a full and constant reciprocity.

As long as we feel no love towards ourselves, we will accept any love. But as soon as we receive the love and are satiated with it, we begin to be more selective and to desire only the feelings of unusually great intensity.

And therein lies the possibility of a constant aspiration to increase the strength of one's love for the Creator. An unwavering, constant, mutual love is possible only if it does not depend on anything.

For this reason, the love of the Creator is concealed from us, and is revealed gradually in the consciousness of the Kabbalist, to the degree that the latter is able to rid himself of egoism, which is the sole cause for the waning of the feeling of mutual love in our world.

We have been created egoists in order to give us the capacity to expand the boundaries of our own feelings by allowing us to increasingly sense the Creator's unveiling love. It is only by sensing the Creator's love, by desiring to unite with Him, that we yearn to be freed of egoism—the common enemy. It can be said that egoism is the third in the triangle of creation (the Creator, us, and egoism), allowing us to choose the Creator.

Moreover, all the acts of the Creator, the ultimate goal of creation and all His actions, irrespective of the way we see them, are formed on the basis of this absolute and constant love. The Light that emanates from the Creator—which constructed all the worlds and which created us, a micro-dose of which is found in our bodies and constitutes our life, reminds us of what our souls will be after their correction. That Light is the feeling of His Love.

The reason for our creation is a simple desire to create good, a desire to love and to gratify, a simple desire of altruism (thus, not understandable for us), a desire that we, the objects of His love, should experience His love in its entirety and find gratification in this, as well as in our own feeling of love for Him. Only a simultaneous sensation of these two feelings, so contradictory in our world, awards that complete pleasure that is the goal of the Creator.

Our entire nature can be denoted by a single word— egoism. One of the most manifest expressions of egoism is the perception of one's own "self." An individual can tolerate anything except the feeling of personal humiliation. In order to avoid humiliation, a person is often ready to die.

In all circumstances, be it poverty, defeat, loss, or betrayal, we always attempt, and actually do, find extraneous causes and reasons beyond our control that are responsible for our condition. Otherwise, we would never be able to exonerate ourselves in our own eyes or in the eyes of others, which our nature will not permit.

It will never allow us to humiliate ourselves, because in that way a part of creation, perceived by us in the form of the "self," will be destroyed and removed from the world.

For this reason, our destruction of egoism is impossible and can only be accomplished with the help of the Creator. It can be replaced voluntarily only by elevating the importance of the goal of creation in our eyes above all else.

23

Spiritual Work

The fact that we ask the Creator for spiritual perceptions, but do not ask Him to solve the various problems in our daily lives, indicates how weak is our faith in the omnipotence and Omnipresence of the Creator. It also signifies our lack of understanding that all of our problems are sent to us with one purpose only: for us to try to resolve them ourselves.

At the same time, we should ask the Creator to help in resolving them, believing all the while that every problem is sent to us to strengthen our faith in His Oneness. If we truly believe that everything depends upon the Creator, then we must turn to the Creator, but not in the hope that the Creator will resolve our problems.

Instead, we should use these problems as opportunities to become dependent on the Creator.

So as not to deceive ourselves regarding our personal motives, we must, at the same time, struggle with these problems on our own, as others around us do.

A spiritual decline is sent from Above to allow subsequent spiritual growth. Since it is sent from Above, it comes to us *instantaneously*, reveals itself in a flash, and thus almost always finds us unprepared.

But the exit from that state, the spiritual ascent, occurs *slowly*, like a healing from an illness, because we must fully grasp the condition of the decline and must attempt to overcome it by ourselves.

If, during our spiritual ascent, we are able to analyze our own bad qualities, to join the left line with the right one, then we will manage to avoid many spiritual declines, leaping over them, as it were. But only those of us capable of keeping to the right line, that is, capable of justifying the actions of the Creator in spite of egotistical suffering, will stay the course and avoid spiritual declines.

This is reminiscent of the rule outlined in the Bible concerning obligatory war (*milhemet mitzva*) and voluntary war (*milhemet reshut*): the obligatory war against egoism, and the voluntary war, if an individual is capable of and desires to exert personal effort.

Our internal work on ourselves, on the struggle to overcome egoism, on elevating the Creator above all else, on strengthening our faith in the Creator's domain, all these we must conceal, just like all other spiritual states we pass through.

Also, we may not advise another with respect to how that other person should act. If we notice the other person exhibiting signs of egoism, that individual must be the one to interpret these signs since there is no one in the world other than the Creator. This implies that all that one sees and feels is the direct result of the Creator desiring that these aspects be seen and felt by the person in question.

All that surrounds us was created solely to make us realize that it is necessary to constantly think about the Creator, to ask the Creator to change the material, the physical, the social, and other conditions of creation.

Each of us possesses an infinite number of deficiencies, all of which stem from our egoism, from the desire to be gratified and to attain comfort under any circumstances. The collection of admonitions (*mussar*) relates to the way in which we should struggle with each deficiency, and scientifically explains its methods.

Kabbalah, even for beginners, introduces us to the realm of the Higher Spiritual Forces, and allows each of us to understand the difference between ourselves and the spiritual objects. In this way, through oneself, one learns who one is and who one ought to become.

Thus, the need for secular upbringing disappears altogether, especially in light of the fact that it does not yield the desired results. Witnessing in ourselves the struggle between two forces—the egoistic and the spiritual—we gradually force the body to desire a replacement of our own nature with a spiritual one, of our own qualities with those of the Creator, without the external pressure of our mentors.

Instead of correcting each of our faults, as it is suggested by the mussar *system, Kabbalah suggests that we should correct our egoism as the source of all evil.*

We experience the past, the present, and the future in the *present*. In our world, all three are perceived in the present, but as three distinct sensations. These are produced as a result of our minds arranging these notions in accordance with their own internal time charts and, thus, yielding an impression of tense.

In the language of Kabbalah, this is defined as the difference in the effects of the "Light-pleasure." The pleasure that is felt at a given moment is considered to be the present. If its internal, direct impact on us has already passed, if the pleasure is gone, gleams from afar and is sensed by us as being distant, then we perceive it as "in the past."

If there was a cessation of Light when the pleasure left us, if we no longer receive it, then we completely forget about its existence. But if it resumes radiating Light from afar, then it becomes the forgotten past that we just remembered.

If we have not yet experienced a certain Light-pleasure, and it suddenly appears to our senses from afar, it will be perceived by us as in "the *future*" ("the Light of Confidence").

In other words, we perceive the present as an internal acquisition, as Light, as information, and as pleasure, whereas we perceive the past and the future as the result of the distant external glow of remembered or anticipated pleasure. But in any case, we do not live either in the past or in the future, but only at the present moment, perceiving the different types of Light, which are interpreted as the different times, or tenses.

If we do not experience any pleasure in the present, we seek the Source that can give pleasure in the future; we await the next moment, which will bring with it a different sensation. Our efforts in the sphere of self-improvement consist of drawing the distant external Light into our present perceptions.

There are two forces acting upon us: Suffering pushes us from behind, and pleasures entice us and pull us forward.

Usually, one force alone is not sufficient; the mere anticipation of future pleasure is not enough to advance forward, since if we have to make an effort to progress, such factors as laziness or fear of losing what we already possess may come into play.

For this reason, it is necessary to have a force that works from behind—the sense of suffering in the present state. All blunders stem from one ultimate blunder—a desire to partake of pleasure.

Usually, those who commit these blunders do not boast of the fact that they could not withstand the temptation, the fact that they were weaker than the enticement. Only the pleasure from anger awards them a sense of open pride because it ascertains their righteousness. It is this pride that immediately brings them down. Thus, anger is the most forceful expression of one's egoism.

When we experience material, bodily, or spiritual suffering, we should regret the fact that the Creator awarded us such a punishment. If we do not regret it, then it is not a punishment, since a punishment is a feeling of pain and regret for a condition we cannot overcome, whether it be health, material needs, etc.

If we do not experience pain from our condition, it means that we did not yet receive the punishment sent by the Creator. Since any punishment is the correction of one's soul, by not experiencing it, we miss an opportunity for correction. But the one who experiences the punishment and is capable of praying to the Creator to alleviate the suffering, undergoes an even greater self-improvement than would be possible had the suffering been borne without prayer.

The reason for this can be found in the fact that the Creator allots punishment to us for completely different reasons than those that induce punishment in our world. Punishment is not given to us for acting contrary to His Will, but in order to form a bond with Him, in order to force us to turn to Him and to come closer to Him.

Thus, if we pray to the Creator to relieve us from suffering, it should not be interpreted as our asking the Creator to be relieved of self-improvement. Offering a prayer to form a bond with the Creator is a step of incomparably greater progress than that allotted through suffering.

"You are coerced to be born, coerced to live, and coerced to die." This is the way it happens in our world. But all that happens in our world is the result of the events that take place in the spiritual worlds. There is, however, no direct analogy or likeness between the two realms.

Thus, we are coerced (against the desires of the body) to be born (born spiritually, receive your first spiritual sensations), implying the start of our separation from our own "self," a separation which the body never agrees to voluntarily. Having received from Above the spiritual organs of action and perception (*kelim*), we then begin to lead a spiritual existence and to understand our new world.

But even in this state, we go against the body's desire to partake of spiritual pleasures, and so, "you are coerced to live." Finally, "you are coerced to die" implies that we perceive being forced to take part in our mundane everyday life as a spiritual death.

In every generation, Kabbalists, through their efforts and books on Kabbalah, create better conditions for attaining the ultimate goal—coming closer to the Creator. Prior to the great Baal Shem-Tov, only a handful could reach that goal. After him, as a result of his work, even simply prominent scholars of Kabbalah could reach the ultimate goal as well.

Furthermore, as a result of the work of Baal HaSulam, Rabbi Yehuda Ashlag in this world, today each person desiring to grasp the goal of creation can do so. The path of Kabbalah and the path of suffering differ in that an individual travels on the path of suffering only until realizing that it is both faster and easier to take the path of Kabbalah.

The path of Kabbalah consists of the process by which we remember the suffering that we have already undergone and that may befall us again. Thus, there is no need to relive the same suffering, because the recollection of it is sufficient to realize and to choose the right path of action.

Wisdom lies in analyzing all that happens, and in realizing that the source of all our suffering is egoism.

As a result, we need to act in such a way as to avoid entering the path of suffering from egoism. Having voluntarily rejected the use of egoism, we must then accept the ways of Kabbalah.

Kabbalists feel that the entire world was created solely for their use, in order to aid them in reaching their goals. All the desires that Kabbalists receive from those around them only help them advance, because they immediately reject the idea of using them for personal benefit.

When one sees the negative in others, it is because the person is not yet free from deficiencies, and as a result, realizes the need for personal improvement. In this light, the entire world is created to serve the ascent of human beings, because it allows them to observe their own deficiencies.

Only by feeling the depths of our own spiritual decline, along with the sense of the infinite distance from that which is ardently desired, can we grasp the miracle rendered by the Creator when He elevates us from this world to Himself, into the spiritual world.

What an immense present the Creator has given us! Only from the depths of our own condition can we fully appreciate such a gift and respond with true love and a desire for unity.

It is impossible for us to obtain any kind of knowledge without making the effort to obtain it. This, in turn, gives rise to two consequences: realizing the necessity of knowledge, which will be proportional to the efforts made to acquire it, and understanding that the onus is on us to acquire that knowledge.

Thus, an effort brings forth two requisite conditions in a person: a desire in our hearts and the thoughts, or mental readiness, to grasp and comprehend the new. For this reason, we are called on to put forth an effort; in fact, it is essential.

It is only this act that truly depends on us, for knowledge itself is granted from Above, and we have no influence over its emergence. Notably, in the realm of acquiring spiritual knowledge and perception, we receive from Above only that for which we ask and for which we are prepared internally. But when we ask the Creator to grant something, are we not using our desires, our own egos?

Can such requests be answered by our spiritual elevation by the Creator? Moreover, how can we ask for something that we have never experienced?

If we ask to be rid of our egos, the source of all suffering, or ask for spiritual qualities, even without knowing what they are prior to receiving them, the Creator will award us the gift we desire.

If Kabbalah centers only on the spiritual work that takes place in our minds and hearts, asserting that our spiritual progress depends solely on these factors, then what is the relation between our observance of religious rituals and the goal of creation?

Since all the commandments of the Bible are actually descriptions of a Kabbalist's spiritual actions when in the higher realms, then by observing them physically in our world—even though it has no impact on the spiritual worlds—we are physically carrying out the Will of the Creator.

Undoubtedly, the Creator's desire is to spiritually elevate His creations to His own level. But the passing of the teaching from generation to generation, the cultivation of the soil from which a precious few great ones will arise, is only possible when the masses carry out certain tasks.

The above is reminiscent of our own world. In order for one great scholar to flourish, all the others are needed as well. The passing of knowledge from generation to generation requires that certain conditions are established. This includes the founding of academic institutions in which the future great one will be reared and educated. Thus, everyone will participate in the achievements of this scholar, and can later partake of the fruits of the great one's labors.

Kabbalists, having been brought up with their peers in an environment in which observing the commandments is mechanical, and faith in the Creator is simple, continue growing spiritually, whereas others remain on the initial levels of spiritual development.

Nonetheless, they, like the rest of humanity, unconsciously participate in the Kabbalist's work, and therefore unconsciously partake of a portion of any spiritual gains the Kabbalist might make.

Moreover, the subconscious parts of their spiritual qualities are also unconsciously corrected, thus allowing for the possibility that in several generations the peers themselves will be capable of conscious spiritual ascent. Even of the students who have come to study Kabbalah (some for general knowledge, others for spiritual ascent), it is said, "a thousand enter the school, but only one exits to teaching." Nevertheless, all participate in the success of the one, and all receive their own portion of correction through their participation.

Having entered the spiritual realm, and having corrected one's own egoistic qualities, the Kabbalist once again experiences the need for others: Living in our world, the

Kabbalist collects the egoistical desires of others, and corrects them, thus helping the rest to gain the ability to be engaged in conscious spiritual work sometime in the future.

If an ordinary person can in any way aid the Kabbalist, even by performing purely mechanical tasks, that person thereby allows the Kabbalist to include his or her personal desires in the correction that the Kabbalist makes.

Hence, it is said in the Talmud that "serving a sage is more useful for a disciple than learning from one."

The learning process entails egoism and employs our earthly reason, while the service of a sage originates in one's faith in the sage's greatness, a feeling that a student cannot perceive. Therefore, the student's service is much closer in essence to the spiritual qualities, and consequently is preferable for the disciple.

As a result, the one who was closer to a teacher and best served that teacher gained a greater chance for spiritual ascent. Accordingly, it is said by the Kabbalists that the way of Kabbalah is not inherited, but rather passed down from teacher to disciple. So it was in all generations, up to the present one.

However, the present generation has fallen so low spiritually that even its leaders pass on their knowledge via family lineage, since all their knowledge is on a bodily level. On the other hand, those who have formed a spiritual bond with the Creator and with the disciples, transfer their legacy only to those who can receive it, that is, to their closest disciples.

When we experience obstacles in our advance toward the Creator, we must ask the following of the Creator:

1. That the Creator remove all the obstacles, which He Himself sends, so that we can overcome them by our own

means, and not be in need of greater spiritual strengths than we already possess.

2. That the Creator grant us a greater desire for spiritual understanding, and impart to us the importance of spiritual ascent. Then, obstacles will not be able to stop us on the path to the Creator. We as individuals are willing to give up everything in the world for our lives, if life is valuable to us. For this reason, we must ask the Creator to grant us a taste of spiritual life so no obstacles will deter us.

A spiritual desire implies a desire to give, and to use one's desire only for the pleasure of others. A desire to please oneself is absent from the spiritual realm. The material world is diametrically opposite to the spiritual world.

But if there is no common ground or common qualities between the spiritual (altruism) and the material (egoism), how can one correct egoism? The spiritual Light, which is able to transform egoism into altruism, cannot enter an egoistic desire.

The reason the world does not perceive the Creator is because the Light of the Creator enters any object only to the degree that the qualities of the object correspond to the qualities of the Light.

Only the Light of the Creator can change an egoistic vessel into a spiritual one by entering it. There is no other way.

Therefore, He created human beings; first, to exist under the influence of egoistic forces and to receive such qualities from them that would separate them from the spiritual; then, to come under the influence of the spiritual forces.

Finally, while working on their own spiritual center in the heart, with the help of Kabbalah they must correct those desires they had received from the ego's forces.

24

Faith

It is told in the Bible that Abraham declared that Sarah was his sister, and not his wife, because he feared that he would be killed so that she could become available to others. Since Kabbalah equates the entire world to one person, because the soul was divided into 600,000 parts only in order to simplify the attainment of the ultimate goal, Abraham is regarded as the personification of the faith within us.

A wife is permitted only to the husband, as opposed to the sister forbidden only to the brother, but not to others. Abraham saw that he himself (faith) was the only one (the only quality of human beings) capable of making Sarah the basis of life.

He also realized that other men (other qualities of a person) could harm him (faith) because they were enthralled by Sarah's beauty and wished to possess her eternally for their own ego's sake. For this reason, Abraham declared Sarah (the goal of creation) as his sister, thus not making her forbidden to other men (the qualities of a person). Consequently, until one's correction is complete, one can only employ Kabbalah to one's own advantage.

The difference between all the spiritual realms and our world is that everything belonging to the spiritual realms is a part of the Creator, and has assumed the shape of a spiritual ladder to make the spiritual ascent of human beings easier.

Our egoistical world, on the other hand, was never part of the Creator, but was generated from nonexistence and will disappear after the ascent of the last soul from our world into the spiritual realm. For this reason, all types of human activity passed on from generation to generation, as well as all that is produced from the materials of this world, are doomed to vanish.

Question: The first creation received the whole Light and rejected it, so as not to feel ashamed; how can such a state be considered close to the Creator, since an unpleasant sensation is supposed to mean a distancing from the Creator?

Answer: In such a spiritual state, the past, present, and future merge into one entirety. The creation did not experience the feeling of shame because it decided to reach such a state of unity with the Creator by its own desires, and so it experienced the decision and its consequences at the same time.

Confidence and the feeling of lack of danger both result from the effect of the Surrounding Light (*Ohr Makif*), and the sensing of the Creator in the present. But since an individual has not yet generated appropriate corrected qualities, the Creator is not sensed as the Inner Light (*Ohr Pnimi*), but as the Surrounding Light.

Confidence and faith are similar concepts. Faith is "the psychological readiness to suffer for a goal."

There are no obstacles to one's desire other than the lack of patience to exert the needed effort and weariness. Thus, a strong person is the one who possesses the confidence, the patience and the strength to suffer. A weak person is the one who feels a lack of tolerance to suffering and gives up at the very onset of pressure exerted by suffering.

To be able to perceive the Creator, one requires intellect and strength. It is known that to attain something highly valuable one needs to put in great effort and to undergo tremendous suffering. The amount of effort we invest determines in our eyes the worth of the object that we seek to attain.

The degree of our patience signifies our life strength. Until the age of forty, we are at the peak of our strength, whereas after that, the life force wanes along with our capacity to believe in ourselves, until our self-confidence and faith disappear completely at the moment of our exit from this life.

Since Kabbalah is the highest wisdom and an eternal acquisition, in contrast to all the other acquisitions of this world, it naturally demands the greatest efforts because it "buys" us the world, rather than something temporary and transitory. Having grasped Kabbalah, we can grasp the source of all sciences in their true, completely revealed state. This in itself shows what kind of effort is needed, since we know how much effort is required to grasp a single science, even in the paltry framework within which we understand it.

We receive the truly supernatural strengths needed to grasp Kabbalah from Above, and are thus able to bear the suffering on the path to grasping this wisdom. At this time, we receive the self-confidence and life strength necessary to comprehend it by ourselves.

But we cannot overcome all the obstacles without the clear help of the Creator (obscured help of the Creator is evident in the fact that the Creator upholds life in every creation). Faith is the strength that determines how ready we are to take action.

At the beginning of our paths, we lack the capacity to perceive the Creator, since we have no altruistic qualities. Nonetheless, we begin to feel the existence of a supreme, omnipotent force governing the world, and we turn to this force in moments of utter despair. We do this instinctively.

We are given this special quality by the Creator so that, even in the face of anti-religious upbringing and outlook, we could begin to discover Him even from the state of absolute concealment.

While we observe generations of scientists uncovering the mysteries of nature, if we undertook a similar effort to discover the Creator, He would reveal Himself to us to the same degree as do the mysteries of nature. In fact, all paths of mankind's search lead us through the revelation of the mysteries of nature.

But where are the scientists examining the goal of creation? On the contrary, scientists are usually those who deny the existence of the Highest Domain.

The reason for their denial rests with the fact that the Creator has bestowed on them only the ability to reason and to engage only in material research and innovation.

But precisely for this reason, in spite of all sciences, the Creator instills in us an instinctive faith. Nature and the universe appear to us to deny the existence of the Higher Domain; thus, scientists do not possess the natural power of faith.

In addition, society expects material results from the labors of scientists, who instinctively obey this expectation. Since the most precious things in this world exist in the smallest quantities and are found only through great effort, and the Revelation of the Creator is the most difficult of all discoveries, a scientist naturally tries to avoid failure and does not embark on the task of revealing the Creator.

Thus, the only way to bring ourselves closer to perceiving the Creator is to cultivate within the feeling of faith, regardless of the opinion of the multitude. The power of faith is not greater than all the other powers inherent to human nature—all of them result from the Light of the

Creator. The particular quality that sets the power of faith apart from all the others is that the power of faith has the potential to bring us into contact with the Creator.

The process of perceiving the Creator is comparable to the process of attaining knowledge.

At first, we learn and comprehend. Then, having achieved that, we begin to use what we have learned.

As always, it is difficult at first, but the fruits are reaped only by those who achieve the final goal: entrance into the spiritual world. At that point, we gain the boundless pleasure of perceiving the Creator, and consequently acquiring an absolute knowledge of all the worlds and those that inhabit them, and the circulation of souls in all time-states from the beginning of creation to its end.

25

The Process of Conforming

to the Creator

Creation, an altruistic action, is the departure from egoism. It consists of setting a limit or a screen (*masach*) to the pleasure coming in the form of a spiritual Light. This screen in turn reflects pleasure back to the Source. By doing this, we voluntarily limit our potential for pleasure, and thus set forth why we accept pleasure—not for ourselves, but for the goal of creation.

The Creator wants to give pleasure to us; therefore by delighting in this pleasure, we in turn delight the Creator, and this is the sole reason why we indulge in the pleasure. Notably, we decide for ourselves that the pleasure we receive should be from this: that we benefit the Creator and thus have the willpower to withstand receiving pleasure directly.

In such a case, our actions and the form of the Creator's actions coincide, and in addition to the original pleasure, we also experience great pleasure from the concurrence of our own qualities with the qualities of the Creator—His greatness, strength, might, full knowledge, and limitless existence.

The level of our spiritual maturity is determined by the size of the screen that we can erect on the path of egoistic pleasure: The greater the strength of our countermeasures to personal interests, the higher the level achieved and the greater the Light we will receive "for the sake of the Creator."

All of our organs of perception are constructed as follows: when they contact incoming information through sound, sight, smell, etc., we can then interpret this information. Until the signal contacts these barriers we can neither sense nor interpret the information.

Naturally, all of our measuring instruments function in accordance with this main principle, since the laws of our world are simply the consequences of spiritual laws. Hence, new phenomena are revealed in our world and, so, too, our first unveiling of the Creator and then every subsequent sensing of Him solely depends on the size of the boundary that we are able to erect.

In the spiritual realm, this boundary is known as a *vessel* (*kli*). What we actually perceive is not the Light itself, but its interaction with the boundary on the path of its dissemination, which is derived from the influence of this Light on the spiritual *kli* of a human being.

Similarly, in our own world, we do not perceive the phenomenon itself, but only the result of its interaction with our organs of perception or with our instruments.

The Creator has endowed a certain part of Himself with an egoistic desire for pleasure, the desire that He Himself created. Consequently, that part stopped perceiving the Creator and senses only itself, its own state, its own desire. This part is called "the soul."

This egoistic part is also a part of the Creator, since only He exists, and there is no vacancy that is not filled by Him. However, because egoism senses only its own desires, it does not perceive the Creator.

The goal of creation is having this part choose to return to the Creator through its own will and its own decision, to again become akin to Him in its qualities.

The Creator completely controls the process of bringing this egoistical part to unite with Him. But this control from the outside is imperceptible. The desire of the Creator manifests itself (with His own concealed help) in the desire to merge with Him that emanates from the depths of the egoistic part.

For the sake of simplifying this problem, the Creator has divided egoism into 600,000 parts. Each of these parts resolves the problem of rejecting egoism gradually, by slowly arriving at the realization that egoism is evil through the repetitive process of gaining egoistic qualities and suffering from them.

Each of the 600,000 parts of the soul is known as "the soul" of a human being. The period of merging with egoism is known as "the life" of a human being. A temporary break of the connection with egoism is known as "the existence" in higher, spiritual realms. The moment at which the soul gains egoistic qualities is known as "the birth" of a human being in our world.

Each of these 600,000 parts of the collective soul must, after a series of fusions with egoism, nevertheless choose to unite with the Creator and to reject egoism, despite the fact that egoism is still within the soul while the soul is still [clothed] within a human body.

The gradual process of conforming to the Creator in qualities; the systematic approaching of the qualities of the soul to those of the Creator is known as "the spiritual ascent." The spiritual ascent occurs along the levels or steps known as Sefirot.

In total, from the very first to the very last step of merging with the Creator, the spiritual ladder consists of 125 steps or *Sefirot*. Every 25 *Sefirot* constitutes a finished stage, known as a "world" or a "realm." Thus, aside from our own state, which is known as "our world," there are 5 worlds.

The goal of the egoistic part is to reach the qualities of the Creator while still existing in us, in this world, so that in spite of our egoism we can still perceive the Creator in everything around us and within us. The desire for unity is a natural desire within us all. It is a desire not influenced by any prerequisites or inferences; rather, it is a deep knowledge about the need to unite with the Creator.

In the Creator, this desire exists as a free wish, but in the creation, it acts as a natural abiding law. Since He created nature according to His own plan, every natural law represents His desire to see such an order in place. Therefore, all our "natural" instincts and desires emanate directly from the Creator, while inferences requiring calculations and prior knowledge are the fruits of our own actions.

If we wish to reach complete unity with the Creator, we must bring that desire to the level of instinctive knowledge, as if it had been received with our own nature from the Creator.

The laws of spiritual desires are such that there is no place for incomplete or partial desires—those that allow room for doubt or for unrelated wishes. For this reason, the Creator heeds only the plea that emanates from our very Depths, and that corresponds with the complete desire of the spiritual vessel on the level at which we exist.

But the process of the birth of such a desire within our hearts occurs slowly and accumulates unknown to us, on a level higher than can be grasped by mere human intellect.

The Creator consolidates all the small prayers we make into one, and upon receiving the final plea for help of necessary magnitude, He helps us.

Similarly, when we enter the sphere of action of the Creator's Light, we receive everything at once, because the Supreme Giver is eternal and does not make calculations based on time and the circulation of lives. For this reason even the lowest of the spiritual levels generates a complete sense of the eternal.

But because we continue to experience a series of spiritual ascents and declines even after reaching the initial spiritual level, we exist in conditions such as the world, the year, the soul.

The dynamic soul, which did not yet complete its own correction, requires a place to move; this place is known as the "world." The sum of all the soul's motions is perceived as time, and is known as a "year."

Even the lowest spiritual level generates the feeling of *complete perfection* to such a degree, that only through the individual's faith above reason do we understand that elevating to the new state is nothing more than overcoming the "spiritual denial" of a higher spiritual level. Only by grasping this concept can one ascend even higher, to the spiritual level that one believed to exist and which one elevated above one's own sense of perfection.

Our bodies function automatically in accordance with the laws of their own egoistic nature and habit. If we constantly repeat to ourselves that we desire only spiritual ascent, then in the end we will desire it. The body, by virtue of these incessant exercises, will accept this desire as a natural one. It is often said that a habit becomes second nature.

In the state of a spiritual decline, we should hold on to the belief that "When Israel is in exile, the Creator is with them."

When we are in a state of apathy and hopelessness, even the spiritual world presents no interest to us, because everything appears to exist on the level at which we exist at that moment.

Therefore, we must believe that this feeling is nothing more than our personal awareness, as we are presently in a state of spiritual exile and thus unaware of the Creator, who is also exiled from our awareness.

The Light that emanates from the Creator goes through four stages before egoism is created. Only the last, the fifth stage *(Malchut)*, is called creation because it perceives its own egoistic desires to delight in the Light of the Creator.

Thus, the first four stages are all qualities of the Light itself, through which He creates us. We accept the highest quality, that of the first stage, or the desire to delight a future creation, as the quality of the Creator Himself. At the end of the spectrum is the fifth stage of development, or the egoistical creation, which desires to counteract its own egoistical nature and to become akin to the first stage. Though attempts are made, they are only partially successful in this endeavor.

The first stage of egoism, which can counteract itself fully, is known as the world *Olam Adam Kadmon.*

The second stage of egoism, is the world *Olam Atzilut.*

The third stage of egoism, which forms a part of the fifth stage that can no longer be compared to either the first or the second stage, is the world *Olam Beria.*

The fourth stage of egoism, which forms a part of the fifth stage, has no strength to withstand itself, so as to be compared to the first, second, or third stages, but can only resemble the fourth stage of the development of Light. It is known as the world *Olam Yetzira.*

The remaining part of the fifth stage has no strength to aspire to be like any of the previous stages. It can only passively resist egoism by preventing itself from receiving pleasure (the action contrary to the fifth stage). This is known as the world *Olam Assiya*.

Every world has five sub-stages that are called *partzufim: Keter, Hochma, Bina, Zeir Anpin*, and *Malchut. Zeir Anpin* consists of six sub-Sefirot: *Hesed, Gevura, Tifferet, Netzah, Hod, and Yesod*. After the creation of the five worlds, our *material world*—the realm below the world of *Assiya* was created and a human being was created in it.

The human being was endowed with a small portion of the egoistic qualities of the fifth stage. If human beings ascend in the process of spiritual development from the bottom to the top within the spiritual worlds, then the part of egoism that is in them and, likewise, all the parts of those worlds that they used for their ascent, become comparable with the first stage, with the quality of the Creator.

When the entire fifth stage elevates to the level of the first, then all the worlds will arrive at the *purpose of creation*.

The spiritual cause of time and space is the absence of Light in the collective soul, where spiritual ascents and declines result in a sensation of time, and the place for the future Presence of the Creator's Light gives an impression of space in our world.

Our world is affected by spiritual forces that impart to us a sensation of time caused by the change of their influence. Since two spiritual objects differing in their qualities cannot be as one spiritual object, they exert their influence one after the other, first the higher and then the lower, and so on. In our world, this produces a sensation of time.

We are endowed with three instruments for the task of successfully correcting our egoism: feelings, intellect and imagination. With regard to the spiritual matter and form, *the matter* is represented by egoism, while its *form* is determined by the opposing forces, corresponding to our own world.

We define delights and suffering as good and evil respectively. But spiritual suffering serves as the only source of development and progress of humankind. Spiritual redemption is perfection, received on the basis of strong negative sensations, which are received as pleasant ones.

Since the left line returns to the right one, the misfortunes, suffering, and pressures are transformed into happiness, pleasure, and spiritual freedom.

The reason for this is that in every object there are two opposing forces: egoism and altruism, which are experienced as remoteness from, or proximity to, the Creator.

There are many examples of this in the Bible: the sacrifice of Yitzhak, the sacrifices in the Temple, and so forth. (In Hebrew sacrifices are *korbanot*, a word that is derived from the word *karov*-—to advance toward something).

The right line represents the essence of the spiritual object, whereas the left line is actually only that part of egoism that can be employed by joining it to one's altruistic intentions.

26
Cognition of the Spiritual World

Much paper has been wasted by philosophers discussing the impossibility of comprehending the Creator. Judaism, as a doctrine founded on the personal experimentation of the Kabbalists, answers the question: How can we discourse on the possibility or impossibility of perceiving the Creator prior to perceiving Him?

Any definite statement implies a certain measure of perception. Therefore, it is first necessary to define what is meant by saying "it is impossible to perceive the Creator or infinity." On what basis can we claim that we understand these notions?

It is clear that when we speak of comprehending the Creator, we imply that such comprehension would be made with our sensory organs and our intellect, just as is done when researching anything else in our world. Moreover, all concepts must be understandable to everyone in our world, just like any other concepts that are being researched. Thus, the ideas must embody something tangible and real, something that can be discerned by our sensory organs.

The closest boundary of perception is found in the organs of tactile sensation, when we come in direct contact with the object's external boundary. As to using our sense of hearing, we are no longer in direct contact with the object itself, but instead come in contact with the intermediary that is transmitting the object (like air), which has had contact with the object's external boundary, be it the vocal cords of a human being, or the oscillating surface that emits a sound wave. Similarly, we use our spiritual organs of perception to perceive the Creator.

A sensation of contact (much like a tactile sensation) with the external boundary of the created being is known as *"prophetic vision."* On the other hand, a contact that has been infracted by a certain other medium that came into contact with the external boundary of the created being, (much like the sensation of hearing) is known as *"prophetic hearing."*

"Prophetic vision" is considered to be the most obvious disclosure (just as in our world, we desire to see an object and consider this to be the most complete perception of the object) because we come into direct contact with the Light emanating from the Creator Himself.

On the other hand, "prophetic hearing" (the voice of the Creator) is defined by the Kabbalists as incomprehensible, as opposed to prophetic vision. It is similar to our ability to hear sound waves, since what we are really sensing are the signals of the intermediary spiritual object that emanate from the contact of the intermediary object with the external boundary of the Creator. We interpret these waves, just as in the case of prophetic vision, as sound waves.

Kabbalists who have attained the prophetic understanding of the Creator first perceive Him through their spiritual counterparts of sight or hearing. Later, they interpret what they perceived. Notably, comprehending visible phenomena gives them complete cognition, whereas it is impossible to comprehend the nature of a purely auditory phenomenon.

But, just as in our world, even simple hearing is sufficient to grasp qualities of the object being studied (even a person blind from birth senses many qualities of those nearby), so spiritual cognition derived through hearing is also sufficient. This is due to the fact that with spiritual hearing, the information that reaches one, contains within it all the other concealed qualities.

The commandment of comprehending the Creator in essence is reduced to the perception of Him by means of spiritual sight and hearing to such a degree that we are absolutely certain that we are conscious of a full visual and audible contact with the Creator, which is called "face to face."

Creation, and the governing of those beings that have been created, occur through two opposing phenomena: the concealment of the omnipotence of the Creator, and the gradual Revelation of His Omnipotence, so that the creations can perceive Him through their corrected qualities.

For this reason, one of the names of the Creator in Hebrew is *Maatzil*, from the word *tzel*, "shadow;" there is another name as well: *Boreh*, derived from the words *bo-re'eh*, "come and see." Consequently, from these words were derived the names of the two worlds: *Atzilut* and *Beria*.

We are incapable of comprehending the true state of creation, but only that which our senses can perceive, whether material or spiritual.

Our consciousness divides everything that exists in the world into either an emptiness or sufficiency. This is so, even though "learned people" insist that there really is no such concept as complete emptiness or a vacuum.

This concept is beyond our comprehension, because we can only understand what is missing through our senses. But we are able to sense an absence or an emptiness if we compare the relation of that which exists in this world to our situation after our death .

However, even while living in this world, we feel as if everything outside our bodies is somehow absent and does not really exist at all. The truth is just the opposite: What exists outside of us is eternal and existing, while we ourselves are nothing and disappear into nothing.

These two concepts are absolutely inadequate because our sensations lead us to believe that everything that exists is connected to us and exists only within that framework; whereas everything outside of us does not carry any worth. But reason points to the opposite—that it is *we* who are insignificant, while everything outside us is eternal.

Grasping Higher Spiritual Levels

The infinitely small portion of the Upper Light that exists in all objects, both animate and inanimate, determining their existence, is known as "the small Light" (*Nehiro Dakik*).

The prohibition against revealing the secrets of Kabbalah stems from the concern that disdain for Kabbalah may arise. Everything unknown elicits respect and is perceived as something valuable. Such is the nature of human beings: A poor person prizes a penny, but once he comes to possess a million, he prizes the million no longer, but seeks two million, and so forth.

The same pattern may be observed in science: the unknown elicits respect and is considered valuable, but once it becomes known and understood, is no longer valued. Then, new unknown objects take the place of the previous objects and become objectives to be pursued,

For this reason, the secrets of Kabbalah cannot be revealed to the masses, because once they grasp them, they will grow to disdain Kabbalah. But the secrets of Kabbalah may be revealed to Kabbalists because they seek to expand their knowledge, just as the scientists of this world do.

Because they do not value their knowledge, that fact in itself prompts them to pursue the understanding of that which is still unknown. Thus, the entire world is created for those who seek to grasp the mysteries of the Creator. Those who sense and grasp the Upper Light of Life that emanates from the Creator (*Ohr Hochma*) nevertheless do not grasp the Creator, or His Essence, in the process.

But this is not true of those who grasp higher spiritual levels. Those who perceive the spiritual levels and the Light particular to those levels not only perceive the Light, but grasp the Creator. Kabbalists cannot attain even the lowest spiritual level if they do not grasp the Creator and His qualities in relation to us that pertain to that particular spiritual level.

In our world, we come to understand our friends according to their actions, both toward us and toward others. After we are familiar with an individual's various qualities, such as kindness, envy, anger, willingness to compromise and so on, we can assert that we "know" that individual.

Similarly, after a Kabbalist grasps all actions and the Divine manifestation in those actions, the Creator is revealed to the Kabbalist by means of Light, in a completely comprehensible way. If the spiritual levels and the Light emanating from them do not carry with them the possibility of perceiving the Creator "Himself," then we consider them impure. ("Himself" implies, just as in our world, that we gain an impression of one through one's actions and do not feel the urge to find out anything else. After all, that which we cannot perceive at all does not elicit in us an interest or a need to be perceived).

Impure forces such as *klipa* and *Sitra Achra*, are the forces that dominate us, preventing us from delighting in every pleasure that comes to us to satisfy us with the little that we experience. In other words, these forces prompt us to be satisfied with the knowledge that we already possess, to be content with the peel (*klipa*) while leaving the actual "fruit" aside.

Therefore, our intellects cannot understand the purpose of working for the sake of the Creator, as the interference caused by impure forces does not allow us to understand the hidden meaning of Kabbalah.

In a spiritual object, the Light that fills its top half, from the *Rosh* (head) to the *Tabur* (Navel), is called "the *past*," while the light that fills its bottom half is called "the *present*." The Surrounding Light that did not yet enter the object, but is still awaiting its turn to be revealed is called "the *future*."

If one has fallen spiritually and the egoistic desires have increased, then the importance of the spiritual decreases in that person's eyes.

But a spiritual decline is sent from Above for a purpose: to impart to one the understanding that one is still in spiritual exile; this should in turn prompt one to pray for redemption.

But we will not find true serenity until we elevate our preordained purpose—the spiritual liberation of ourselves and of all mankind—above all else. *Exile* is a spiritual concept.

Galut is not the physical enslavement that was experienced by all nations at some point in their history. *Galut* is the enslavement of each of us by our worst enemy—egoism. Moreover, this enslavement is so sophisticated that we are not aware of the fact that we are constantly working for that master—that external force that has possessed us and now dictates its own wishes to us.

We, like insane people, do not realize this and strive with all our efforts to carry out all of the ego's demands. Truly, our state can be likened to that of the mentally ill who perceive imaginary voices either as commands or, worse yet, as true personal desires, and who carry out these commands and desires.

Our *galut* is our exile from the spiritual, our inability to be in contact with the Creator and to work for Him alone. Becoming aware of being in this state is a vital precondition to our liberation from it.

At first, the ego is inclined to study Kabbalah and to put forth the effort needed to understand the spiritual, as it sees certain benefits to having spiritual knowledge. However, when we begin to realize all the implications of the real work "for the sake of the Creator," and when we are forced to ask for our liberation, then we push away such redemption, convincing ourselves that it is impossible to succeed in such work.

Thus, once again, we become the slave of our own reason, that is, we return to the ideals of the material life. Our redemption from such a state can only be found in acting according to faith above reason.

A spiritual descent does not imply the loss of faith.

By revealing more to us about our egoism, the Creator grants us the possibility of making an extra effort and, in so doing, increasing our faith. Our former level of faith was not lost, but when we consider the work ahead, we experienced it as having been on a spiritual decline.

Our world is created in likeness to the spiritual one, with the exception that it is formed from egoistic matter. We can gain significant knowledge from the surrounding world if not about the qualities of the spiritual objects, then at least about their interrelation, by comparing them with our world.

The spiritual world also contains such concepts as the world, a desert, a settlement, countries, etc. All spiritual actions (commandments) may be maintained on any level, except for the commandments of love and fear. These commandments are revealed only to those who have attained the spiritual level of the Land of Israel (*Eretz Yisrael*).

Within the level of *Eretz Yisrael* is a sub-level known as Jerusalem (*Yerushalayim*), derived from the words *yir'ah* (fear) and *shalem* (complete): the desire to experience trepidation before the Creator, which helps us free ourselves from egoism.

27

Stages of Correction

Human beings must unwillingly carry out all actions that are necessary to sustain physical life in the body. For example, even when we are ill and lack the desire to eat, we still force ourselves to take food, knowing that we will not become healthy otherwise. This is because, in our world, reward and punishment is clearly discernable for everyone; thus, all must obey the laws of nature.

But regardless of the fact that our souls are ill and can be cured only by performing altruistic efforts, when we are unable to see apparent rewards and punishments, we cannot force ourselves to undertake the process of healing.

Therefore, the healing of the soul is completely dependent on our faith .

The lower half of the Higher Spiritual Object is found within the upper half of the lower spiritual object. In the lower object, the screen (*masach*) is found in the eye area. This is known as "spiritual blindness," because in such a state only the lower half of the higher object is visible to us, since the screen of the lower spiritual object conceals part of the Higher Spiritual Object.

The Higher Spiritual Object drops its screen to the lower one, then it reveals itself to the lower object, which in turn begins to view the higher object as the higher one views itself. As a result, the lower object receives the state of fullness (*gadlut*). The lower object, then, sees that the higher one is in a "great" state, and realizes that the higher object's prior concealment and apparent manifestation as the "small" state *(katnut)*, was done exclusively for the benefit of the lower one. In this way, the lower object could become aware of the importance of the higher one.

All consecutive states that we experience on our paths can be compared to being inflicted by the Creator with an illness, which the Creator Himself eventually cures. When we perceive this illness (for example, as hopelessness, weakness, and despair) as the Will of the Creator, this transforms these states into the stages of correction and we can progress toward unity with the Creator.

As soon as the Light of the Creator enters an egoistical desire, that desire immediately submits to the Light and is ready to be transformed into altruism. (It has been said many times that Light cannot enter an egoistical desire, but there are two kinds of Light: the Light that comes to correct a desire, and the Light that brings pleasure; in this case we mean the Light that brings correction.)

Thus, when the Light enters these desires, they are changed into their opposites. In this manner, even our biggest sins are transformed into merits. But this occurs only if we return because of our love for the Creator, when we are able to receive the entire Light of the Creator not for our own sake. Only then do our former actions (desires) become transformed into vessels that can receive Light.

Such a state cannot come about, however, prior to the final correction. Until then, we may receive only a part of the Creator's Light, not for our own sakes, but according to the principle of the middle line.

There are several ways of receiving: by charity, by a gift, or by forcefully taking it (demanding because one is entitled). When one receives charity, one may be ashamed of it, but one still asks from necessity. On the other hand, one does not ask for a gift. Rather, a gift is given to one who is loved. One who demands does not consider having received either as charity or as a gift, but by right.

This latter feeling is characteristic of the righteous who demand of the Creator, thinking that they are entitled to something intended for them in the very design of creation. Thus, it is said: "The righteous take by force."

Abraham (the right line: faith above reason) was ready to sacrifice Yitzhak (the left line: reason and control of one's spiritual condition) in order to constantly progress only along the right line. Consequently, he advanced to the middle line, which combines the two.

Simple faith is an uncontrolled faith and is usually known as "*faith below reason.*" Faith that is checked by reason is known as "*faith within reason.*" But *faith above reason* is possible only after one has analyzed one's state.

Thus, if we, seeing that we accomplished nothing, still chose faith as if everything had been accomplished, and continued to uphold this belief up to the critical point, then this is considered to be "faith above reason," because we had ignored reason. Only then do we become worthy of the middle line.

There are three lines of spiritual behavior: the right line, the left line, and the combination of the two—the middle line. If the individual possesses only one line, it can neither be considered the right nor the left, since only the possession of two opposite lines can determine which is which.

There is also the straight line, known as the state of perfection, along which travels every believer, this is the one path according to the laws of which we are brought up and along which we travel through our entire lives.

Every person traveling this path knows exactly how much effort must be exerted, according to their own calculations, in order to feel that they fulfilled all obligations. Thus, they feel satisfaction from the work. Moreover, they feel that every passing day adds further merits and benefits, since several additional commandments have been observed.

This line of action is called "the straight line." Those who were guided along this path while young cannot wander from it because they were taught to behave in this manner from childhood, without having to exert self-control or engage in self-criticism. Therefore, they travel straight for their entire lives, and every day increases their own merits.

Those who travel along the *right line* must act as those who travel along the straight line. The only difference is that those traveling the straight line lack self-criticism of their spiritual state. Those who travel the right line take every step with difficulty, as the left line neutralizes the right, awakening spiritual thirst, and hence bringing no satisfaction from the attained spiritual state.

When we travel the *straight line*, we do not critically scrutinize our own state, but constantly add new merits to the past ones, since we have a sound base to rely on. Meanwhile, the left line erases all former efforts.

Faith, the Only Antidote to Egoism

The most important determinant of the perception of pleasure is the thirst for pleasure, which in Kabbalah is known as a *"vessel."* The size of the vessel is determined by the degree to which one feels the need for the lack of pleasure.

For this reason, if two separate vessel-people receive the same pleasure, one will receive a feeling of absolute satiation, while the other will feel no sense of possessing anything and, thus, be very depressed.

Therefore, every person must strive to live in the given moment; taking knowledge from the previous states; with faith above reason in the present state, we have no need for the future.

The perceiving of *Eretz Yisrael* ("Land of Israel") and, consequently, the Revelation of the Creator, is awarded to those who have reached the spiritual level of *Eretz Yisrael.* In order to reach this level, one must rid oneself of the three impure forces, which signify the spiritual circumcision of one's egoism, and voluntarily take upon oneself the condition of restriction *(tzimtzum),* in order that the Light will not enter egoism.

If Kabbalah says that something is "forbidden," it actually implies that something is impossible even if one desires it. The objective, however, is not to desire it. For example, if an individual works in a certain job for an hour a day, and does not know any other workers who have already been rewarded for their work, that person will worry whether there will be pay for the performed task, but much less than the person who works ten hours a day.

The latter must have much more faith in the boss, but must also endure greater suffering at not seeing others being rewarded. And if one wishes to work day and night, then that person feels an even greater awareness of the concealment of the boss and of the reward. This is because the worker has a greater need to know whether there will be the promised reward in the end.

However, those who travel by *faith above reason* develop in themselves an immense need for the Revelation of the

Creator, and along with it, an ability to confront the revelation. At that point, the Creator will unveil the entire creation before them.

The only way to avoid the use of egoistic desires is to advance by the path of faith.

Only if we refuse to see and know from fear of losing the capacity to work altruistically will we be able to continue to receive strong feelings and knowledge to the degree that advancement on the path of faith will not be impeded.

It thus becomes clear that the crucial point of *not* working for the sake of the self emanates from the necessity to abandon the limited egoistic possibilities of attaining pleasure. Instead, one must seek to gain the unlimited possibilities of receiving pleasure outside the narrow boundaries of the body. Such a spiritual "organ" of perception is known as "faith above knowledge."

Those who reach the level of spiritual development at which they can work without receiving any reward for egoism become compatible in qualities with the Creator (and therefore, achieve closeness with Him, because in spiritual realms it is only the difference in qualities that separates objects, as there exist no concepts of space and time).

Endless pleasure is also gained, unlimited by feelings of shame as when one receives charity. When we perceive the all-encompassing, invisible presence of the Upper Intellect, which permeates the entire universe and holds domain over everything, we receive the truest sense of support and confidence. Therefore, faith is the only antidote to egoism.

Human beings by nature only have the power to do that which they comprehend and sense. This is known as "faith within reason." Faith is called an upper, confronting power, which gives one the ability to act even when we do not yet realize or understand the essence of our actions;

that is, faith is a force that does not depend on our personal interest, egoism.

It is said that in the place where a *ba'al teshuva* (one who wishes to return and draw near the Creator) stands, a complete righteous person cannot stand. When one corrects a new desire, one is considered to be completely righteous. When one is incapable of correction, one is called a "sinner."

But if one overcomes oneself, then one is called "a returning one." Since our entire path leads only toward the goal of creation, each consecutive new state is higher than the preceding one and the new state of the "returning one" is higher than the previous state of "the righteous one."

We perceive the Creator as a Light of Pleasure.

Depending on the qualities and the level of purity of our own altruistic vessel (our organ of perception of the spiritual Light), we perceive the Light of the Creator in different ways. In view of this, though there exists only one Light, we assign different names to it, based on our own perceptions of it and its effect on us.

Light that brings Correction

There are two kinds of Light of the Creator: the Light of knowledge, reason, and wisdom (called *Ohr Hochma*), and the Light of mercy, confidence, and unity (called *Ohr Hassadim*). In turn, *Ohr Hochma* comes in two types according to its action upon us.

At first, when the Light arrives, we discover our own evil. Then, when we have discovered the evil, and realize that we should not use egoism, this same Light imparts strength towards those egoistic wishes, so that we can work (take pleasure) with them, but not for our own sake. Finally, when we gain the strength to overcome our own egoism, this same Light makes it possible for the corrected, formerly egoistic desires to take pleasure in altruism.

On the other hand, *Ohr Hassadim* bestows on us the desire "to give" rather than "to take" pleasure. For this reason, from the 320 uncorrected desires of the soul, the action of *ohr hochma* separates the 32 parts of *Malchut* (which are gradually sensed as spiritual ascents take place, just as the individual gradually comprehends the full depths of his evil and shudders at the realization of his own essence) from the desire to receive personal pleasure, because we have realized that egoism is our worst enemy.

The remaining 288 desires have neither an egoistic nor an altruistic direction, as they are simply sensations (like those of hearing, sight, etc.), which can be employed in any way we choose: either for ourselves or for others. Under the action of *Ohr Hassadim*, we develop a desire to work altruistically with all 288 sensations. This occurs after *Ohr Hochma* has replaced the 32 egoistic desires with the 32 altruistic desires.

A correction under the influence of the Light occurs without a sensation of pleasure derived from it. One only senses the difference in qualities between one's own egoism and the magnificence of the Light. This alone is sufficient to break free of bodily desires. It is thus said, "I have created in you egoistical tendencies, and I created Kabbalah as its cure."

But then, having corrected one's desires, one begins to receive the Light in order to delight the Creator. This Light, also known as "Torah," is called "The Names of the Creator," because the individual receives into one's self and soul a part of the Creator, and assigns names to the Creator in accordance with the pleasures received from the Light.

We can enter the spiritual world only by becoming completely unselfish (hafetz hesed).

This is the minimal prerequisite to ensure that no egoistic desires could ever seduce us and thereby cause harm, because we want nothing for the self.

Without the protection of the altruistic tendencies with the quality of *Ohr Hassadim*, when we begin to receive the unbounded pleasure from the Upper Light, we will inevitably desire to gratify ourselves, and thus will bring about personal ruin; we will never be able to leave egoism for altruism. Our entire existence will consist of pursuing these pleasures, which are inaccessible to our egoistic desires.

But *Ohr Hassadim*, which imparts on us a striving toward altruism, cannot shine its Light into our egoistical desires. Egoistic desires are sustained by a spark of the Light within us that was forcibly put there by the Creator to resist the laws of the nature of spirituality. This enables us to maintain life in us because, without receiving any pleasure, human beings cannot survive.

If this spark of the Upper Light disappeared, we would immediately perish. Only by doing so could we break away from egoism and from our unfulfilled desire to be gratified, thereby bringing us absolute gloom and despair.

What is the reason that *Ohr Hassadim* cannot enter egoism? As was demonstrated earlier, the Light itself carries no distinction between *Ohr Hochma* or *Ohr Hassadim*, but the individual determines this distinction. An egoistic desire can begin to take pleasure in the Light, regardless of the Light's origin; that is, it can begin to take pleasure in *Ohr Hassadim* for its own sake. Only a desire that has been prepared for altruistic actions can receive the Light in order to take pleasure in altruism; that is, to receive the Light as *Ohr Hassadim*.

An individual receives pleasure from three types of sensations: past, present, and future. The greatest pleasure is derived from the sensations of the future, because an individual begins to anticipate the pleasure in the present, that is, the pleasure is experienced in the present. In this way, anticipating and thinking about objectionable deeds are worse than the deeds themselves, because the anticipation prolongs the pleasure and occupies the thoughts of the individual for a long time.

Present pleasure is usually short in its span, in light of our petty and easily satisfied desires.

Past pleasure, on the other hand, can be repeatedly recalled in one's mind and enjoyed. Thus, prior to engaging in an act of goodness, it is necessary to dedicate a lot of time to thinking and preparing for it. This allows us to take in as many different sensations as possible, so that later we can remember them in order to recreate our aspirations toward the spiritual.

Because egoism is the essence of our nature, we desire to delight in our lives. So if we are given from Above, into our desires, a small seed of a soul, which by its nature wishes to and tries to exist on anti-egoistical pleasures, then egoism can no longer motivate these types of actions. Thus, there is no more gratification from such a life.

This is because the soul gives us no rest, constantly reminding us that we are not living a true full life, but merely existing. As a result, we begin to see life as unbearable and full of suffering, because regardless of our actions, we are incapable of receiving pleasure. At the very least, we cannot be satisfied by anything, because the soul does not allow us to be satisfied. Thus it continues until egoism itself decides that there is no other solution but *to listen to the voice of the soul,* and to follow its directions. Otherwise, we will never be at peace.

This situation can be described as "the Creator bringing us back to Him against our will." It is impossible for us to perceive even the smallest pleasure if we did not feel the lack of it beforehand. This lack of a desired pleasure is defined as "suffering."

The ability to receive the Upper Light also requires a prior desire for it. For this reason, when we are learning, and during other actions, we should ask to feel a need for the Upper Light.

"There is none else but Him." Everything that transpires is His desire, and all creations carry out His Will. The only difference is that there is a small group of people who carry out His Will because they so wish. The experience of unification of the Creator with the created is only possible when there exists a congruence of desires.

"A blessing" is defined as an outpouring of the Light of Mercy (*Ohr Hassadim*) from Above, which is possible only when we are engaged in altruistic acts. It is said by the Kabbalists: "The needs of your people are great, but their wisdom is slight." The needs are great precisely because the wisdom is slight.

Rabbi Yehuda Ashlag said: "Our state can be likened to the state of the King's son, who was placed by his father in a palace filled with all kinds of treasures but with no light with which to see it all. So the son sits in the darkness and lacks only the light in order to possess the riches. He even has a candle with him (the Creator sends him the possibility to begin the advance toward Himself), as it is said: 'The soul of a human being is the candle of the Creator.' One needs only to light it by his own desire."

Rabbi Yehuda Ashlag said: "Although it is said that the goal of creation is incomprehensible, there is a great difference between its incomprehension by the wise man, and the ignorance of the simpleton."

Rabbi Yehuda Ashlag said: "The law of the root and the branch implies that the lowest must reach the level of the highest, but the highest does not have to be like the lowest."

All our work consists of the preparation to receive the Light. As Rabbi Yehuda Ashlag said: "The most important is the *kli-vessel*, even though *kli* without light is as lifeless as the body without the soul. Thus, we should prepare our *kli* in advance, so that when it receives the light it works properly. This can be likened to a man-made machine that operates on electricity. The machine will not work unless it is plugged into the electrical source, but the result of its work depends on the way the machine itself is made."

In the spiritual world, all laws and desires are diametrically opposite to those of our world.

Just as in our world, it is extremely difficult to act contrary to knowledge and understanding, so in the spiritual world it is extremely difficult to progress with knowledge.

As Rabbi Yehuda Ashlag said: "It is said that when everyone stood during the service at the Temple, it was very crowded, but when everyone prostrated themselves, there was plenty of room." The act of standing symbolizes the state of "greatness" of *partzuf*, the receiving of Light; whereas the act of prostrating is a state of "smallness" and represents the lack of Light.

In this lower state there was more room and a greater feeling of freedom, because in the state of the Creator's concealment, those in the process of spiritual ascent feel the potential to advance against their reason, and this is the source of joy from their work.

Rabbi Yehuda Ashlag used to tell the story of a great Kabbalist of the last century, Rabbi Pinchas, from the village of Korits. Rabbi Pinchas had no money even to buy Ari's *The Tree of Life*, and was forced to teach children for half a year in order to earn the money needed to purchase this book. Even though it may appear that our bodies are an obstruction to our spiritual ascent, it only seems this way because we are not aware of the functions that the Creator assigned to them.

As Rabbi Yehuda Ashlag said: "Our body is like an *anker* (a part in a watch); even though the *anker* stops the watch, without it the watch would not work, it would not move forward."

At another time, Rabbi Ashlag said: "In the barrel of a long-range shotgun there is a special threading which makes the exit of the bullet difficult, but precisely because of this threading the bullet flies farther and is more accurate." In Kabbalah such a state is known as *kishui*.

Rabbi Yehuda Ashlag said: "Everyone is so accustomed to interpreting the Bible in accordance with the concepts of this world, that even when it is explicitly stated in the Bible, 'Guard your souls,' it is still understood to mean the health of the body."

Rabbi Yehuda Ashlag said: "An individual is in the spiritual state to the extent that he realizes that his egoistic desires are, in essence, the impure force."

Rabbi Yehuda Ashlag said: "The lowest of the spiritual levels is attained when the spiritual becomes most important and comes before the material."

Rabbi Yehuda Ashlag said: "In only one thing can a person display haughtiness; that is, in asserting that no one else can please the Creator more than he himself."

Rabbi Yehuda Ashlag said: "The reward for keeping a Commandment is in gaining the perception of the One who commands it."

Rabbi Yehuda Ashlag said: "The worries of this world are of no concern to those engaged in spiritual ascent, just as the person who is seriously ill does not worry about getting his salary, but only about surviving the illness."

Rabbi Yehuda Ashlag said: "In the spiritual, as in our physical world, if something occurs to us because of circumstances that were beyond our control, this fact itself will not save us. For example, if someone inadvertently falls off a cliff, the mere fact that he fell, even though he did not want to fall, will not save him from dying.

The same is true in the spiritual world. When Rabbi Yehuda Ashlag was sick, a doctor was called to come and see him. The doctor prescribed rest and peace, suggested that it was important to calm down the patient's nerves, and remarked that if he was to engage in learning, he should choose something uncomplicated like The Psalms.

When the doctor left, Rabbi Yehuda commented, "It seems that the doctor thinks it possible to read The Psalms superficially, without looking for a deeper meaning."

Rabbi Yehuda Ashlag said: "There is no place in between the spiritual, altruistic 'giving' and the material, egoistic, impure 'receiving.' If at every single moment a person is not bound to the spiritual, he forgets about it altogether and remains in the impure and physical state."

It is said in the book, *Hakuzari*, that the King Kuzari, when it came time to select a religion for his people, turned to a Christian, to a Muslim, and finally to a Jew. When the King heard the Jew, he remarked that the Christian and the Muslim both promised him eternal heavenly life and great rewards in the world to come, after his death. On the other hand, the Jew spoke of the rewards for the observance of the Commandments and the punishment for disobeying them in this world.

But it seemed to the King that it was more important to be concerned with what he would receive in the world to come, after death, than with the way he should live his life in this world.

The Jew then explained that those who promise reward in the world to come, do so because they want to distance themselves from the falsehood in this manner, to conceal the lie and the meaning in their words. In a similar fashion, Rabbi Yehuda Ashlag explained that the words of Agra, the concept of *yehudi* ("Jew") is the name for one who attained the entire spiritual world, the whole world to come, while in this world.

This is what Kabbalah promises us as a reward. All of the rewards of Kabbalah must be received while a person is in this world, specifically while in the body, to feel everything with one's entire body.

Rabbi Yehuda Ashlag said: "When a person feels that the impure forces, that is, egoistic desires, begin to press him, this is the beginning of his spiritual liberation." Rabbi Yehuda Ashlag said, commenting on Kabbalah "All is in the hands of God, except the fear of God": In respect to everything that a person asks of the Creator, the Almighty decides whether to grant that person what is asked of Him or not to grant it.

However, the request to grant one the 'fear of Heaven' is not decided by the Creator, but if a person truly yearns to have the fear of God, he will surely be granted this request."

28

Not for One's Self

Life is considered to be a state in which we perceive desires for attaining pleasure, either from receiving or from giving. If the desire to attain pleasure disappears, then the new state is that of unconsciousness, fainting, or death. If we are in such a state that we clearly see and feel that we cannot receive any more pleasure, for example because of the shame that we feel for past actions.

If we suffer so much that even the smallest pleasure we get out of life is neutralized, then we will no longer feel like living. Thus, by means of the surrounding environment, enemies, bankruptcy, or failure in one's work, those who are ascending spiritually may experience sensations of hopelessness, despair, and a complete lack of meaning of existence.

Therefore, we must put all our efforts into receiving pleasure from performing deeds that are considered good in the eyes of the Creator, and in this manner bring happiness to Him. Such thoughts and actions contain such tremendous pleasure, they can neutralize the greatest suffering in this world.

We may already be at the stage of being able to perform altruistic acts. Whatever action we may be engaged in, we will not be calculating personal gain, and will think only of the well-being of the One for whom the act is done (i.e., for the Creator).

However, if at the same time we do not receive pleasure from our altruistic actions, then such actions will be considered as pure giving. For instance, observing the commandments only for the sake of the Creator will not accord us the Light of the Creator (the pleasure) that corresponds to each commandment. This is because the process of self-improvement is not yet complete.

Having received the pleasure from the unobstructed Light of the Creator, one would be at risk of awakening one's egoism and, then, having that egoism demand to receive pleasure at any expense for reasons of self-gratification. at that point, the person would not be able to resist this pleasure, and would obtain it not for the reason of pleasing the Creator, but from the sheer force of the desire to attain pleasure.

Kelim, with which we perform altruistic acts, are known as "vessels of bestowal." A spiritual object has a structure similar to that of the physical body, and consists of 613 organs.

In general, the design of the spiritual forces is similar to the physical structure of our bodies.

For this reason, 248 vessels of bestowal are located above the upper torso of the spiritual object and correspond to positive spiritual acts, which each person is obligated to perform.

The Light that is received by one who observes the above spiritual acts is known as the "Light of Grace" (*Ohr Hassadim*), or "concealed grace" (*hassadim mehusim*). The Light of Wisdom (*Ohr Hochma*) is concealed from the recipient.

One with strong willpower will rectify one's feelings to such an extent, that this individual will be able to perform altruistic acts as well as receive pleasure from them for the sake of the Creator, that is, to receive pleasure into the past egoistic desires. This process is known as "Receiving for the sake of Giving."

Consequently, that person will be able to receive the Light that is contained in every spiritual act.(The commandments of the Bible are spiritual acts. Because every person in our world is obligated to fulfill these commandments regardless of their spiritual level these are a necessary preliminary stage in accordance with their primary spiritual goal: to bring pleasure to the Creator).

The first stage we go through when trying to understand the purpose of creation is working on ourselves for personal gain ("not for His name") since there are many ways to feel pleasure—eating, playing games, receiving honors and glory, etc. These methods, however, allow us to feel only small and fleeting pleasures. The motivations behind such actions are "for the self."

We can attain much greater pleasures by having faith in the Creator; in the fact that He is Almighty; in His Oneness with respect to ruling over the entire world, including everything that happens to each of us, in His Dominion over everything that concerns each of us, in His Willingness to help, when hearing our prayers and in having faith in all of the above.

Only after we have accomplished the first stage of this work will we receive very different, special sensations of a higher spiritual state. As a result, we will no longer be concerned with whether or not we will gain personally from our actions. On the contrary, all our thoughts and calculations will be directed toward attaining spiritual truth. Our thoughts and intentions will focus on yielding to the essence of the true laws of creation, to perceiving and carrying out only the Will of the Creator, which itself will ensue from our perception of His grandeur and power.

Then, we will forget about our past motivations and will realize that we have not the slightest inclination to think or worry about ourselves, that we completely surrender to the grandeur of the all-transcending Supreme Reason, and cannot hear the voice of our own reason at all. Our main worry will center on how to do something pleasing and agreeable for the Creator. Such a state is known as "not for oneself."

The underlying cause of faith is the fact that there is no greater pleasure than to perceive the Creator, and to be filled with Him. But in order for us to be able to receive this pleasure unselfishly, we need the Creator to be concealed; the state of concealment allows us to observe the commandments without receiving any pleasure in return. Such an act is considered "not for the sake of the reward."

When we reach this state and create such a spiritual vessel, we immediately begin to see and perceive the Creator with our entire being. The reason that earlier prompted and convinced us to work for the Creator for the sake of personal benefit disappears, and is even compared to death, because we were once connected to life, and attained this feeling by virtue of faith.

But if we begin to work on attaining faith above reason when we are already in the corrected state, we receive back our souls, the Light of the Creator.

Obtaining "*lishma*"

The Kabbalistic names, though they were taken from our world, signify completely different objects and actions in the spiritual world, unrelated to those of this world. It is true that the spiritual objects are the immediate sources of the objects found in this world [see "*The Language of Kabbalah*," part 1; "*The Names of the Creator*," part 3].

From this incongruence, and the dissimilarity of the spiritual cause and the effect found in our world, it can once again be seen how remote the spiritual objects are from our egoistic concepts. In the spiritual world, a name signifies a particular disclosure of the Creator's light to a person through an action, which is assigned that particular name.

Similarly, in our world, every word discloses something not of the object itself, but of our perception of that object. The phenomenon or the object itself is completely outside the realm of our perception. It is an entity in itself, absolutely incomprehensible to us.

Undoubtedly, the object possesses forms and qualities absolutely different from those that can be detected by our instruments or senses. One can confirm this concept with the example of seeing an object through one's vision vs. seeing one obtained through x-rays or heat frequencies.

In any case, an object and the perception of that object exist separately.

The latter arises out of the qualities of the person perceiving the object in question. Thus, the combination of the object (that is, of the true qualities of the object) and of the qualities of the one who perceives the object (the perceiver), give rise to a third entity: a depiction of the object formed by the perceiver. This is based both on the general qualities of the object itself, and on the qualities of the perceiver.

In the process of working with the spiritual Light, there are two distinct states of a person who wishes to receive and receives the Light: the perception and the qualities of a person prior to receiving the Light, and after receiving it.

There are also two states of the Light that fill the vessels-desires of a person: the state of the Light prior to coming in contact with the feelings and desires of the person, and the state of the Light after it has come into contact with the perceiver.

In a prior state, the Light is known as Simple Light, because it bears no connection to the qualities of the perceiver. Since all the objects, other than the Light of the Creator, desire to receive and to be gratified by the Light, there is no actual possibility to perceive, to examine, to sense, or even to imagine the Light outside of ourselves.

Thus, if we refer to the Creator as the Strong One, it is because at that moment we feel (one who truly feels!) His strength. But not having perceived any quality of the Creator, it is impossible to refer to Him by any name, because even the word "Creator" connotes the fact that a person perceived this particular quality of the Light.

However, if a person pronounces the names of the Creator (that is, enumerates His qualities), without having perceived these qualities through the senses, then this act implies that a person assigns names to the simple Light prior to sensing the meaning of these names in oneself, which is equal to lying, since a simple Light has no name.

Those of us who strive to ascend spiritually must *avoid extraneous influences* and protect personal convictions that have not yet matured, until we receive the necessary perceptions that can support us. The main defense and distancing must be aimed not at those people who are far from Kabbalah, since they can only transmit indifference or utter, at most, negativity, indicating a great divergence from the state of the person involved in spiritual ascent. The defense must be aimed at the people who are supposedly close to Kabbalah.

On the other hand, a beginner need not be concerned with the people who are far from Kabbalah, because it is evident that there is nothing that one can learn from them, and hence they do not pose a threat of spiritual enslavement.

Our egoism allows us to progress only when it feels fear.

Then, it pushes us into all kinds of actions, just to neutralize that feeling. Therefore, if a person could feel fear of the Creator, one could develop the necessary strength and the desire to work.

There are two kinds of fear: the fear of transgressing a commandment, and fear of the Creator. The first is a fear that prevents an individual from sinning, otherwise that individual would sin. However, if a person has no fear of sinning because all actions are carried out solely for the sake of the Creator, that person will observe all the commandments anyway, not out of fear, but because this is the Will of the Creator.

The fear of transgression (sin) is an egoistic fear, because it is prompted by the concern of doing harm to the self. Fearing the Creator is considered to be an altruistic fear, because it is prompted by a concern of not fulfilling the desire of the Creator, out of feelings of love.

But despite one's tremendous yearning to fulfill all that brings joy to the Creator, it is nevertheless very difficult to observe the commandments of the Creator (actions that are desired by the Creator) because one does not see the necessity of fulfilling them.

The fear emanating from the feeling of love must be stronger than the egoistic fear. For instance, when one anticipates that one will be seen at the moment of committing a crime, or simply a transgression, that person experiences feelings of suffering and shame.

Similarly, a Kabbalist develops in the self a feeling of anxiety, that not enough is done for the Creator. This feeling is just as constant and as great as the egoist's fear of punishment for obvious transgressions.

"A person learns only that which one desires to learn." ("A person learns only at the place where his heart desires.") Starting from this supposition, it becomes clear that a person will never learn to observe certain rules and norms unless that person desires it. But who wants to listen to moralizing, especially since, most often, one does not perceive one's own shortcomings? How, then, can anyone, even the individual aspiring to self-correction, attain that goal?

A human being is created in such a way that there is only one desire: to gratify the self. Thus people learn only for the sake of finding a means to satisfy their desires, and will not learn something that does not concern gratifying themselves, because that is our nature.

Therefore, in order that those who wish to approach the Creator can learn how to act "for the sake of the Creator," they must ask Him to grant them new hearts, replacing egoism with altruistic desires. If the Creator will grant this request, then wherever they learn, they will find ways of pleasing Him.

However, we will never perceive anything that is in contrast to our hearts, be it altruistic or egoistic, and will never feel obligated to do something that will not please our hearts. But once the Creator alters the egoistic heart to an altruistic one, we will immediately realize our obligations, in order to be able to correct ourselves with the aid of the newly acquired attributes, as well as to discover that there is nothing more important in this world than to please the Creator.

In addition, the qualities that we had seen as our shortcomings will transform into virtues, because by correcting them we bring pleasure to the Creator. But those who are not yet ready to correct themselves will not be able to see their own shortcomings, because they are revealed to us only to the degree that we are able to correct them.

All human actions with respect to the gratification of personal needs, as well as all the work "for the sake of the self," disappear when one departs from this world. All that one cared about and suffered for vanishes in one moment.

Therefore, if we are able to evaluate whether it is worth it to work for something in this world and then lose it in the very last moment of our lives, then we may conclude that it is preferable to work "for the sake of the Creator." This decision will make us realize the necessity of asking the Creator for help, especially if we have invested a great amount of effort into observing the commandments with the anticipation of gaining some personal benefit from doing so.

One who did not toil greatly in Kabbalah has a lesser desire to transform one's actions into actions "for the sake of the Creator," since this person does not have such a great deal to lose, while the work of transforming the self requires great effort.

For this reason, a person must endeavor with all the means at one's disposal to intensify efforts in the work, *lishma* , "not for the Creator's sake," because this will subsequently lead to the development of the desire to return to the Creator, and then to work, *lishma*, for His name.

29

Transformation of Our Nature

Every feeling we have emanates from Above. If we experience a striving, a love, and a pull towards the Creator, it is a sure indication that the Creator is experiencing the same feelings towards us (in accordance with the rule that "Man is a shadow of the Creator"). Thus, whatever a person feels toward the Creator is the same as what the Creator feels toward that person, and vice versa.

After Adam's spiritual fall as a result of his sin (which symbolizes the spiritual descent of the primordial soul from the world of *Atzilut* to the level known as "this world" or "our world"), his soul divided into 600,000 distinct parts. These parts clothed themselves into the human bodies that are born into this world. Each part garbs itself in a human body as many times as it is necessary for it to correct itself completely.

When all the distinct individual parts complete their independent process of correction, they will once again merge into one collective soul, known as "Adam."

In the alternating of the generations there is the cause, known as "the fathers," and the effect, known as "the sons." The reason for the appearance of sons is to continue the correction of that which has not been corrected by the fathers, meaning the souls of the previous incarnation.

The Creator brings us close to Him not because of our good qualities, but because of our feelings of lowliness and our desire to cleanse ourselves of our "filth." If we were to experience pleasure from the state of spiritual exhilaration, we might reason that it is worthwhile to serve the Creator to gain such sensations.

Therefore, the Creator usually removes pleasure from one's spiritual state in order to reveal why one is seeking spiritual elevation: either from the wish to serve, to receive the pleasures that would come while doing so, or because of one's faith in the Creator. In this manner, a person is given a chance to act for other than the sake of pleasure.

The removal of pleasure from any spiritual state immediately plunges one into a state of depression and despair, in which there is no desire for spiritual work. However, it is in this state that one gets a real chance to move closer to the Creator by virtue of faith above reason.

Feeling despair helps one realize that the present lack of attraction towards the spiritual is merely one's subjective perceptions. In reality, there is nothing greater than the Creator.

From the above, we can conclude that the Creator deliberately prepares a spiritual fall to elevate us quickly to an even higher level.

This is also an opportunity to increase our faith. Thus, it is said: "The Creator prepares the cure before the illness" and also, "With the same thing that the Creator strikes, He also cures."

Although every endeavor to remove our life force and our life interest shakes our entire being, if we truly desire to ascend spiritually, we will welcome the chance to uphold faith above reason. By so doing, we will affirm our wish to liberate ourselves from personal pleasures.

A human being is usually self-absorbed, focusing on personal feelings and thoughts of suffering and pleasure. But when striving to attain spiritual perception, we must refocus our interests on selfless matters, into the space filled by the Creator, so that the existence and desires of the Creator are one's total life focus.

We must correlate all that happens with His design; we must transfer ourselves into Him, so that only our bodily shells remain within the physical bounds.

However, our inner feelings, the essence of the person and of the self, all that is designated as the soul, must be transferred "outside" the body. Only then will we constantly feel the force of goodness that permeates all of creation. This feeling is akin to faith above reason, because we attempt to transfer all our feelings outside, beyond the boundaries of our bodies.

Once we attain faith in the Creator, we must remain in this state regardless of the obstacles that the Creator may send, to increase our faith and gradually begin to receive the Light of the Creator into the vessel created through faith.

The entire creation is built on the interaction between two opposite forces: egoism, the desire to receive pleasure, and altruism, the desire to please. The path of gradual correction is the experience of transforming our egoistic desires into the opposite desires, and this path is built by combining the two forces.

Gradually, small quantities of egoistic desires merge with the altruistic desires and are thereby corrected. This method of transforming our nature is known as "the work in three lines." The right line is called "the white line" because it contains no faults or defects.

After we have gained possession of the right line, we can obtain the greatest part of the left line, the so-called "red line," which contains our egoism. There is a prohibition against the use of egoism in spiritual actions, since it is possible for us to fall under its influence.

The impure forces/desires strive to receive the Light of Wisdom, *Ohr Hochma*, for their own sake, to perceive the Creator and to indulge in self-gratification, using these perceptions to satisfy egoistic desires. If we, by virtue of faith above reason, (by striving to receive, but not into our egoistic desires), refuse the possibility of perceiving the Creator, His actions, and His domain, and refuse the gratification from His Light; if we decide to go beyond our natural aspirations to know and to experience everything, to get prior knowledge of everything, to know what reward we will receive for our actions; then we will no longer be bound by the prohibition of using the left line.

When we choose this course, it is called "the creation of a shadow," because we are isolating ourselves from the Light of the Creator. In this case, we have the option of taking a small part of our left desires and connecting them with the right.

The resulting combination of strengths and desires is known as "the middle line." It is precisely in this line that the Creator reveals Himself. Subsequently, this whole process repeats itself on a higher spiritual level, and so on, until the end of the path.

The difference between hired help and a slave is that in the process of working, the hired help thinks of the reward that will be received for the work; the size of the reward is known, and it serves as the reason for that person's work. The slave, on the other hand, does not receive any reward, but only the bare necessities for survival. A slave owns nothing; the master owns all. Therefore, if a slave works hard, it indicates the slave's desire to please the master, to do something nice for him.

Our goal is to feel towards our spiritual work the way a slave does who works without any reward.

Our spiritual journey should not be influenced by any fear of punishment or any anticipation of reward, but only by a selfless desire to carry out the Will of the Creator.

Moreover, we should not even anticipate perceiving Him as the result, because that, too, is a form of reward. We should carry out His Will without wanting Him to know that we did it for His sake, without even thinking that anything special has actually been done for His sake, without seeing the results of our work, but only having faith that the Creator is pleased with us.

If our work should truly be as described above, then we should eliminate notions of reward and punishment completely from consideration. In order to understand this, it is necessary to know what Kabbalah means by the notions of reward and punishment.

We receive a reward when we exert a certain amount of effort to obtain something we desire. As a result of these efforts, we receive or find that which is desired. A reward cannot be something that exists in abundance in our world and is accessible to everyone else. Work translates into our efforts towards receiving a particular reward, which we cannot obtain without these efforts.

For instance, one can hardly claim to have performed "work" by finding a stone, if stones are in abundance all around. In such a case, there is no work and no reward. On the other hand, in order to possess a small precious stone, one must exert a great effort, because it is very hard to find. In such a case, real efforts are made, and a reward is received.

30

Fear of the Creator

The Light of the Creator fills all of creation. Although we swim inside this Light, we cannot perceive it. The pleasures that we feel are but tiny rays, which, with the Creator's mercy, reach us; since without any pleasure we would end our existence.

We feel these rays as forces that attract us to certain objects, into which the rays enter. The objects themselves are of no consequence, which becomes evident to us when, at some point, we stop being interested in things that once posed a great attraction to us.

The reason for receiving only the small amount of Light, rather than the entire Light of the Creator, is that our egoism acts as a barrier. If our egoistic desires are present, we cannot perceive the Light, due to the law of the congruence of qualities, the law of likeness.

Two objects can perceive each other only to the degree to which their qualities coincide.

Even in our own world, we can see that if two people are on completely different levels of thought and desire, they cannot understand each other.

Thus, an individual possessing the qualities of the Creator would simply be immersed in the unbounded ocean of pleasure and complete knowledge.

But if the Creator fills everything with Himself, and there is no need to look for Him as for some precious object, then, evidently, He does not merit consideration as a "reward." Similarly, we cannot apply the concept of work to the search for Him, since He is around us and inside us.

We may not perceive Him, but He is within us, within our faith. At the same time, once we perceive Him, and receive pleasure from Him, it cannot be said that we were rewarded. After all, if there is no work done, and the object in question is found in abundance in the whole world, then this object cannot be considered a reward.

The question remains, then, what is our reward for resisting our egoistic nature?

First, we must understand why the Creator instituted the law of congruence. As a result of this, though He fills everything, we are unable to perceive Him because He conceals Himself from us.

The answer to the question: "What is our reward for resisting our egos?" is as follows: The Creator instituted the Law of Congruence. This enables us to perceive only those objects on our own spiritual level. Thus, we are prevented from experiencing the most dreadful feeling from our egoism (that is the nature of the creations) when we receive pleasure from Him—since along with the pleasure the feelings of shame and humiliation set in.

Egoism cannot withstand this feeling. If we are unable to justify bad actions to ourselves or to others; if we are unable to find any extraneous circumstances that have supposedly forced us, against our will, to carry out the bad deed; then we prefer any other punishment except the feeling of humiliation of the "self," because the "self" is the pillar of our existence. Once it is humiliated, the "self" disappears spiritually; it is as if we had disappeared from this world.

But when we reach such a level of understanding that our only desire is to give everything to the Creator, and when we are constantly preoccupied with the thought of what else we can do for the sake of the Creator, then we will discover that we were created in order to receive pleasure from the Creator, and the Creator desires only that. At that point, we receive all possible pleasures because we want to carry out the Will of the Creator.

In such a case, there is no place for feelings of shame, because the Creator shows us that He wishes to give us pleasure, and He wants us to accept it. Thus, by accepting, we are carrying out the Will of the Creator, rather than personal egoistic desires. As a result, we become analogous to the Creator in qualities, and the screen disappears. All this ensues because we have reached the spiritual level at which we can give pleasure, just like the Creator.

From the above, we can conclude that our reward for efforts made should consist of receiving new, altruistic qualities—desires to "give" and aspirations to provide pleasure—similar to the desires of the Creator toward us. This spiritual level and these qualities are known as "fear of the Creator."

Spiritual, altruistic fear, like all other anti-egoistic qualities of spiritual objects, is completely unlike any of our qualities or perceptions. "Fear of the Creator" is the fear of being pushed away from the Creator. This arises not from calculations of selfish benefit, nor from fear of being left with egoism, nor from fear of becoming similar to the Creator. All of these are based on notions of personal benefit and take into consideration only one's own state.

The fear of the Creator is a selfless concern about not being able to do something that could have been done for the sake of the Creator. Such fear is itself an altruistic quality of a spiritual object, in contrast to our egoistic fear, which is always connected to our inability to satisfy our own needs.

Attaining the quality of fearing the Creator should be the cause and the goal of our efforts.

We should put all of our strength into this endeavor. Then, with the aid of the attained qualities, we can receive all the pleasures that were in store for us. Such a state is known as "the completing of the correction" (*gmar tikkun*).

Our fear of the Creator should precede our love for the Creator. The reason for this is as follows. In order for us to fulfill our obligations from a sense of love; in order to recognize the pleasure contained in the spiritual actions known as "commandments"; in order for these pleasures to invoke the feeling of love (since in our world we love that which brings us pleasure, whereas we hate that which brings us suffering); we should first attain the fear of the Creator.

If we observe the commandments from fear, rather than from feelings of love or pleasure, it means that we do not perceive the pleasure that is concealed in the commandments, and that we are carrying out the Will of the Creator from fear of punishment. The body does not resist this task because it also fears punishment, but it constantly asks about the reason for performing the tasks at hand.

In turn, this gives us a reason to increase our fear and our belief in punishment and reward inherent in the Creator's domain, until we begin to constantly perceive the existence of the Creator. Having acquired the feeling of the Creator's existence, that is, having attained faith in Him, we can begin to carry out the Will of the Creator from a feeling of love, since we have acquired the taste for, and found pleasure in, observing the commandments.

On the other hand, if the Creator permitted us to observe the commandments from the feeling of love from the very beginning, thus bypassing fear and only receiving pleasure from the task, we would never develop faith in the Creator.

We can compare this to the people who spend their entire lives chasing worldly pleasures, and have no need for faith in the Creator to observe the commandments (the laws) of their nature, since their nature compels them to this task by promising a reward.

Therefore, Kabbalists who perceived the pleasure to be attained from following the spiritual laws of the Creator from the very beginning, would involuntarily observe them, just as others would rush to fulfill the Will of the Creator just for the sake of the tremendous rewards concealed in the way of Kabbalah. Then, no one would ever be able to come closer to the Creator.

For this reason, the pleasures contained in the spiritual laws and in the way of Kabbalah as a whole, are concealed. (The Light is the pleasure that is hidden in each spiritual law; the Light of the Creator is the sum of all the spiritual laws). These pleasures are revealed only when one attains a state of constant faith in the Creator.

31

A Seed of Altruism

How can a human being—who was created with the qualities of absolute egoism; who feels no desires save those dictated by the body; who cannot even imagine anything outside of one's own perceptions—how can a human being proceed beyond the desires of the body and grasp something that exists outside the realm of one's natural sensory organs?

We are created with a longing to fill our egoistic desires with pleasure. Given such a condition, we have no possible way to alter ourselves and transform our egoistic qualities into opposite ones. In order for us to create the possibility of transforming our egoism into altruism, the Creator, when devising egoism, placed into it a seed of altruism, which we are capable of cultivating by studying and acting according to the methods of Kabbalah.

When we feel the dictating desires of our bodies, we are unable to stand up to them. Thus, all our thoughts are directed toward carrying out the commands of the body. In such a state, we have no freedom of will to act, or even to think about, anything other than self-gratification.

On the other hand, during our spiritual elevation we experience aspirations toward spiritual growth and toward departure from the physical desires that pull us down. At these times, we do not even perceive the desires of the body and, hence, do not require the right to a free choice between the material and the spiritual.

Consequently, by remaining in the state of egoism, we do not possess the strength to choose altruism. But once we perceive the grandeur of the spiritual, we no longer face a choice, since we already desire the spiritual.

Therefore, the entire notion of free will consists of a choice: Which force will dominate us, egoism or altruism? But when does such a neutral state occur in which we are able to make a free choice?

Thus, there is no other path for us but to attach ourselves to a teacher, to delve into Kabbalah books, to join a group that aspires to reach the same goals, to open ourselves to the influence of thoughts about altruism and spiritual strength. Consequently, the altruistic seed will awaken in us the seed, which was implanted in each of us, but which sometimes remains dormant for many life cycles.

This is the essence of our free will. Once we begin to feel the awakened altruistic desires, we will try to perceive the spiritual without much effort. A person who strives to attain spiritual thoughts and actions, but is not yet firmly attached to certain personal convictions, must protect himself from contact with people whose thoughts are rooted in their egoism.

This is especially true of those who aspire to live by faith above reason. They must avoid all contact with the opinions of those who travel through life within the bounds of their reason, because they are opposite in philosophy to Kabbalah. It has been said in the books of Kabbalah that the reason of ignoramuses is opposite to the reason of Kabbalah.

"Thinking within the bounds of our own reason implies that, first and foremost, we calculate the benefits of our actions. On the other hand, the reason of Kabbalah—faith above human reason—assumes that our actions will not be connected in any manner with the egoistic calculations of reason, or with the possible benefits that may ensue from these actions.

Those who need help from others are considered to be poor. Those who are happy with what they have are considered to be rich. But when we recognize that egoistic desires *(libba)* and thoughts *(moha)* drive all our actions, we suddenly understand our true spiritual state, and realize the power of our egoism and the evil inside us.

Our feelings of bitterness when we realize our true spiritual state give rise to the desire to correct ourselves. When this desire reaches the required degree of intensity, then the Creator sends His Light of Correction into the *kli* (vessel), and thus we begin to ascend the levels of the spiritual ladder.

People in general are raised in agreement with their egoistic natures, including observing the commandments of the Bible, and they continue to automatically uphold the notions they acquired from their upbringing. This makes it unlikely that they will ever depart from this particular level of connection with the Creator.

Thus, when our bodies (desire to receive) ask why we are observing the commandments, we reply that this was how we were brought up; it is the accepted way of life for us and our community. With upbringing as our base, habit has become second nature, and we require no effort to perform natural actions, since they are dictated both by body and mind.

Thus, there is no risk of transgressing that which is most familiar and natural. For example, an observant Jew will not suddenly have a desire to drive on Saturday. But if we wished to behave in a way unnatural to our upbringing, and not perceived by our being as a natural need of the body, even the least significant action would generate from the body the question: Why are we engaging in this activity and what prompted us to leave the state of relative tranquility to do so?

In this case, we will be confronted by a test and a choice, because neither we, nor the society from which we come, engages in the actions that we plan to undertake. There is no one who could serve as an example and no one to support our intentions.

It is not even possible to gain comfort in the thought that others also think along the same lines as we do. Since we cannot find any example either in our own upbringing or in society, we must come to the conclusion that it is the fear of the Creator that prompts us to act and think in a new fashion. Thus, there is no one to turn to for support and under-standing, except the Creator.

Since the Creator is One and is our only support, we are also considered to be unique, and not part of the masses among which we were born and raised. Since we can find no support in the masses and are solely dependent on the mercy of the Creator, we become worthy of receiving the Light of the Creator, which serves to guide us along our path.

Every beginner comes across one common question: Who decides the direction of one's path, the person or the Creator?

In other words, who chooses whom: *Does a person choose the Creator, or does the Creator choose the person?*

From one point of view, one must say that it is the Creator Who chooses an individual by virtue of what is known as *"personal providence."* As a result, one must be thankful to the Creator for providing an opportunity to do something for His sake.

But on considering why the Creator chose this particular individual, offering this unique opportunity, the question arises: why observe the commandments? For what purpose?

Now, the individual concludes that this opportunity was given to encourage action for the sake of the Creator, that the work itself is its own reward, and that distancing from this work would be a punishment. Taking on this work is now the person's free choice, to serve the Creator; therefore, one is prepared to request help from the Creator—to strengthen the intention that all actions undertaken will benefit the Creator. This is the free choice that a person makes.

32

Battling for the Perception of the Creator's Oneness

In Kabbalah, the masses are known as the "homeowners" (*ba'al bait*), because they aspire to build their own house (an egoistic vessel, *kli*) and fill it with pleasure. The desires of one who is ascending spiritually stem from the Light of the Creator, and focus on the task of building a home for the Creator in one's heart, in order for it to be filled with the Light of the Creator.

We discern all notions and all events according to our own perceptions. We assign names to the events that take place in accordance with the reactions of our sensory organs. Thus, if we speak about a particular object or action, we are expressing how we personally perceive it.

Each of us determines the level of evil in a particular object according to the degree to which that object obstructs our reception of pleasure. In certain cases, we cannot tolerate any proximity to a certain object. Thus, our level of understanding of the importance of Kabbalah and its laws will determine the evil that we will discern in that which stands in the way of our observance of the spiritual laws.

Therefore, if we wish to reach the level of hatred toward all evil, we must work on extolling Kabbalah and the Creator in our minds. In this way, we will cultivate within us love toward the Creator, and to the same degree we will develop hatred toward egoism.

In the Passover reading, there is a story of four sons, each of whom asks a question in regard to one's spiritual work. Though all four qualities are present in each of us, and though Kabbalah usually speaks of a single composite image of a person in relation to the Creator, nevertheless, the four qualities can be examined as four distinct types of personalities.

Kabbalah is given to help us focus on our struggle with egoism. If we have no questions about our own nature, it means we have not yet come to realize our own evil; and hence have no need for Kabbalah. In this case, if we believe in reward and punishment, we can be aroused by the idea that there is a reward for observing the spiritual laws.

But if we already act in order to be rewarded, but still do not feel our own egoism, we cannot correct ourselves because we have no sense of our own defects. Then, we need to learn to observe the commandments selflessly. As a result, our egoism will appear, and will ask:

"What is the purpose of this work?"

"What will I gain from it?"

What if it goes contrary to my wishes?"

At that point, we will need the help of Kabbalah to begin the work against our egoism, since we have begun to feel the evil in ourselves.

There is a particular spiritual force—an angel—that is responsible for generating suffering in a person in order to make it clear that one cannot be satisfied by gratifying one's egoism. This suffering prompts one to digress from the bounds of egoism and thus avoid remaining a slave to it forever.

It is said that prior to giving the Bible to Israel, the Creator offered it to all the other nations of the world, and they all refused it. Each of us is like a miniature world that consists of a multitude of desires, which are called "nations."

We must know that none of our desires are suitable for spiritual ascent, except the desire to advance toward the Creator; this desire is known as "Israel" (from the Hebrew words *yashar*, straight, and *El*, God, meaning "straight to the God"). Only by choosing this desire over all the others can that individual receive the hidden wisdom of Kabbalah.

The concealment of one's spiritual level is one of the imperative conditions of a successful spiritual ascent.

Concealment of this type implies the performance of actions so that they are not noticeable to others.

Most important, however, is the concealment of a person's thoughts and aspirations. If a situation arises in which a Kabbalist must express a point of view, it must be blurred and expressed in very general terms, so that the Kabbalist's true intentions do not become clear.

For example, let us suppose that a person makes a large donation in support of Kabbalah lessons, but also puts forth a condition that a public acknowledgment of the donor be printed in the newspaper. Mention would also be made of the large sum of money given, in order for the donor to receive fame and thereby to receive pleasure.

However, even though it seems clear that honor is the main desire of the donor, it is also possible that the donor wishes to disguise the fact that the newspaper article will advance the spreading of Kabbalah. Thus, concealment generally takes place in intentions, rather than in actions.

If the Creator must send a Kabbalist a feeling of spiritual decline, then, first, He will take away the Kabbalist's faith in other great Kabbalists. Otherwise, the Kabbalist could receive encouragement from them, and thus never come to experience the spiritual decline.

The multitudes that observe the commandments are only concerned with their own actions, but not with their intentions. It is clear to them that they observe for the sake of the reward, either in this world or in the next. They always have a justification for their actions and they perceive themselves to be righteous.

On the other hand, a Kabbalist who works on correcting innate egoism attempts to control every intention to observe the commandments. While the desire may be to carry out the Will of the Creator selflessly, the body will oppose this, along with constantly obstructing thoughts. Consequently, the Kabbalist will feel like a sinner.

All this is done for a purpose. The Creator wants to prompt the Kabbalist to engage in constant correction of both thoughts and intentions. Thus, the Kabbalist will not remain enslaved by egoism; and not continue to toil for the sake of the self, as do others, and will realize that there is no other way to carry out the Will of the Creator, except for His sake.

It is from this process that the Kabbalist derives a very intense feeling of being worse than the masses. For the masses, their inability to grasp their true spiritual state is the underlying cause of the physical observance of commandments.

But a Kabbalist is obligated to transform egoistic intentions to altruistic ones—or be unable to observe the commandments altogether.

For this reason, the Kabbalist sees himself as even worse than the masses.

An individual is constantly in a state of war for compliance with his desires. But there is a war of an opposite nature, in which an individual battles against the self in order to relinquish the entire territory of the heart to the Creator, and to fill the heart with one's natural enemy—with altruism.

The aim of this battle is to ensure that the Creator should occupy the entire being of the person, not only because this is the Divine Will, but also because this is desired by the person; thus, the Creator should govern and guide us because we request this of Him.

In such a battle, we must first and foremost *stop equating the self with the body*, and realize that the body, the intellect, the thoughts, and emotions—all these are external attributes sent by the Creator to get us to turn to the Creator for help; to ask the Creator to overcome these attributes; to plead for the Creator to strengthen the idea of His Oneness; to reinforce the knowledge that it is He Who sends all thoughts to us; to pray that the Creator should send faith and the feeling of His Presence and His Dominion.

In this way, all thoughts to the contrary will be silenced. No longer will we believe that everything is dependent on the individual, or that in this world there is a will and a force other than the Creator.

For example, irrespective of the fact that we might know that the Creator created everything and has dominion over everything (the right line), we may still think that a certain other person did something bad to us, or may do something bad (the left line).

On the one hand, we are convinced that all actions emanate from a single Source—the Creator (the right line). On the other hand, we cannot suppress the thought that someone else is affecting us, or that the outcome of an event is conditional on something other than just the Creator (the left line).

Such internal collisions between opposing perceptions occur for various reasons, depending on our social ties, until the moment the Creator helps us attain the middle line. The battle takes place for our perception of the Creator's Oneness, while the obstructing thoughts are sent to battle precisely these thoughts. We battle for victory with the help of the Creator, and for the attainment of greater perception of His Dominion, that is, the attainment of greater faith.

Our natural war centers on gratifying our egoism and on seizing greater gains, like all wars in our world. However, the meta-war—the war against our own nature—focuses on relinquishing the domain over ourselves to the "enemy"—the Creator. The meta-war attempts to surrender the entire territory in our minds and hearts to the control of the Creator, so that the Creator could fill the territory with Himself, and conquer the entire world, both the little world of the individual, and the greater world as a whole, and endow all creations with His qualities, but in accordance with their will.

A condition in which the desires and the qualities of the Creator occupy all a person's thoughts and desires is known as "an altruistic condition." This includes: a condition of "giving," a condition of surrendering one's physical soul to the Creator, and a condition of spiritual return (*teshuva*). All these conditions come under the influence of the Light of Grace (*Ohr Hassadim*), which emanates from the Creator and gives us strength to withstand the obstructing thoughts of the body.

The above condition may not necessarily be constant. We may overcome certain obstructions in our thoughts, but then a new wave of thoughts may push us back. We may, once again, fall under their influence and develop doubts with respect to the Creator's Oneness; once again, we will have to struggle with these thoughts; once again, we will feel the need to turn to the Creator for help and to receive Light, in order to overcome these thoughts, and to surrender them to the Rule of the Creator.

The condition in which we receive pleasure for the sake of the Creator, that is, not only surrender to our "enemy," the Creator, but also switch to His side, is known as "receiving for the sake of the Creator." The natural order of our choice of actions and thoughts is such, that either consciously or subconsciously, we always choose the path that will award us greater pleasures. A person will scorn smaller pleasures for the sake of the greater ones.

There is no free will or free choice in this process. The right to choose and the freedom to decide appear only at the time when we decide to reach decisions based on the criterion of truth, rather than on pleasure. This occurs only when we decide to proceed by way of truth, despite the suffering it brings.

However, the natural inclination of the body is to avoid suffering and seek pleasure by any means.

This tendency will obstruct a person from making decisions based on the principle of truth. The person who aspires to carry out the Will of the Creator must place all personal desires below the desires of the Creator.

Instead, one must *constantly* concern oneself with perceiving the grandeur of the Creator to gain sufficient strength to carry out the Will of the Creator, rather than one's own will.

The degree to which we believe in the greatness and strength of the Creator will determine our ability to fulfill the Creator's desires. Thus, we must concentrate all our efforts on grasping the grandeur of the Creator. Since the Creator wishes us to feel pleasure, He created in us the desire to be gratified. There is no other quality in us besides this desire. It dictates our every thought and action and programs our existence.

Egoism is known as an evil angel, an evil force, because it regulates us from Above by sending us pleasure, and unwittingly we become its slaves. The state of compliant submission to this force is known as "*slavery*," or "*exile*" (*galut*) from the spiritual world.

If egoism, this evil angel, had nothing to give, it would not be able to attain dominion over a human being. At the same time, if we could forsake the pleasures offered by egoism, we would not be enslaved by those pleasures. Thus, we are not able to depart from the state of slavery; but if we attempt to do so, which is considered to be our free choice, then the Creator will help from Above by removing the pleasures with which egoism entices us.

As a result, we can depart from egoism's domain and become free. Moreover, by coming under the influence of pure spiritual forces, we experience pleasure in altruistic actions and become instead a servant of altruism.

Conclusion: We as individuals are slaves to pleasure. If we derive our pleasure from receiving, then we are slaves of egoism (of pharaoh, of the evil angel, etc.). If we derive our pleasure from bestowing, then we are servants of the Creator (of altruism).

But we cannot exist without receiving some form of pleasure. This is the human essence; this is the way the Creator has designed human beings, and this aspect cannot be altered. All we must do is ask the Creator to bestow upon on us a desire for altruism. This is the essence of our free will and of our prayer.

33

Receiving for the Sake of Giving

A correct (effective) way to address the Creator is composed of two stages. First, one must understand that the Creator is absolutely kind to all beings, without exception, and all His actions are benevolent, irrespective of how unpleasant they may appear.

Therefore, the Creator sends us only what is best for us, and fills us with all that is most necessary.

Thus, we have nothing to ask of the Creator. We should be content with what we receive from the Creator, regardless of the state we may be in. We must also be thankful to the Creator and must glorify Him: There is nothing that can be added to our personal state, because we should be happy with our lot.

We must always first thank the Creator for all that we have received in the past. Then, we can ask for the future. But if we feel a lack of something in life, then we are removed from the Creator to the same degree as our perception of deficiency. This occurs because the Creator is absolutely perfect, whereas we might see ourselves as unhappy.

Thus, when we begin to feel that what we have is the best that we could have, since this is precisely the state that the Creator has sent us, then we come closer to the Creator, and can ask for something for the future.

The state of "being happy with one's lot" may arise in us simply by realizing that the circumstances of our lives are not a consequence of our own actions, but are sent by the Creator. This state may also arise because we realize that we are reading a book that deals with the Creator, with immortality, with the supreme goal in life, with the benevolent purpose of creation.

It also deals with the method of asking the Creator to alter our lives, as well as the realization that millions of other people in this world do not receive the opportunity to experience all these things. Thus, those who want to perceive the Creator, but have not yet been awarded this objective, should be content with their condition because it comes from the Creator.

Since these people still have unfulfilled desires (despite being content with what the Creator has decided to give them, and are thus close to Him), they become worthy of receiving the Light of the Creator, which will bring them full knowledge, understanding, and pleasure.

In order to separate ourselves spiritually from egoism, we must come to realize our own insignificance, the baseness of our interests, aspirations, and pleasures; we must also be aware to what extent we are willing to do everything just for our personal success, as well as, in all our thoughts, how we pursue only personal gain.

What is important when we feel our lowliness is that we recognize the truth: that personal gratification is more important to us than the Creator is, and if we do not see any personal benefit from our actions, we cannot carry these actions out, either in thought or in deed.

The Creator receives pleasure by giving pleasure to us. If we delight in the fact that it gives the Creator a possibility to delight us, then both we and the Creator coincide in qualities and in desires, because each is happy with the process of giving: The Creator gives pleasure, and we create the conditions to receive it. Each thinks of the other, but not of themselves, and this is what defines their actions.

But since human beings are born egoists, we are incapable of thinking about others, but only about ourselves. We can give only in the situation where we see immediate benefit from it, greater than the benefit being given away (as in the process of trade or bargaining). With respect to this quality, a human being is utterly distant from the Creator, and does not perceive Him.

This ultimate separation of a human being from the Creator—the Source of all pleasures—is caused by our egoism, and is the source of all our suffering. Realizing this is known as "the realization of the evil," because in order for us to be repelled from egoism by a hatred toward it, we must fully feel and recognize that it is all of our evil, the single most deadly enemy, that stands in the way of our being able to attain perfection, pleasure and immortality.

Thus, in all of our actions, be it the study of Kabbalah, or the observance of commandments, we must set as our goal the departure from egoism and the advance toward the Creator by virtue of coinciding in qualities. Only then will we be able to receive the same pleasure from altruistic acts as we received from our egoism.

If, with help from Above, we begin to receive pleasure from altruistic deeds, and in this we find happiness and our greatest reward, this state is known as "giving for the sake of giving" without any expected reward. Our gratification comes only from having the ability to do something for the Creator.

Once we have attained that spiritual level and wish to give something to the Creator, it becomes apparent to us that the Creator desires only one thing: to give pleasure to us. Then, we are ready to receive pleasure because such is the Will of the Creator. Actions of this nature are known as "receiving for the sake of giving."

In the spiritual states, one's intellect (reason, wisdom) corresponds to the Light of wisdom (*Ohr Hochma*). One's heart, desires, and feelings correspond to the Light of Mercy (*Ohr Hassadim*). Only when our hearts are ready to listen, can reason affect them. *Ohr Hochma* can illuminate only in the place where *Ohr Hassadim* is already present. If *Ohr Hassadim* is not present, then *Ohr Hochma* does not illuminate. Such a state is known as "darkness," or "night."

But in our world, that is, in an individual who still remains in the enslavement of egoism, reason can never hold domain over the heart, because the heart is the source of all desires. It, alone, is the sole master of the individual, whereas reason has no power to counter the desires of the heart.

For example, a person who wants to steal asks advice from reason, to determine how to carry it out. Thus, reason becomes the executor of the heart's desires. On the other hand, if a person decides to do a good deed, once again reason helps, just like all the other parts of the body. Hence, there is no other solution but to cleanse the heart of egoistic desires.

The Creator intentionally shows a person that His desire is to have that person receive pleasure, in order to offer the person the possibility to become freed from the shame of receiving. One forms a strong impression that by receiving pleasures "for the sake of the Creator;" one truly pleases Him, That is, the person gratifies the Creator, rather than receives pleasure from Him.

There are three types of work done by a person in Kabbalah and the commandments. In each type there are good aspirations and evil ones:

1. One studies for one's own sake, such as to become famous, so that those other than the Creator will pay honors and money for one's efforts. For this reason, one publicly engages in the study of Kabbalah in order to receive a reward.

2. One studies for the sake of the Creator to gain reward from the Creator in this world and in the world to come. In such a case, in order that people should not see one's work, all studies are done in private to avoid being given a reward for one's efforts. The only reward sought is from the Creator. Such a student would fear that rewards from others would become a distraction from the intention to be rewarded only by the Creator.

These intentions of one doing spiritual work are known as "for the sake of the Creator" because one works for the Creator, and observes the commandments of the Creator, to receive the reward only from Him. This is like the first case, in which a person was working for the people, fulfilled people's expectations by doing the work, and then demanded a reward for the performed tasks.

In both cases, the common dominator is the expectation and desire for a reward for work done. In the first case, one worked for people and expected a reward for the work done. In the second, one worked for the Creator and expected a reward from Him.

3. After the first two stages, a person realizes the degree of enslavement to the ego. The body (desire to receive) then begins to inquire: "What type of work is this? Where is the reward for it?" But one does not receive an answer to this question.

In the first stage, egoism does not pose any questions because it sees the reward for the work done from others' reactions. In the second stage, an individual can respond to egoism by stating that one desires a bigger reward than can be received from other people, that is, one desires eternal spiritual pleasures both in this and in the other world.

But in the third stage, when the Creator wants to bestow upon a person, one begins to realize the degree of one's enslavement to egoism, and can make no reply to the body. And the fact that the Creator wants only to give leads one to wish to do the same, and this will be the reward for one's actions.

A "reward" refers to that benefit which people desire to receive for their work. In general, we refer to it as "pleasure," whereas by "work" we mean any intellectual, physical or moral exertion of the body. A reward may also come in the form of money, honors, fame, etc.

When we feel that we lack any strength to withstand the body, that there is no energy to perform even the lightest of tasks, because the body cannot make any effort without seeing some reward in return, then there is no other alternative but to turn to the Creator for help. We must pray for some supernatural power that would allow one to work against one's nature and reason.

Thus, the most important problem is to believe in the fact that the Creator is able to help despite natural laws to the contrary, and that He is waiting for such requests. However, this decision can be reached only after one is completely disillusioned with one's own abilities.

The Creator desires that each person choose what is right, and should distance himself from what is wrong.

Otherwise, the Creator would have made a human being with His own qualities, or, once having created egoism, He himself would have transformed it into altruism without the process of bitter exile from the state of Upper Perfection.

34

Suffering Sent As Absolute Kindness

Free will is the personal, independent decision of human beings to choose that the Creator should rule over us rather than Pharaoh. The power of Pharaoh consists of demonstrating to us the rewards we can receive. We clearly perceive the rewards that can be gained from our egoistic actions; we comprehend these rewards with our reason, and see them with our eyes. The result is known from the start; and is approved by society, by the family, by the parents, and by the children.

Hence, the body asks Pharaoh, "Who is the Lord that I should obey His voice?" (Exodus 5, 2), meaning, "What do I gain from work like this?"

We are thus correct when we see that it is impossible to advance against our own nature. But advancement itself is not the ultimate goal, but only the act of having faith in the Creator's ability to change us.

The Light of the Creator, His disclosure to a human being, is known as "life."

The first instance of the permanent perception of the Creator is known as "the spiritual birth" of a person. But just as in our world a person possesses a natural desire to live, so in the spiritual world one is obligated to develop the same aspiration in oneself.

This is necessary if one truly desires to be born spiritually, in accordance with the principle "the suffering for pleasure determines the pleasure that is received." Therefore, we must study Kabbalah for the sake of Kabbalah; that is, to reveal the Light and the Creator. If one does not attain this objective, one feels tremendous suffering and bitterness. This condition is known as "a life of suffering." Yet one must, nevertheless, continue to exert effort. The fact that one did not attain the Revelation of the Creator should prompt that person to increase efforts until the Creator will reveal Himself.

It is clearly seen that it is human suffering that gradually gives rise to the real desire to attain the Revelation of the Creator. Such suffering is known as "the suffering of love." This suffering is worthy of anyone's envy! When the vessel is sufficiently filled with this suffering, the Creator will reveal Himself to the Kabbalists, those who acquired this desire.

Quite often, in order to complete a business deal, there is a need for a middle man, who can convey to the buyer a message that a certain object is worth even more than the price that is placed on that object. In other words, the seller is not inflating the price at all.

The entire method of "receiving admonition" (*mussar*) is based on this principle, which attempts to convince an individual to leave aside material considerations for the sake of the spiritual. All the books of *mussar* teach that all the pleasures of our world are spurious, and carry no value in them. Therefore, an individual is not really giving up anything significant when turning away from spiritual pleasures.

The method of Rabbi Baal Shem-Tov is somewhat different. A greater emphasis is placed on the object that is being bought. An individual is shown the infinite worth and grandeur of the spiritual acquisition. It is conceded that there is certain value in the pleasures of this world, but it is preferable if one would refuse them, since the spiritual pleasures are incomparably greater.

If an individual could remain in egoism and, at the same time, receive spiritual pleasures with the material ones, then the desires of that individual would constantly increase. As a result, the individual would move further away from the Creator due to an increasing disparity in qualities and their magnitude. Because the individual would not perceive the Creator, there would be no feelings of shame from the act of receiving pleasure.

One can receive pleasure from the Creator only by virtue of becoming similar to Him in qualities, which will immediately be countered by the body. This resistance will be experienced in the form of questions that will arise, such as:

"What did I gain from this work, even though I spent so much effort on it? "Why should I study so hard at night?"

"Is it truly possible to attain the perception of the spiritual and of the Creator to the degree that the Kabbalists describe?"

"Is it a task that can be carried out by an ordinary person?"

All that our egoism suggests is correct: A human being is not able to attain even the lowest of the spiritual levels without help. However, it can be done with the help of the Creator. The most difficult aspect, however, is to have faith in the Creator's help until it is received. The Creator's help in countering egoism comes as a Revelation of His grandeur and power.

If the grandeur of the Creator were revealed to everyone in our world, each person would do nothing but strive to please the Creator, even without any reward, because the opportunity to serve Him would be considered a reward in itself, and no one would request a reward. They would even refuse any additional reward.

But since the grandeur of the Creator is concealed from our eyes and senses, we are not able to accomplish anything for His sake. The body (our reason) considers itself more important than the Creator, since it senses only itself. Thus, it logically argues that if the body is more important than the Creator, then one should work for the body and to receive rewards.

But one should not work if there is no perceived benefit from the completed work. However, in our world we observe that only children during their games, or emotionally unstable people, are ready to toil without the anticipation of reward. In both cases, this occurs because people in both categories are forced into this line of action by their nature: children, for the sake of their development; emotionally unstable people, for the sake of correcting their souls.

Pleasure is a derivative of the desire that preceded it: appetite, suffering, passion, and hunger. A person who possesses everything is terribly unhappy because there is nothing more worth seeking for gratification. Hence, one may become depressed. If we were to measure a person's possessions by the perception of happiness, then poor people would be the richest, because even the most insignificant things please them.

The Creator does not reveal Himself immediately and all at once; this is so that a person will develop a complete and correct desire for His Revelation. This is precisely the reason that the Creator conceals Himself, in order that a person will develop a feeling of urgent necessity for the Creator. When one decides to advance toward the Creator, instead of feeling fulfillment from this choice and an enjoyment of the process of spiritual attainment, one plunges into circum-stances full of suffering.

This occurs specifically to prompt us to cultivate faith in the Creator's kindness above our own feelings and thoughts. Regardless of the suffering that suddenly descends upon us, we must overcome our thoughts about this suffering through internal exertion and force ourselves to think of the goal of creation. We should also consider our part in the scheme of things, even though neither the mind nor the heart are inclined to think of these issues.

We should not lie to ourselves and say that this is not suffering. But along with this we should believe, despite feelings to the contrary. This requires trying not to perceive the Creator or His Revelation, nor seeking clear knowledge of His thoughts, actions and plans in sending us the suffering. This could be similar to a bribe, a reward for the endured pain.

But all actions and thoughts should be directed not to the self or into the self; they should not be concentrated on the feelings of suffering, or on the thoughts of how to escape it. Instead, we should transfer our perception to outside our bodies, as if moving from the inside out. We should attempt to perceive the Creator and His design, not through our own hearts, but from the outside, distancing the self from the process, placing ourselves in the shoes of the Creator, accepting this suffering as the necessary precondition for increasing our faith in the Supreme Dominion, so that we do everything only for the sake of the Creator.

Having accomplished the above, we can earn the Revela-tion of the Creator, the perception of the Divine Light and of His true Dominion. This is because the Creator reveals Himself only to altruistic desires; only in thoughts other than those about self and personal problems; only in "outside" concerns, because only then is there a congruence of qualities between the Creator and ourselves.

But if we, in our hearts ask Him to spare us suffering, then we are in the state of a beggar, an egoist.

For this reason, we must discover positive feelings for the Creator. Only then can we receive a personal Revelation of the Creator.

It is necessary to remember that the concealment of the Creator and our suffering are the consequences of our egoistic shells, because the Creator emits only pleasure and clarity.

He does this on the condition that we create altruistic desires and completely reject egoism as a departure from our nature and from the feeling of the "self," the "I." All our sins stem from the refusal to advance by means of faith above reason. Consequently, we undergo constant suffering because the ground is being pulled from under our feet.

It is natural that, having invested much effort into our studies and into working on ourselves, we await a good reward. Instead, we receive only painful feelings of despair and critical situations. It is harder to resist pleasures from our altruistic deeds than from our egoistic deeds, because the magnitude of the pleasure itself is incomparably greater.

It is very difficult, even for an instant, to see intellectually that, in fact, this is the help of the Creator. The body, against all reasoning, cries of the necessity to rid itself of such a state. Only the help of the Creator can save us from the sudden problems that arise, but not by asking for a solution.

The answer is in praying for an opportunity, regardless of the demands of the body, to acquire faith above reason, to attain the feeling of agreement with the actions of the Creator, as it is only He Who has the domain over everything, and it is

He Who creates all circumstances in order to ensure our ultimate spiritual well-being.

All earthly torments, spiritual suffering, shame, and reprimands need to be tolerated by a Kabbalist on the path to the spiritual unification with the Creator. The history of Kabbalah is full of examples: Rashbi, Rambam, Ramchal, The Ari, etc.

But as soon as we are able to have faith above reason against our own perceptions; as soon as the suffering is interpreted as absolute kindness and the Will of the Creator to bring a person closer to Him; as soon as we accept our state and stop wanting to alter it so we can be filled with feelings pleasant for egoism; as soon as all these conditions take place, the Creator will reveal Himself to us in all His grandeur.

35

The Evil Inclination

According to Kabbalah, our bodies are only a temporary casing for an eternal soul that descends from Above, and that the cycle of life and death can be compared to the change of clothing by a person in our world. The soul changes one body for another just as easily as a person changes one set of clothes for another.

The definition of the Creator's selfless fulfillment of His Will, as well as the definition of being an altruist in both thought and action, embodies the process of self-evaluation and self-assessment, regardless of unpleasant events, feelings, or incidents that are purposely sent by the Creator to the person.

The process of self-evaluation should bring one to see how low one's state truly is, yet keep that person committed to the fulfillment of the Creator's Will, and to the aspiration of carrying out the direct and just laws of the spiritual world, contrary to one's "personal" well-being.

The desire to be similar to the Creator in one's qualities may derive from the suffering and trials one experiences, but it can also emanate from the perception of the Creator's grandeur. Then, an individual's choice involves asking the Creator for advancement by means of Kabbalah.

All the actions we undertake must be motivated by our intention to perceive the grandeur of the Creator, so that the perception and the realization of this aspect could help us become purer and more spiritual.

In order to advance spiritually, we must, at every level, be concerned with the development within us of our perception of the Creator's grandeur. We must realize that to attain spiritual perfection or even to remain at the spiritual level at which we exist, we need to cultivate a deeper understanding of the Creator's grandeur.

The worth of the gift is determined by the importance of the one who gives it. This is true to a great degree. For instance, an object that belongs to someone considered famous and important by society is often worth millions.

The worth of Kabbalah is also determined by the prominence of the One Who awards us Kabbalah. If one does not believe in the Creator, then Kabbalah is worth no more to that person than any other historical or literary document. But if one does believe in the power of Kabbalah and in its usefulness because one believes in the Upper Power, then the value of Kabbalah is immeasurably higher.

The more we believe in the Creator, the more value Kabbalah presents for us.

Consequently, every time we voluntarily submit to the Dominion of the Creator in accordance with the magnitude of our faith in Him, we also grasp the significance of Kabbalah and its inner meaning. In this manner, it can be said that each consecutive time we reach a higher spiritual level, we receive a new Kabbalah (Light), as if from a new Creator.

The above process refers only to those who receive a new Revelation of the Creator's Light as they ascend on the spiritual ladder. For this reason, it is said that "The righteous person lives by his faith"—the magnitude of one's faith determines the amount of the perceived Light.

It is written in the books of Kabbalah, "Every day is he awarding of the new Light." For a Kabbalist, every "day" (the time when the Light of the Creator radiates) is a new Light.

We may be brought up to observe the commandments, but it is impossible to educate us with the need to assign our actions particular altruistic intentions, since this cannot become part of our egoistic nature that could automatically be carried out just like our physical needs.

If we are permeated by the feeling that our war against egoism is a war against the forces of darkness, against the qualities that are opposite to those of the Creator, then in this manner we remove these forces from ourselves, and do not associate oneself with them; avoid them in our thoughts, as if departing from the desires of our own bodies.

Continuing to feel these desires, we begin to despise them, as one despises an enemy. In this manner, we can triumph over egoism, and at the same time find comfort from its suffering. An action of this type is known as "the war of vengeance for the sake of the Creator" (*nikmat hashem*). Gradually, we can get used to perceiving the right goals, thoughts, and intentions, regardless of the desires and egoistic demands of the body.

If, while studying, we do not see any personal benefit and begin to suffer from this lack of perceived benefit, this is known as "the *evil inclination*" (*yetzer ra*). The degree of evil is determined by our level of perception of evil, by the extent of our suffering from our lack of attraction to spirituality, unless we perceive in it a personal benefit.

The more we suffer from the unchanging situation, the greater the degree of our perception of evil. If we understand by reason that we are not yet succeeding in spiritual advancement, but this does not cause us pain, it means that we do not yet have an evil inclination (*yetzer ra*), since we are not yet suffering from evil.

If we do not feel evil, we must engage in the study of Kabbalah. But if we perceive evil in ourselves, we need to rid ourselves of it by faith above reason.

The definitions given above require explanations. It is written in the books of Kabbalah: "I created the evil inclination (force, desire) and I also created the *Torah* as a *tavlin* ("spice") for it (for its correction). *Tavlin* means spices, additives, supplements that make the food tasty and acceptable for consumption.

We see that the primary creation is the evil, the egoism. Kabbalah is only an addition to it, that is, the means that allows us to taste and to use evil. This is very peculiar, because it is also stated that the commandments are given only for the purpose of purifying the soul with their aid. This implies that once a person is purified, there will no longer be a need for commandments (spiritual acts in order to correct).

The true goal of creation is for the Creator to give pleasures to His created beings. For this purpose, the creatures are endowed with the desire to receive pleasure. In order for the creations not to experience feelings of shame when they receive pleasure, which would spoil the pleasure itself, the creations are given the opportunity to correct the feelings of shame.

This can be achieved if the created beings wish to receive nothing for themselves, but wish only to please the Creator. Only then will they not feel shame at receiving pleasure, since they will receive it for the sake of the Creator, rather than for their own gratification.

But what can be given to the Creator that would give Him pleasure? For this, the Creator gave us Kabbalah and the spiritual laws, so that we could observe them "for His sake." Then He can send us pleasures we can receive, that will not be diminished by feelings of shame and the insinuations of charity.

If we behave according to the spiritual laws, i.e. for the sake of the Creator, we are similar to the Creator in our actions, which are aimed at giving us pleasure. As our desires, acts, and qualities gain greater resemblance to those of the Creator, we and the Creator advance closer to one another. The Creator desires that we should give to Him, as He gives to us, in order for our pleasures not to be overshadowed by shame, and not to be seen as charity.

The spiritual desire—a desire that possesses all the conditions necessary to receive the Light determines the magnitude and type of pleasure that is received, because the Light of the Creator includes everything in itself, each one of our desires to be gratified by something. It isolates from the entire Light that which we desire.

The Creator prescribes precisely 613 commandments for the correction of the evil (in us) into the good (for us), because He created our desire for gratification from precisely 613 parts, and each commandment corrects a certain part or quality. For this reason it says, "I created the evil, and the *Torah* for its correction."

But what is the purpose of observing the *Torah* (the spiritual laws) after the correction of evil? The spiritual laws are given to us:

1. When we are still under the enslavement of our own nature and are unable to act for the sake of the Creator, because we remain distant from the Creator, due to the disparity in qualities. The 613 spiritual laws allow us to have the strength to depart from egoism.

2. At the end of the correction, when we are in a state of unity with the Creator due to the congruence of qualities and desires, we then become worthy of the Light of the *Torah*:

613 spiritual laws become a part of our spiritual body; they become the vessel of our soul, and into each of the 613 desires, we receive the Light of Pleasure.

As we see, at this stage, spiritual laws transform from the means of correction to the "place" of receiving pleasure (the vessel, *kli*).

36

The Work Along the Three Lines

In the left line, which brings about suffering as a result of the absence of the desired, is awakened a need for the help of the Creator, which comes in the form of Light of the soul. In the right line, in a state when a person desires nothing for the self, there exists only the Light of Mercy (*Ohr Hassadim*), the joy from the similarity in spiritual qualities. But this state is not perfect, because it lacks knowledge and the understanding of the inner meaning. In the left line is no perfection because the Light of Wisdom can illuminate only if there is congruence in qualities between the Light received and the recipient of the Light.

The congruence results in *Ohr Hassadim*, which is found in the right line. Spiritual gains can be made only by having a desire. But the right line has no desire for anything. All the desires are concentrated in the left line. However, the desired cannot be received into the egoistic desires.

Thus, it is necessary to unite these two qualities so that the Light of knowledge and pleasure of the left line can enter the Light of altruistic qualities of the right line, and the Light of the middle line will illuminate the created being. Without the Light of the right line, the Light of the left is not revealed and is perceived only as darkness.

Even when we are still enslaved by our own egoism, the work in the right and the left lines still takes place. However, we do not yet control our desires. Instead, the desires dictate our thoughts and actions, and prevent us from being filled with the Light of congruence with the Creator (*Ohr Hassadim*) and the Light of ultimate comprehension (*Ohr Hochma*).

Rather, we are only capable of pronouncing the names of the worlds, the *Sefirot* and *kelim*. In such a state, it is especially effective to study the construction of the spiritual worlds and their effects, that is, Kabbalah, to help us develop the desire to come closer to the Creator. In the process, we begin to desire to resemble the objects that are being studied, and hence, draw upon ourselves grace from the upper realms, though we do not perceive this process, due to the lack of spiritual senses.

But the spiritual forces affect us only if we are studying for the sake of coming closer (in qualities) to the spiritual. Only in this case do we bring upon us the purifying effect of the Surrounding Light. It can be observed in numerous cases, though, that without the proper guidance, we may know what is contained in the Kabbalah books, and may even engage in "meaningful" discussions on the topic.

Nevertheless, we may never truly grasp the emotional essence of what we learned. But those who attain spiritual levels through their own work, even the most insignificant, already exist in the shell of our world, and are engaged in the task for which they descended into this world.

On the other hand, the knowledge and the memory of the "smart ones" often increases their egoism and doubts, and thus pushes them further away from their goal.

This is because the Light derived from the study of Kabbalah can be a life-saving medicine (sam hachaim), or a deadly poison (sam hamavet).

Beginners cannot discern between those who truly perceive (Kabbalists) and those who study Kabbalah as just another social science. For beginners, *the work along the three lines* is focused on analyzing their own states, rather than on attaining the Upper Light, the focus of those who already perceive.

In the right line, also known as the state of "giving," *hesed*, or faith above reason, we are happy with the lot that was given to us, with our fate, and with what the Creator has given us, since we regard this as our greatest gift. This is regardless of the fact that we carry out the commandments of the Creator without grasping their inner meaning, but rather based on our own upbringing or the acceptance upon ourselves of certain obligations and self-education.

But this state is not yet considered as the right line because the left line is absent. Only when the opposite state appears can we speak of either one of the lines. Thus, only after we are inclined towards critically assessing ourselves, only after we appraise our own achievements, only after we determine the true goals of our lives, only when we critically appraise the results of our own efforts, only then will we obtain the left line.

What is important here is the goal of creation. We determine that, in essence, our goal is to receive pleasure from the Creator. At the same time, we feel that we have not experienced this even once.

In the course of our studies, we learn that this can occur only when a congruence of qualities exists between us and the Creator. Thus, we are obligated to examine our own desires and aspirations, to judge them as objectively as we can, to control and analyze everything, in order to determine if we are truly moving toward renouncing egoism and acquiring love for other people.

If as students we see that we remain in the state of egoistic desires and have not progressed toward a better condition, we often feel despair and apathy. Moreover, we sometimes discover that not only do we remain amidst our egoistic desires, but we find that they have increased since we acquired desires for pleasure that once we considered as low, petty, ephemeral, and unworthy.

It is clear that in this state it becomes difficult to continue to observe the commandments and to study with our previous joy; rather, we fall into despair and disappointment, and regret the time wasted, as well as efforts we made and deprivations we have suffered. We thus rebel against the goal of creation.

This state is known as "the left line" because it is in need of correction. We have now perceived our own emptiness and must turn to the right line, to the feelings of completeness, satisfaction, and full happiness with our lot. Previously, it was not considered that we were in the right line because we were still in one line, simply because there was no second line, and thus, no self-criticism existed.

But if, after a genuine realization of personal imperfection in the second line, we return to the first line, that is to the feeling of perfection (against our actual state and feelings), then we are considered to be acting along the two lines, not simply the first and the second, but along two opposite lines— the right and the left.

The entire path of renouncing egoism and departing from the narrow boundaries of personal interests is built on the basis of the right line. It is said that we must break away from "our own" interests, which are the ephemeral, petty and constantly changing desires of our bodies. They were given to us from Above not for accepting them as the goal of life, but so that we would renounce them for the sake of attaining eternal, supreme, absolute perceptions of spiritual pleasure, and uniting with the ultimately Supreme that exists in the universe, that is, with the Creator.

But to break away from personal thoughts and desires is impossible, since we do not perceive anything other than ourselves. One thing in our condition we may believe is in the existence of the Creator, in His complete Dominion, in the goal of His creation, in the necessity to reach this goal despite the complaints of our bodies.

A faith in that which is not perceived—the faith in something that is above our understanding—is known as "faith above reason."

Precisely after the left line it is time for us to pass into such a perception of reality as explained above.

We are happy to have merited carrying out the Will of the Creator, despite the fact that as a result of our egoistic desires, we have attained no pleasure or enjoyment from this. However, despite these feelings, we do believe that we have received a special gift from the Creator.

Thus, even though we are in such a state, nonetheless we are able to carry out the Creator's Will specifically in this manner; and not like most people who do it either to receive pleasure or as a result of their upbringing and education, without even being conscious of their mechanical acts.

We also realize that we are acting contrary to our bodies, that is, we are internally on the side of the Creator rather than on the side of the body. We believe that everything emanates from Above, from the Creator, through a special connection to us. Therefore, we value such a gift from the Creator, and draw inspiration from it, as if we were awarded the highest spiritual perception.

Only in such a case is the first line known as the right line, as perfection, because the joy comes to us not from our own condition but from the relation of the Creator to us that allowed us to act outside the boundaries of selfish egoistic desires. In such a state, though we may still be enslaved by egoism, we can receive spiritual illumination from Above.

Although the Upper Illumination has not yet entered us because Light cannot enter egoistic desires, this Light nevertheless surrounds us (*Ohr Makif*) and bonds us with the spiritual. It also helps us realize that even the most minute connection with the Creator is already a great reward and pleasure. As for the perception of the Light, we must tell ourselves that it is not in our power to appraise the actual value of the Light.

The right line is also called "the truth" because we can clearly understand that we have not yet attained the spiritual level, and do not lie to ourselves. Rather, we say that what we received comes from the Creator, even our most bitter conditions. Thus faith above reason is very valuable, because there is a contact with the Creator.

We can see, then, that the right line is built on the clear realization of the absence of spiritual perception and on the bitter feeling of personal worthlessness. This is followed by our departure from egoistic calculations toward actions based on the principle, "not what I will gain, but what the Creator desires."

If we realize that we are the object of special attention from the Creator, and that we possess a special relation to Kabbalah and to the commandments, while most others are busy with petty calculations related to the mundane concerns of life, then our considerations are reasonable.

Still, these considerations are the products of the intellect. They are not above reason. We must, however, tell ourselves that even though we are happy in the present state, we must proceed by faith above reason, so that our delight may be built on our faith.

The left line, on the other hand, is built on verifying the genuine nature of our love for other human beings; on determining if we are capable of altruistic actions, and of selfless deeds. It is also built on checking if we truly do not wish to receive any reward for our efforts.

If, after such calculations, we see that we are incapable of giving up our interests even to a small degree, then we have no choice but to beg the Creator for redemption. For this reason, the left line brings us to the Creator.

The right line gives us the possibility of thanking the Creator for the feeling of His perfection. But it does not give us a perception of his true state—the state characterized by absolute ignorance, and by the complete absence of the connection to the spiritual. Thus, it does not bring us to prayer, and without prayer it is impossible to comprehend the Light of Kabbalah.

In the left line, however, we attempt to overcome our true state with our own willpower, and thus come to realize that we do not possess sufficient strength for such a task. Only then do we begin to discern our need for help from Above, since we see that only supernatural powers can help us. Only through the left line can we attain the desired end.

But it is important to understand that the two lines must be balanced so that each is utilized equally. Only then will a middle line emerge, combining the right and the left line into a single line.

If one line is greater than the other, it will prevent the two from merging, since that line will perceive itself as more beneficial in a given situation. Thus, the two lines must be absolutely equal.

The benefit from this difficult task of increasing the two lines equally is in this, that on their foundation a person receives the middle line, the Upper Light, which is revealed and perceived specifically on the experiences of the two lines.

The right gives perfection because one believes in the perfection of the Creator. Since the Creator governs the world, just He and no one else, then if egoism were not to be taken into account, then a person is in perfection.

The left line gives a critical evaluation of one's state and a feeling of one's imperfection. It is of critical importance to be concerned that the left line should under no circumstances remain greater than the right. (In practical terms, an individual should spend 23.5 hours a day in the right line, and allow oneself only one half-hour to activate the egoistic deliberations).

The right line should be so pronounced that there should be no need for any other attributes in order to attain the feeling of absolute happiness. This process symbolizes the controlled departure from personal egoistic delibera- tions. Thus, it signifies perfection, since it requires nothing else to feel joy.

This occurs because all considerations pertain to all that is outside of the body—all that is together with the Creator, rather than to the inner needs of the body. Shifting to the left line involves a transition from the right line to the left, and back. We should consciously undertake it at a certain set time, and with certain preset conditions, not just according to our mood.

We then find that not only have we not progressed in our perception and understanding of the spiritual, but our normal daily lives have become worse than they had been previously. Instead of moving forward, we then withdraw even more to our egoism.

In such a state, we must immediately shift to prayer to correct our situation. On this, it is said in the Bible that the exodus from *Egypt* (egoism) occurred when they were in the very last, forty-ninth state of impure desires. Only when we completely realize all of the depth and evil of our egoism and cry for help, does the Creator elevate us, and give us the middle line, bestowing upon us a soul, Light of the Creator, from Above. This begins to illuminate us and gives us the powers to shift to altruism and to be born in the spiritual world.

37

Understanding Our True Nature

In order to attain the goal of creation, we need to feel a "hunger," without which we cannot taste the whole depth of the pleasures that are sent by the Creator, and without which we cannot bring gratification to the Almighty. Therefore, it is crucial to correct egoism. This would permit us to experience pleasure for the sake of the Creator.

In times of fear, we must understand the reason for which the Creator sends us these feelings. There is no force or power that rules in the world except the Creator; no enemies, or dark forces. However, it is the Creator Himself who forms in us a sensation like this, in order for us to wonder why we felt it so suddenly.

Then, as a result of our searching, we will be able, through an exertion of faith, to say that the Creator Himself sends this to us. If, after all our efforts, our fear does not subside, we must interpret it as an example of the degree to which we should experience the fear of the grandeur and the power of the Creator. To the same degree that our bodies are shaken by an imaginary source of fear in our world, so must we shudder at the fear of the Creator.

How can we determine precisely what spiritual state we are in? When we feel confident and happy, it is usually the result of having faith in personal strength, and thus not feeling that we are in need of the Creator. This state implies that, in fact, we are completely buried in the depths of our own egoism and are distanced from the Creator.

On the other hand, when we feel completely lost and helpless, we then experience a sharp need for the support of the Creator. At that time, we enter a much better state with regard to our own well-being.

If, after having exerted ourselves, we perform an act that appears to be "good," and consequently experience a feeling of satisfaction with ourselves, we immediately fall prey to our own egoism. We do not realize that it is the Creator who gave us a possibility to perform an act of goodness; thus, by feeling good about ourselves, we only increase our egoism.

If we, day after day, exert effort in our studies and try to return in our thoughts to the goal of creation, and we still feel we do not understand anything, nor correct ourselves to some degree, and if in our hearts we reproach the Creator for the state we are in, then we move further away from the truth.

As soon as we attempt to shift to altruism, our bodies and our reason immediately rise against such thoughts, and in every way possible try to push us away from this path. Hundreds of thoughts, excuses and urgent tasks immediately appear, since altruism, that is, anything not connected with some sort of benefit for the body, is hateful to us. It is not possible for our intellect to bear such aspirations for even a moment, and they are immediately suppressed.

Therefore, thoughts about nullifying egoism seem very difficult and not within human power. If, however, they are not perceived as such, it indicates that somewhere deep in them is concealed some benefit for the body, which allows us to think and to act in a certain manner, by deceiving us into thinking that our thoughts and deeds are altruistic.

Thus, the best test for determining whether a given thought or action comes as a result of a concern for the self or from altruism is: Do the heart and reason allow this thought to be sustained somehow, or even to make a slight movement based upon it? If we find agreement, then it is self-deception, not true altruism.

The moment we concentrate on thoughts that are not concerned with bodily needs, questions immediately arise such as, "Why do I need this?" and "Who benefits from it?" In such situations, although we feel that the barriers are coming from the body (our desire to receive pleasure), the most important thing for us to discover is that ultimately it is not the body that poses these questions and prohibits us from engaging in anything beyond the limitations of its interests.

This is the action of the Creator Himself. He forms within us these thoughts and desires, and does not allow us to break away from the desires of the body, and there is nothing else beside Him.

Just as He draws us closer to Himself, so He Himself places obstacles on the path to Him, so that we would learn to understand our own nature and be able to react to our every thought and desire during our attempts to break free from them.

Undoubtedly, such states can happen only among those who strive to attain Divine qualities, and to "break through" into the spiritual world—to such individuals the Creator sends various obstacles, which are felt as thoughts and desires of the body that push them away from spirituality.

All this is done so that we may discover our true spiritual state and relation to the Creator. To see how much we justify the acts of the Creator despite the objections of reason, how much we hate the Creator, who takes away all the pleasures from our lives, once filled with wonder and Light, and then thrown into the abyss of despair, because the body cannot find even an ounce of pleasure anymore in the altruistic conditions.

It appears to us that it is the body that is objecting, and not the Creator Himself who acts upon our feelings and reason by giving us thoughts and emotions that are received either positively or negatively. The Creator Himself forms specific responses of the heart and mind in order to teach us, and to acquaint us with ourselves.

A mother teaching her baby shows him something, lets him taste it, and immediately explains it to him. Similarly, the Creator shows and explains to us our true attitude toward spirituality, and our inability to act independently.

The most difficult aspect of spiritual ascent is the fact that within us are two opinions, two forces, two goals, two desires, all of which constantly collide. Even with respect to the goal of creation: on the one hand, we must attain unity in our qualities with the Creator, just so, on the other hand, we would beget a single desire to part with everything for the sake of the Creator.

But the Creator is absolutely altruistic and has no need of anything, wishing only that we should experience absolute pleasure. That is His goal in creation. However, these goals appear contradictory; first, we must relinquish everything to the Creator, while simultaneously being gratified and attaining ultimate pleasure.

The answer to this seeming contradiction is that one of them is not a goal but a means to achieving the goal. First, we must reach the condition where all thoughts, desires and actions are situated outside the boundaries of egoism, when they are ultimately altruistic, solely "for the sake of the Creator." But since there is nothing in the universe other than man and the Creator, everything that falls outside the boundaries of our five senses (body) is automatically of the Creator.

Once we have attained the correction of creation, that is, the congruence of our personal qualities with the qualities of the Creator, then we begin to grasp the goal of creation, to receive from the Creator the unlimited pleasure, unbounded by the limits of egoism.

First, we need to achieve the correction of the creation, that is the congruence of our personal qualities with the qualities of the Creator, and only then can we begin to achieve the goal of creation, to receive from the Creator unlimited pleasure, unbounded by the limits of egoism.

Before the correction, we possess only the desire for selfish gratification. As we progress in correcting ourselves, we start to favor the desire to give everything away over the desire to receive pleasure for ourselves.

However, at this stage we are still incapable of receiving pleasure from the Creator.

Only upon completing the process of self-correction can we begin to receive unbounded pleasure, not for the sake of our own egoism, but for the sake of the goal of creation.

The gratification that we receive not for the sake of our own egoism does not generate feelings of shame, because by receiving, by grasping, and by perceiving the Creator, we are happy for the pleasure He receives. Thus, the more we receive from the Creator and are pleased by Him, the happier we are that the Creator experiences pleasure as a result.

We can make an analogy between light and darkness in our world by referring to perceptions of the spiritual Light and darkness (day and night). This is the feeling of presence or absence of the Creator, of the presence or the absence of the

Creator's supervision; or, "the presence or the absence of the Creator" within ourselves.

In other words, if we were to ask something of the Creator and receive it immediately, this is denoted as "Light", or "Day". But if we are plagued by doubts about the existence of the Creator and about His management of the universe, this situation is called "darkness," or "night."

To better phrase it, the concealment of the Creator is known as "darkness, "since it arouses in a person doubts and incorrect thoughts, which are felt by him as the darkness of the night.

Our true goal should not be to perceive the Creator and grasp His actions, since this, in itself, is a purely egoistic desire. A human being will not be able to withstand the enormous pleasure resulting from the attained perceptions and will return to the egoistic state.

The real objective should be the desire to receive from the Creator the strength to proceed against the yearnings of the body and the mind, that is, to attain faith that will be greater than the human intellect and bodily desires. Having grasped and perceived the Creator and His absolute benevolent dominion, as well as His power in the entire creation, we should choose not to see the Creator in all His glory, because this would undermine our faith.

Rather, we should proceed by virtue of our faith and against the desires of the body and human intellect. All that we can desire is the strength to believe in Him and in His Dominion of the universe. The possession of such a belief is known as "Light," or "Day," since we can begin to receive pleasure without fear, being free from the desires of the body, and not being enslaved by our bodies and our reason.

When we achieve this new nature, that is, when we are capable of carrying out acts independent of our bodily desires, the Creator gives us pleasures from His Light. If darkness descends on us, and we do not feel any joy in the work of attaining the spiritual nor the ability to feel a special relation with the Creator and to feel fear and love for Him, then we have but one alternative: the crying of the soul.

We must pray to the Creator so that He should have pity on us and remove the black cloud that darkens all of our feelings and thoughts, concealing the Creator from our hearts and eyes. This is because the cry of the soul is the most powerful prayer.

When nothing can help, when we are convinced that all our efforts, knowledge, experience, physical acts and endeavors are inadequate to help us enter the Upper Spiritual Realm; when with our entire being we feel that we have exhausted all possibilities and all powers, only then do we realize that only the Creator can help; only then do we come to cry out to the Creator and pray to Him for personal redemption.

But before this time, no extraneous hardships will induce us to cry out to the Creator genuinely and from the bottom of our hearts. Only when we feel that all the options before us are already closed will the "gates of tears" open, so that we may enter the Higher World, the dwelling of the Creator.

Because of this, after we have tested all possibilities to attain spiritual ascent by ourselves, a state of absolute darkness will descend upon us. There is only one escape—only the Creator can help us. But still in the breaking of the egoistic "I," when we have not yet achieved the perception that there is a Force that guides and directs us, when we have not yet been cured by this truth and have not yet apprehended the state, our bodies will not yet allow us to call out to the Creator.

And because of this we are obligated to do everything in our strength we can, and not to wait for a miracle from Above. This is not because the Creator does not wish to take pity on us and is awaiting a "breaking point."

When we try out all our options, we gain experience, understanding and perception of our own nature. The feelings we have passed through are necessary because it is in them that we receive, and it is with them that we sense, the Revelation of the Light of the Creator and the Upper Intellect.

38

Kabbalistic Quotes

The most important aspect of the process of self-improvement is the cultivation of one's sense of humility before the Creator. This, however, should not be an artificial undertaking, but a goal of one's efforts. If, as a result of working on the self, an individual gradually starts to develop this quality, then it means that he is proceeding in the right direction. (Talmud, Avodah Zarah)

A human being is born as an absolute egoist, and this quality is so visceral that it can convince him that he has already become righteous and has rid himself of all egoism. (Talmud, Hagiga)

The *Torah* is the Light of the Creator, and only a person who receives this light is considered as *learning Torah* (rather than just acquiring mere wisdom). (Zohar, Metzorah)

The *Torah* is concealed. It is only revealed to those who have reached the level of the righteous. (Talmud, Hagiga)

When a person, by means of his studies, reaches the level at which he wants nothing but spiritual elevation and at which he accepts only the bare necessities of life in order to sustain his physical existence, not for pleasure's sake, this is the first step of his ascent to the spiritual world. (Talmud, Psachim)

The lower a person feels, the closer he comes to his true state and to the Creator. (Talmud, Sota)

It is forbidden to study Kabbalah for any purpose other than spiritual elevation. (Talmud, Sanhedrin)

A person's highest spiritual potential is to reach the level of *maaseh merkavah* ("the act of rule"). He is able to correct himself to such an extent that Divine Providence over the world can be executed through that person. (Talmud, Suka)

A necessary condition for spiritual elevation is a continuous quest for a bond with the Creator. (Rambam, Ilchot Yesodot Torah)

Do not despair once you have entered the path, for the Creator assures us of success if the direction of our aspirations is correct. (Talmud, Psachim)

The most important aspect of a person is his aspirations, rather than his achievements, because it is egoism that requires achievements. (Talmud, Yavamot; Talmud, Sota)

Just as a person should strive to feel the insignificance of his inborn characteristics, so too should he be proud of his spiritual work and purpose. (Talmud, Brachot)

A person who strives toward the Creator is known as His child (Talmud, Shabbat), in contrast with those who want to be rewarded for their studies (by respect, knowledge, or money).

Grasp the Creator. Kabbalah is known as the teaching of the hidden (*nistar*) because it can only be grasped by a person to the degree that he is able to alter his inner qualities. Therefore, he cannot pass along his perceptions to others, but he can and should help others to overcome the same path. (Rambam, Ilchot Yesodot Torah)

Who can imagine a world that is not filled by the Creator? (Talmud, Shabbat)

An individual must imagine that he is alone in the world with the Creator. The various characters and stories in the Bible signify the different qualities of one person and of all people and the different stages of this person's spiritual path. The qualities and the stages are denoted by people's names, their actions, and geographical locations. (Talmud, Kidushin)

An individual need not despair when, as he studies and works on improving himself in an effort to attain spiritual elevation, he comes to see himself as being in an even worse condition than prior to studying Kabbalah. The true nature of egoism is revealed to a person whose level is higher than that of others, and for this reason a person becomes worse in his own eyes, even though he has actually become better. (Talmud, Megillah)

Do not pay attention to the fact that the entire world is continuously chasing pleasures while only a few ascend to the Creator. (Talmud, Rosh Hashanah)

The most important aspect of a person's spiritual progress is a plea for help addressed to the Creator. (Talmud, Yomah)

The worst manifestation of egoism is arrogance and conceit. (Talmud, Sota)

A person must draw strength from the understanding of the purpose of creation, rejoicing in advance in the inevitable reformation of the entire world and the arrival of peace for humanity. (Talmud, Truma)

Faith is the only way to redemption. In all other qualities a person can become confused by egoism, but faith is the only basis for a person's ascent to the spiritual realm. (Talmud, Makot)

Faith cannot manifest itself in a person without being accompanied by fear, for egoism bows only to fear. (Talmud, Shabbat)

Even if an individual is not doing anything, his egoism urges him to commit all kinds of evil deeds. Thus, a person who has not sinned can be compared to a person who has done good deeds. (Talmud, Bava Metziah)

An individual's unification with the Creator can only be achieved through the congruity of their qualities. (Talmud, Sota)

39

Rabbi Laitman's Search for

Kabbalah

There is a question that is commonly addressed to me at various lectures and interviews with regard to how I came to Kabbalah. Probably, if I was engaged in something different and far removed from Kabbalah I could understand the validity of this question. But Kabbalah is the teaching about the goal of our lives; a subject that is so close and relevant to each of us! I believe a more correct question would be, "How did you discover that the questions about the self and about life are in Kabbalah? How did you discover Kabbalah?" rather than, "Why are you preoccupied with it?"

While still in childhood, like many others, I asked the question, "Why do I exist?" This question perturbed me constantly, if, of course, it was not suppressed by the pursuit of pleasures.

However, many times the question arose, though I did try to quell it by various spurious goals; to attain an interesting profession and to drown myself in it; or to immigrate to my own country; a goal that I pursued for many years.

Having arrived in Israel (1974), I continued to struggle with the same question about the meaning of life; I tried to find a reason that would be worth living for. Having rehashed the previous possibilities at my disposal (politics, business, etc.) to be like everyone else, I still was not able to terminate the persistent question, "For what reason do I continue to do all this? What do I gain by being similar to everyone else?'

Spurred by material and moral hardships, as well as by the realization that I could not cope with reality, I decided to turn to the religious way of life (1976), hoping that this course, and the thoughts and ideas that would ensue from it, would suit me better.

I never felt a particular inclination to the humanities; I was never fascinated with the study of psychology; nor could I truly appreciate the depth of Dostoevsky. All my studies in humanities were on a mediocre level. They did not stand out due to particular depth of thought or of feeling.

From early childhood, however, I had a strong reverence for science, which seemed to be very beneficial. At one point I came across an advertisement for a Kabbalah class. I signed up immediately, and dived into it with the usual eagerness. I bought loads of books (1978) and began to delve into them to get all the answers, even if it would take weeks at a time.

For the first time in my life I was affected to the core, and I understood that this was my area of interest because it dealt with all the issues that had been plaguing me for years.

I began to search for real teachers. I looked through the entire country and took many lessons. But somehow, an inner voice kept telling me that all that I came across was not the real Kabbalah, because it did not speak of me but of some distant and abstract issues.

Abandoning all teachers, I got one of my friends interested in the subject. Together, we spent evenings studying all the Kabbalah books we could find. This went on for months. On one cold, rainy winter evening in 1980, instead of sitting down as usual to toil over *Pardes Rimonim* and *Tal Orot*, out of desperation, and to my own surprise, I suggested to my partner that we go and search for a teacher in Bnei Brak.

I justified it by arguing that if we were to find a teacher, it would be convenient to attend classes there. Prior to that day I had visited Bnei Brak only two or three times, in my search for Kabbalah books.

That evening in Bnei Brak was just as cold, windy, and rainy. Reaching the intersection of Rabbi Akiva and Hazon-Ish streets, I opened the window and yelled to a man across the street, dressed in long black attire: "Could you tell me where they study Kabbalah around here?"

For people who are not familiar with the atmosphere and the society of the religious quarter, I must explain that my question sounded strange, to say the least. Kabbalah was not taught in any of the institutions of learning or yeshivas.

Rarely would anyone have the boldness to declare that one had an interest in Kabbalah. But the stranger across the street, without a hint of surprise, gave me an answer: "Turn left, proceed until you reach a citrus plantation, there you will see a synagogue. They teach Kabbalah there."

Reaching the described destination we found a dark building. Upon entering, we noticed a long table in a side room. There were four or five white-bearded men at the table. I introduced myself and explained that we were from Rehovot, and we wanted to learn Kabbalah. The elderly man sitting at the head of the table invited us to join and suggested that we could discuss our issues after the class ended.

Then, the class proceeded with the weekly reading of the chapter from the book of Zohar, with the commentaries of the Sulam, and with the muffling of words and with half phrases in Yiddish, as people who understood each other from half a glance. Seeing them and listening to them I came to the conclusion that this bunch was simply biding their time until their old age, and if we hurried, we could still find another place to study Kabbalah that evening.

However, my friend held me back, declaring that he could not behave so tactlessly. In a few minutes the lesson was over, and the elderly man, having established who we were, asked for our phone numbers. He said that he would think of whom to suggest as a teacher for us, and he would get back to us.

I was very reluctant to even give my number, thinking that this endeavor was the same waste of time as all the previous attempts that we had undertaken. Sensing my reluctance, my friend gave his phone number. We said good-bye and departed.

The very next evening my friend came to my house and declared that the elder had called him and offered us a Kabbalah teacher. He also informed me that a meeting was already set and it was to take place that same evening. I did not want to spend another night in vain, but I succumbed to the appeals of my friend.

We arrived. The elder called another man, slightly younger than himself, but also with a white beard; he said a few words in Yiddish to the younger man, and then left us alone with him.

The latter suggested that we should sit down and start studying right away. He recommended starting with an article titled "An Introduction to Kabbalah," which on numerous occasions my friend and I had tried to understand. We sat down at one of the tables in the empty room of the Beit-Knesset (synagogue).

The man began to read paragraph by paragraph, and to explain the meaning of each. It is always difficult for me to recall that moment; that sharp sensation that after a lengthy search I had finally found what I was seeking for so many years and could not find anywhere else. At the end of the lesson we set up our next class for the following day.

The next day I came equipped with a recorder. Learning that the main classes take place between 3 and 6 in the morning, we started attending them every night. We also came to the monthly feasts to celebrate the new moon, and like everyone else, we contributed our monthly donations.

Prompted by a desire to discover everything for myself, and in general being more aggressive, I often got into arguments. All the information about us constantly streamed to the main elder, who, as it turned out, inquired about us quite often.

One day, our teacher informed me that after the morning prayer, around 7 a.m., the main elder could study the "Introduction to the Book of Zohar" with me. However, seeing that I did not understand, after two or three lessons, the elder, through our own teacher, announced that the lessons would stop.

I would have continued to study, even though I felt that I did not understand anything. I was ready to read everything mechanically with him, prompted by the necessity to under-stand the meaning deep inside the lines. However, he must have known that my time had not come yet, and ended the lessons, though I was terribly offended.

Several months passed, and through our regular teacher, the main elder asked me if I could drive him to see a doctor in Tel Aviv. Of course, I agreed. On the way there he talked a lot about various subjects. I, on my part, tried to ask questions pertaining to Kabbalah.

It was then that he said to me that while I have no understanding of anything, he could talk with me about everything, but in the future, when I begin to understand, he would stop being so frank with me.

It happened just as he described. For years, instead of the answers, I would hear the same reply: "You already have Whom to ask," meaning the Creator, "demand, ask, plead, do whatever you want; address everything to Him, and demand everything from Him!"

The visits to the doctor did not help, and the elder had to be placed in the hospital with an ear infection for an entire month. Over time I had accompanied the elder many times on his trips to the doctor; the day he went into the hospital I decided to stay with him there overnight.

During the entire month I would come to the hospital at 4 a.m., climb over the fence, quietly pass through the building, and then study. For the entire month! From that time, Baruch Shalom Halevi Ashlag, the eldest son of Baal HaSulam, became my Rabbi.

After his release from the hospital we regularly made trips to parks and took long walks. Returning from these trips, I would sit down and feverishly write down all that I heard from him. These frequent trips, lasting three to four hours a day, transformed into a habit with time.

In the first two years I kept asking the Rabbi for permission to move closer to him, but he always answered that he saw no necessity in the move, since my trips from Rehovot represented efforts that brought spiritual benefit to me.

However, when two years later the Rabbi himself suggested that I should move to live in Bnei Brak for some reason, I was in no hurry to do so. So unhurried was I that my Rabbi went out and got an apartment for me close to himself, and started pressing for my move.

Still living in Rehovot, I asked my Rabbi for permission to conduct several classes in one of the places where some time ago I had attended and met other people who were attempting to study Kabbalah. He received the news without great enthusiasm, but later questioned me about my classes.

When I told him that there was an opportunity to invite several young men to join us in Bnei Brak, the Rabbi cautiously agreed. Thus, many dozens of young men joined our synagogue, and the quiet secluded place transformed into a lively establishment.

The first six months witnessed nearly ten weddings. The life of the Rabbi, all his days, received new meaning. He was delighted by the influx of people who wanted to study Kabbalah. Our day usually started at 3 a.m.; a study group took place until 6 a.m., and then a prayer until 7 a.m. Every day, from 9 until 12, we made trips to the park or to the sea.

Upon returning, I would retire home in order to work. From 5 p.m. until 8 p.m. we would continue to study, breaking only for prayers. Then, we would part, and meet again at 3 a.m. This routine went on for years. I taped all classes, so by now the collection of tapes exceeds a thousand.

In the last five years (from 1987) my Rabbi decided that it would be a good idea for us to travel to Tiberias once every two weeks for a couple of days. These trips, which took us away from everyone else, fostered a closeness between us.

However, with the years, the perception of the spiritual gap that separated us, became greater in me, though I did not know how to bridge it. I clearly perceived this gap every time I watched him experience delight at the slightest possibility of suppressing some physical need.

For him, a reached conclusion became law, where the schedule and the timetable were followed strictly, irrespective of fatigue or illness. Almost collapsing from exhaustion, he would carry out all that was planned for the day to the last detail, never diminishing the task that he took upon himself. Breathless from fatigue, suffering from shortness of breath, he never cancelled even one appointment or class; he never shifted any of his responsibilities to another person.

Constantly observing his behavior, I would lose confidence in myself and in my own possible success, even though I understood that this supernatural strength emanated from the realization of the grandiose task before him, and from the help from Above.

I cannot forget even one moment that I spent with him during our trips to T'veria and Mount Meron, when I would spend long evenings sitting across from him, absorbing his glance, his speeches, his songs. These recollections live deep inside of me, and I hope that, even today, they determine and guide my path. The information that was collected in the process of daily interactions with him, in the span of twelve years, lives and operates independently.

Very often, my Rabbi would utter something unintelligible after a speech, sometimes adding that he said the phrase in order to ensure that what was said would enter the world, and would live and operate in this world.

Since group meetings have been practiced by Kabbalists from ancient times, I asked the Rabbi to organize such groups for newcomers, and to outline the plan of such meetings in a written form. This led to his writing weekly articles, which he continued to do almost until his last days.

As a result, we were left with a legacy of several volumes of extraordinary material, which together with the audiotapes that I made over the years, comprise a great collection of commentaries and explanations of the entire Kabbalah.

In the days of the New Year celebration, my Rabbi suddenly became ill and started feeling pressure in his chest. Only after extensive persuasion did he agree to undergo a medical examination. The doctors did not find anything wrong, but early in the morning, on the fifth day of Tishrei, 5752 (1991) he passed away.

Dozens of students that joined the group in the last several years continue to study Kabbalah and search for the inner meaning of creation. The Teaching lives on, just as in all previous centuries.

Rabbi Yehuda Ashlag and his elder son, Rabbi Baruch Ashlag, my Rabbi, through their efforts, have developed and adapted this Teaching to the needs of this generation, to the type of souls that descend into this world at the present time.

Spiritual information is passed to the Kabbalist from Above without the use of words, and it is received simultaneously by all sensory organs, as well as by the intellect. Thus, it is grasped in its entirety instantly.

This information can be transferred by a Kabbalist only to another Kabbalist, who must be on the same or on a higher spiritual level. It is impossible to convey the same information to a person who has not yet reached the right spiritual level, or has not yet been introduced to the spiritual realms, because such a person lacks the necessary instruments of perception.

Sometimes a teacher may resort to an artificial spiritual elevation of the student to the teacher's spiritual level by means of a screen of the teacher (*masach*). In this case, a student may acquire a certain idea about the essence of the spiritual forces and actions. In passing information to those who have not yet entered the spiritual realm, standard means of transmitting information are employed: printed text, speech, direct contact, personal example.

As we know from the description of the meaning of letters (from the article titled *The Names of the Creator*), they can be used to transmit more than just the literal meaning; they can also be used to convey the spiritual, inner content of information.

But until an individual acquires the perceptions that correspond to the spiritual meaning of the names and of actions, the reading of words can be compared to placing empty plates on the table, and attaching to them tags with the names of fancy dishes.

Music presents a more abstract type of transmitting information. Just like visible light, it consists of the seven primary forces-qualities-tones, in light of the fact that the spiritual entity (*partzuf*) that governs our world, known as *partzuf Zeir Anpin de Atzilut*, consists of the seven parts, or *Sefirot*.

Depending on one's particular condition, a person will discern various spiritual states of the composer in a given Kabbalistic melody. That person does not necessarily have to be on the same spiritual level as the composer of the melody; rather, the inner meaning can be grasped to the degree that one's personal spiritual level will permit.

In 1996, 1998, and 2000, three CDs of the Baal HaSulam and Rabash music were recorded and published. The melodies are presented as Rabbi Michael Laitman heard them from his Rabbi, Rabbi Baruch Ashlag. Some of the melodies were composed for texts from psalms, while others originated from fragments of our prayer texts.

In addition to the words, the sounds of the melodies carry a great amount of Kabbalistic information in them.

Other Books by
Rabbi Michael Laitman

An Interview With The Future

"Kabbalah is not about researching an ancient mystical body of knowledge, but is rather the most modern science that is closest to man. It is the science of the 21st century that researches the forces that we do not see, forces that govern our world and influence every moment of our lives. This is a science that will change the future of each and every individual, and all of mankind. The sources explain very clearly that once this process is underway, the entire world will gradually elevate itself to a higher state of being."

Rabbi Michael Laitman

According to Rabbi Laitman, ours is the first generation on earth with the ability to draw the future closer so that we can experience our time here in a much more pleasant manner. But what is hard for us to grasp is that that we do not necessarily need to know what the future holds in order to reach that state. And in our current state, we do not even have the ability to comprehend what that future form will feel like.

So we can either continue to advance as we have been doing since the beginning of time, or use this infinite source of knowledge to control our destiny. We can actively embrace this ultimate Source of fulfillment to reduce suffering in the world, or continue to wait and see what happens next.

Since a Kabbalist is a person who has attained the spiritual realm, they are completely aware of the processes influencing our world. *An Interview With The Future* by the Israel based Kabbalist Michael Laitman, is the defining book of the decade. It is a meeting with destiny that provides the key to safeguarding the future of the entire human race.

The Kabbalah Experience

The wisdom of Kabbalah teaches us how to live in the reality that is spread before us. It is a systematic method that has evolved over thousands of years through a handful of unique individuals in every generation. During all that time it was concealed from the public eye that was not yet ready to receive it, until the current generation—the generation, for which this method was specifically developed. That is why it is written in the Zohar, that from 1995 onward Kabbalah will become a way of life, open to all with no restrictions.

Why our generation? Because the souls that descend to this world and dress in our bodies evolve from generation to generation, until they come to a state where a question awakens in them about the meaning of their very existence. If we contemplate reality as it is described in the books of Kabbalists who speak of 'the end of days'—which we are at the threshold of—there arises a profound fear that without Kabbalah, we will not be able to secure the safe passage to the higher level of being that awaits us.

Kabbalah allows us to come to know the spiritual world—the very system that monitors and leads reality, including the reality of this world, the whole of humanity and each and every one of us at any given moment. Through this method, we can control the system of the worlds and determine how to conduct our daily lives.

A Guide to the *Hidden Wisdom of Kabbalah*
with TEN COMPLETE KABBALAH LESSONS

Kabbalah deals with the unseen forces of the upper worlds, the roots of all our thoughts and feelings, which are just beyond our grasp. Since we have no control over the worlds, we have no idea how and why our thoughts and feelings are formed. We wonder at experiences that are bitter, sweet, pleasant or rough. Yet so far, we have been unsuccessful at creating tools for accurately examining our feelings, even in the realms of psychology, psychiatry and other social disciplines. Behavioral factors remain hidden from our understanding.

Kabbalah provides a systematic method for evaluating our feelings: It takes the total of our feelings and desires and provides the perfect formula for each and every phenomenon, at each level, for attaining every type of perception and feeling known to human beings.

The wisdom of Kabbalah is an ancient and proven method that has been adapted to suit the sophisticated souls of this generation. Through it, we can receive a higher awareness and attain spirituality, which is our true goal for being here.

A Guide To the *Hidden Wisdom of Kabbalah* is designed to satisfy the needs of those searching for a deeper meaning to life. The text gently guides the reader to begin traversing the initial stages of spiritual ascent toward attaining the highest level of human development. Now that the secret is out, the Israel based Kabbalist Michael Laitman encourages you to join thousands of people around the world who are actively engaged in reaping the rewards of this fulfilling path.